Authentic Arabian Horse Names

Volume II

Authentic Arabian Horse Names

Volume II

An Extended Collection of Authentic Arabic Names

and Arabian Tales from the Desert

By Bachir Bserani

with Kellie Kolodziejczyk

Foreword by
Nasr Marei

Paintings by
Ali Al Mimar

Painting (endsheets) by Horace Vernet

Photography by
Gigi Grasso, Darryl Larson, Nasr Marei, Rik Van Lent Jr.,
Gary Kenworthy, Kellie Kolodziejczyk, Robin Lee

Copyright 2011 Bachir Bserani and Kellie Kolodziejczyk

All Rights Reserved.
Except for brief quotations for book reviews, no part of this work may be reproduced
in any form or by any means, electronic or mechanical, including photocopying,
recording by information storage and retrieval systems or otherwise,
without prior written permission from the copyright holders.

Printed in the United States of America by
Josten's Printing and Publishing, Topeka, Kansas

ISBN# 978-0-9763022-4-7

Design and Production: Kellie Kolodziejczyk, Bachir Bserani and Cyndi Greathouse
Graphics by GREATHOUSE & HARDWICK, LLC

Published by, Al Moussami, LLC
PO Box 245, Lycoming, NY 13093
Website: www.al-moussami.com

Front Cover: *Maan Ela Al Abad*. Painted 2007. Back Cover: *Harakat Hourrah*. Painted 2002.
Paintings by Ali Al Mimar, Iraqi artist , b. 1965
Front and Back Cover Design: Kellie Kolodziejczyk and Cyndi Greathouse.
Endsheets: *The Gathering of the Members of the Parliament*, Painted 1834.
by Horace Vernet, French artist, (1789-1863) © Art Resource, NY/Réunion des Musées Nationaux

From the man for whom horses are a source of pride and friendship, I dedicate this book to each one of my friends, and especially to my lovely Heather and my two angels Bahiyeh and Dounia. May peace and Allah's blessings be always your life's companions.

– Bachir Bserani

Dedicated in memory of my beloved Autumn and Kacey. Thank you God for keeping them safe, and for your guidance in finding the strength and courage to accept that which I cannot change; and to persevere where change is possible.

– K. Kolodziejczyk

Contents

Acknowledgements 8
About the Authors 10
Foreword 13
The Bedouin Custom of Naming 17
    the Arabian Horse
Hikayat Al Hadiya 22
    (the story of the gift)
Hikayat Al Mousabakat 31
    (the story of the race)
Hikayat Al Mahrousseh 43
    (the story of the protected one)
Hikayat Al Inteesar 51
    (the story of the conquest)
A Pure and True Translation of an 58
    Authentic Bedouin Pedigree
The Arabian Dancing Horse 60
Authentic Arabian Horse Names, Vol. II 69
Using the Dictionary 71
Guidelines to Follow when Choosing an
    Arabic Name 72
Arabic-English 75
English-Arabic 143
Picture Credits 211
About the Artists and Photographers 212

Acknowledgements

Since my first publication in 2004, I have been pleased
and encouraged by the substantial changes Arabian
horse owners and breeders from around the world have made
with regard to following the true Bedouin traditions of naming their foals.
Personally, I have witnessed this.
I have been to many Arabian horse shows in the US, Europe
and the Middle East and have listened to the beautiful Arabic names
being called by the announcers as the horse is to enter the show ring. This
alone has brought joy and pride to this author.
Following the recommendations of many native Arabic speakers
and my readers around the world, I decided to publish my second book
to give the Arabian horse owners and lovers
more choices in continuing this true desert tradition.

I am grateful to my friends and many readers
who allowed me to share my humble knowledge of the Arabic
language with them as they read and listen to my stories.
I would also like to especially thank my close friends,
artist Ali Al Mimar and Dr. Nasr Marei of Albadeia Stud,
for their ongoing support and encouragement with regard to this book.
I am highly honored and proud to hear the true Arabic names of
Arabian horses chosen from my publication being spoken
as these beautiful creatures are admired not only for their beauty,
but also for their true heritage that the name carries with them.
Shoukran, thank you.

Bachir Bserani
Al Moussami – The Giver of Names

About the Authors

Bachir Youseph
Gergi Bserani

Born in Aleppo, Syria near the area of the Shomar and Thai tribes, Bachir Bserani's passion for horses was passed to him through his father, a cavalry member who often traveled on horseback through the regions of Deir el Zoor, Hasakeh, and Hama. From a young age Bachir was naturally drawn to horses. He traveled many journeys with his father, visiting the Bedouin tribes to solve a problem, or to discuss a bargain or two. As a young boy he always, as is the custom in the desert, watched and listened to the elders, but never asked questions except to his father. And it is through these travels during the scorching daytime heat of the desert, and from beneath the bright stars in the cool desert evening that his knowledge about Arabian horses came to him.

In 1970 Bachir arrived in the United States, married, and in 1973 was told that he was entitled to U.S. citizenship. During the process of obtaining US citizenship Bachir was asked to change his name to a common American name. Of course he politely declined to change his name, as what name could compare to the beautiful name given by his parents ... Bachir (*The One Who Brings Good News*). He would keep his birth name, and speak his name with pride of his heritage and of the Arabian Desert from where he was born.

Bachir's first book *Authentic Arabian Horse Names* by Bachir Bserani with Kellie Kolodziejczyk was published in 2004. In 2008 he released a self titled companion audio CD based on the Arabic-English section of this book. On the CD Bachir recites each name individually in his native Arabic tongue and then gives the English translation. Other credits include educational seminars and articles on the Bedouin tradition of naming foals. On occasion, Bachir will make appearances for book signings at various Arabian horse and Saluki dog events.

Kellie Crane Kolodziejczyk

Many people have asked how all this came to be, but it was simply a matter of circumstances that caused the paths of Bachir Bserani and Kellie Kolodziejczyk to cross. Previously unknown to each other, they quickly discovered the love and passion each had for the Arabian horse. Kellie was immediately intrigued by Bachir's way of speaking with his rich Middle Eastern accent, his compassion when giving his advice on the Arabic custom of the naming of the Arabian horse, and of course, she was taken by the wonderful stories that he told. This chance meeting has transcended well beyond her expectations. With the publication of Volumes I and II of *Authentic Arabian Horse Names*, as well as the companion audio CD to Volume I, this has given her an overwhelming sense of pride to be a part of such a wonderful project that is educational and entertaining to so many people throughout the world. She has also been inspired by the young children in her family, especially Michaela, Molly, Leah, Colin, RJ, Joey, and Jay, whose pure kindness and affection towards animals has been a natural part of their being since a very early age.

Kellie continues to reside in upstate New York with her husband Perry on their breeding farm Abmor Acres. They specialize in black Arabians, and Pintabians. Horses from their breeding program have been sold throughout the United States and Europe.

For additional information about Bachir Bserani and Kellie Kolodziejczyk, please visit the Al-Moussami website at www.al-moussami.com.

Foreword

*" ... I can remember many hours
spent watching the foals with their
dams trying to learn what are
the special characteristics of that baby.
It has always been important
to me to have an authentic name
which captures the heritage
and the personality of
each individual horse."*

– Nasr Marei

The quotation, "What's in a name?" is one of the most famous passages from Shakespeare's play *Romeo and Juliet*. Juliet completes the thought by saying, "That which we call a rose by any other name would smell as sweet." This implies that the name of something is not as important as its essence. An Arabian horse breeder would not agree with this.

To anyone with passion for the Arabian horse, the name given to a foal is extremely important. Many believe that the name should capture the essence of the horse and therefore they may wait a bit to decide on the name. Often it is a derivation of the name of the sire or the dam. Frequently, it is a combination of both or a slightly distorted version of one or the other.

Some names are an attempt to use an Arabic word without a clear meaning of the word itself. Trying to be clever in a different language can occasionally be amusing or in a worst case scenario, an embarrassment with an untoward meaning in the Arabic language. Sadly, there are even names that make no sense in any language.

Originally names given by the Arabs in the desert were not personal. Most horses were named in a functional way with the name of the tribe and/or the strain. This did not reflect poorly on the great affection and bond between the owner and the horse. It was just that this was a practical way to handle the situation. It was a way to insure that there was no confusion as to the actual horse by using what might have been a name that could have been misunderstood by others outside the immediate group. Since there were no written records, oral tradition had to be exact and clear.

This does not mean that there were not instances when personal names were used by the owners. It would not be realistic to assume that all was cut and dried when there was such a tradition of poetry, myth and romance in the Arab culture with the Arabian horse. From what we know of the close connection between all members of the family to the horse and the fact that the horse was often protected and lived in the tent, one would have to believe that this closeness included personal or even pet names for the horse.

In all the years that I have been involved with and breeding the Egyptian horse, I can remember many hours spent watching the foals with their dams trying to learn what are the special characteristics of that baby. It has always been important to me to have an authentic name which captures the heritage and the personality of each individual horse. At times, it can take a while to come up with just the right name. Other times, it comes in a flash. Either way, I am always happy with the name that captures what the horse and I want to say.

The Arabic language is one of the most precise and nuanced in the world. Words have a very specific meaning and deserve the respect of being used properly. Arabs all throughout history have treasured the words of their poets and writers. The oral tradition can still hold people in a spell. One word can trigger an emotional response that carries on through many layers.

That brings us to the importance of this book, *Authentic Arabian Horse Names, Volume* II. In the first volume, Bachir Bserani and Kellie Kolodziejczyk provided a great source of help to Arabian breeders who are striving to be correct and authentic in naming their horses. In a world where so much information is instantly available and sadly not always with correctness, it is important to have these books to help with one of the special tasks and treats of breeding. Naming your horse should be something that gives you pleasure and adds to the history of your farm. The research that has gone into these books takes us a long way in achieving something special to ourselves and all those who meet the horse along its way.

– Nasr Marei

For additional information about Nasr Narei and his Egyptian Arabian breeding program please visit the Albadeia Stud, Egypt website at www.albadeia.net.

The Bedouin Custom of Naming the Arabian Horse

*"It is not the horse that
makes the name,
nor the name
that makes the horse,
it is the name and the horse
that complement each other."*

– Bachir Bserani

One can travel across the Arabian Desert from North to South and from East to West and the Bedouins, from whatever tribe they belong to, will follow the same guarded ritual of naming foals. To the Bedouin a name is a blessing from *Allah* that his foal will carry for life.

Sometimes a foal will be up to five months old before a name is chosen for this beautiful creature. Until this time the young one will be called Son (I*bn*) or Daughter (B*int*) before the name of the sire or dam, for example, I*bn Halima* or B*int Al Ajouz*. Time will be taken to name the foal, but the foal will have a name before he is weaned from his dam.

Every night when the sun begins to set, the tribe members will gather under the tent, sipping tea and smoking the nargileh, discussing the day's most urgent matters. One of them will be the behaviors of the new foals, their colors, their temperament, and their good and bad habits.

The younger men will listen as the elder tribesmen will discuss suitable names for each foal, and once the majority agrees, a name is chosen and given to a foal by the elder. The elder will then announce the name of the foal to the tribe by shouting the name aloud.

The foal is then brought in to the tent and the chant of the name will echo a minute or more through the tribe. And so it is said many times the name of the foal, for example "L*atif*, L*atif*, L*atif*." The foal, which had been called I*bn Halima* as he was the son of *Halima*, is now bestowed with the name L*atif*. The excitement is rampant, and even the young children will be shouting out the name "L*atif*" while running between the tents.

For you it will be difficult to follow the true customs of the Bedouin in naming your horses exactly as it is done in the Middle East, but most importantly we must ensure that a suitable Arabic name is given to our Arabian foal to honor this divine creature, a cherished gift from God.

Indeed, the Arabian horse is a gift from God, a creature that we cherish not only for their beauty, but also for their intelligence, their pride, their gentle nature, and most of all for their loyalty. As many of my readers will recall from Volume I of my book, *Authentic Arabian Horse Names*, I had shared with you a story about R*heemah*, the first

Arabian horse I ever owned. In Arabic, *Rheemah* means *Morning Dew*.

She will be forever in my heart and in my mind. I will never forget her. She was such a beautiful mare, an exquisite dapple-gray from the *Seglawiyah* strain. I had bought her in the desert from an old wise man named Abou Mahmood.

This mare was the most special horse to me. She touched my heart and my soul. I felt that it was important to share with you this continuation to my special story of *Rheemah*, to show you how our horses remain a part of our being even after they are gone.

…And so, after a time when I returned with *Rheemah* to my stable in Damascus I had started schooling her with the help of my French riding instructor. Right away we did notice that this mare's learning abilities went far beyond description.

Sometimes people discuss the intelligence of horses, some will say that the horses are intelligent, some will say they are not a very intelligent creature, but in my opinion, they have an excellent memory, and this is how they are able to learn so quickly. Whatever the belief is, I know *Rheemah* learned at a faster pace than any horse I had trained in my entire life.

On one day in particular, a very hot day, I was gently schooling *Rheemah*, just walking and trotting her and teaching her the aides, and teaching her how to be supple, when suddenly I heard my stable assistant Mohammed shout, "Master Bachir, Master Bachir, a rider is coming; I see him approaching from the distance."

Mohammed had the eyes like an eagle. And before long, galloping through a cloud of dust, there appeared a rider on a beautiful Arabian horse. The horse was breathing heavily, and his coat glistened with sweat under the hot sun. The rider approached towards me, dismounted from his horse, and he said, "May I speak to Master Bachir?"

I stopped *Rheemah*, and then said, "I am Bachir." He looked at me, and then asked, "You are riding *Rheemah*?"

I replied, "Yes, this is *Rheemah*." He said. "Mashallah, May *Allah* bless you. She looks to be very well cared for." I said, "Stranger, you are tired. Do you want to sit down? Do you want to have a drink, a sip of water, perhaps something to eat?"

He said, "No thank you. Your hospitality is very generous. I must tell you that I am the grandson of Abou Mahmood, and I do apologize for not visiting earlier. After you parted with R*heemah*, my dear grandfather lasted only one month, and we had to bury him. But before his death, while he lay dying next to me, I made a promise to him.

He asked me to come to Damascus and ask of you, Master Bachir, to provide a piece of the forelock, a piece of the mane, and a piece of the tail hair of my grandfather's beloved R*heemah*, so it could be put with him in his grave, in memory of his devotion and love for R*heemah*."

I was so moved that I immediately dismounted R*heemah*. I then asked Mohammed to get me a knife. When he returned I cut a piece of the forelock of the mare, and a piece of her mane, and a piece of the hair of her tail. I next removed the kafiya from my head and wrapped the pieces gently within it, then carefully handed it to the grandson.

I said, "This hair from R*heemah* I give to you in honor of your dear grandfather. It is now that you may fulfill his dying wish. May his soul rest in peace."

Again I asked the grandson to come so we could offer him and his horse something to eat and to rest.

He replied, "Shoukran, thank you Master Bachir, this is a long journey for me, and I must return to my tribe soon, but I will stay a short while to eat and rest, and to water and rest my horse, but then I must be on my way."

Mohammed brought the horse to the well to drink, and let the horse stand to rest for awhile and to eat. In some time the young man got back on his horse holding tightly to the hair from R*heemah* in the kafiya, and then disappeared into the desert. And I never was to see the grandson of Abou Mahmood again.

I hope by including the remainder of my story of R*heemah*, it will show to my readers all the love and devotion the people of the desert have for their horses.

Even at our death we long to have a part of our cherished Arabian horse with us. And this I felt was important to share. I would like to add that, please, after carefully choosing a name for your foal be proud of that name.

Tell everyone who listens what the name means and why you chose this particular name. Behind every name should be a story!

Mabrouk! Congratulations!

– Bachir Bserani
with Kellie Kolodziejczyk

Hikayat Al Hadiya

The Story of the Gift

To the Bedouin
the Name is
a Blessing from
Allah that his foal
will carry
for life.

In a time long ago past, in a place in the hot desert of the Middle East, a beautiful black filly was born to a lovely Seglawiyah mare named Maaroofah. This prized desert mare, Maaroofah, belonged to the head of the Hanazah tribe which roamed the area of northern Syria. The Sheik gave this valuable filly as a wedding gift to his only son Omar. The happiness in this young man's eyes could never be described. He truly loved this special young foal and sat for hours watching her grow and develop into a beautiful, eye catching filly.

They came from near and far to admire the beautiful bint al Seglawiyah (the daughter of the Seglawiyah mare) as she was referred to. Omar pondered a name for this divine filly but he had not yet bestowed upon her the blessed Arabic name that she will carry for life. He had been instructed by his father to study carefully the personality and traits of the filly so that he could select a suitable and honorable name as was the Bedouin custom. He was told to not select a name of another famous horse, or to name the filly after a person as this was not looked upon in a favorable manner by the tribes.

A few weeks went by when one evening while everyone was around the fire, Omar declared to all who are present that he chooses the name "Leila" for his filly. When he was asked why he chose the name "Leila", he said that this was the name of his new bride, and he could not think of a better way to express his love to his new wife Leila. Although Omar had been instructed on the proper custom of selecting a name for his beloved filly, being young and naïve, Omar did not follow the instruction of his father.

The uncle of Omar, who was a quiet man, suggested to Omar that he wait for his grandfather, who was the eldest and most wise of the tribe, to return from his journey so that he could choose a name for this filly. The young man, thinking he knew better, refused to abide by the request of his uncle and asserted to everyone that Leila will indeed be the name of the filly. When the grandfather returned and was told about the defiance, and the decision that his grandson took in naming his filly, he immediately summoned all the elders of the tribe as well as his grandson Omar.

When all had arrived at the tent the wise man spoke. "My grandson Omar, is it true that you have decided to not obey the teachings of your elders, and to name this beautiful filly, this beautiful gift from your father, to name her Leila, after your wife?"

Omar responded, "Yes, Grandfather this was my decision. I wanted to honor the beauty of my filly with the name of the woman who is most beautiful to me."

The grandfather, to the surprise of everyone present said, "Then it will be Leila. Leila will be name of your filly."

And so the grandfather accepted the name given to the filly by Omar. Gasps and whispers of discontent could be heard throughout the tent. In a slow motion, the grandfather raised his outstretched arm above his head without a word being said. And as the voices in the tent had risen, so they were quiet. And not another word was spoken.

Several months went by and a delegation from a nearby peaceful tribe came to visit. Omar was at the well allowing his cherished filly Leila to drink the pure water that rose from its confines. One of the young visitors passing by noticed Omar at the well with the filly and went to speak to him.

He said to Omar, "How beautiful your Leila is. Her kind eyes have mesmerized me. I love her gentleness. I do wish so that Leila could be mine."

And he kept on with showering his praises of Leila. Omar got very upset and stormed away from his new friend. He walked directly to the grandfather enraged and complained that a man insulted him by praising Leila, his wife, and wishing to take her away from him. The wise grandfather patted him on the back in a kind and reassuring manner, then took his hand within his own and carefully told him, "This, Omar, that has happened is by your own doing, not by the doing of your new friend. My dear grandson, when your friend was praising Leila, he was endeared to your young filly Leila, not your new wife.

As he passed by here he had seen you at the well with your filly. His breath was taken away by the beauty of this creature, and he asked me her name. Her name, I told him, is Leila."

The grandfather then told Omar, "You must be willing to accept many mixed messages from other visitors as well since you have made the decision to name your filly after your wife Leila."

Omar said, "Grandfather, I beg your pardon; I now see the wisdom in your advice to me, and I now know that I have made a mistake by not listening to you, my elder. With your permission I would like to change the name of my filly to Ihteram (meaning Respect), because this has been the lesson I have been taught by my most beautiful and beloved filly."

And so it was done.

Hikayat Al Mousabakat

The Story of The Race

"I look between the ears of my white horse and his forelock seems as if the night deposited a star between his eyes."

– al-Mutanabbi

I have learned through hearing many stories through the years that the Banu Zahl Bedouin tribe was the best in caring for their horses. It was said also many times that they appreciated their horses more than their own children. Abdullah Bin Habban, a high ranking member of the Banu Zahl tribe had acquired an exquisite mare named Moubarakat, meaning Blessings. At first glance one would know why she was bestowed with such a name. She was a kind and gentle, purely white mare, possessing a delicateness to her that could not be explained, but only seen with one's own eye. She had produced a colt that year, from the stallion Al Haejj, his name meaning The Excited One. He was a very tall and proud steed, well muscled and strong. The colt was born very much in his likeness but with a bright red chestnut coat color. The beautiful name given to him was Al Hadeer meaning The Roaring of the Waterfall.

Abdullah Bin Habban wanted to give this foal called Al Hadeer to his son Azeez, who had a limp since the day

when he started walking. Now at age 12 sadly, he was like an outcast among his peers. But Azeez did not mind as he spent all his time with his beloved colt Al Hadeer. The boy's father helped him take care of his horse and showed him the proper way to raise and train him. Many a time Azeez would take Al Hadeer for a long ride, and wander through the open desert until they were both exhausted.

Travelers passing through came to admire Al Hadeer to the point of offering big sums of money to acquire him, but Azeez was never going to part with his beloved horse. In time, Al Hadeer had matured into a strong and beautiful horse with his chestnut coat turning to purely white as was his dam's, and with the pure muscle and stamina of his sire.

During one of the visits by the Bin Wathel tribe, a group of young boys approached Azeez as he returned from a ride, and was leading Al Hadeer back to the tent to cool him. One of the boys, the son of the tribe elder, began to brag to his friends about his own horse, a great Arabian stallion that was black as the night.

He shouted, "My steed is from the most cherished of blood lines, and runs so swiftly it is as though he is carried by the wings of a mighty falcon."

He then pointed to Al Hadeer and said, "This horse, however, tall and proud he may be is no match for my Arab, a stallion born of divine blood."

Of course Azeez was not going to stand for such an insult. Al Hadeer, too, was born from the finest and swiftest of bloodlines. The boys continued to shout back and forth, and then fighting ensued. Azeez was so angered that in the scuffle he put a big gash in the head of the guest.

Both tribes rushed to stop the fighting, and then gathered around the tent trying to make peace between the two boys. By the law of the land, the visiting tribe who had the injured son must demand retribution. Their demand was harsh, that Al Hadeer be given to them. At first the father of Azeez agreed to their demands, but then he had a change of heart telling them you may take my son, punish him, but you cannot take the horse.

The visiting tribe was allured by the decision and

spoke amongst themselves for some time. They knew the love the father had for his son, yet he was willing to sacrifice his son rather than surrender the Arab horse. After sipping their coffee and smoking their nargileh, the tribe decided that the two boys will have to race each other in front of both tribes and if Al Hadeer loses the race, the son of the visiting tribe will own him outright, and if Al Hadeer wins then the debt of retribution will be completely forgotten. They would have thirty days to prepare for this great race.

Azeez went to his father and implored him to tell him how to train Al Hadeer for such a race. He had heard confirmation through messengers that the black stallion of his competitor, his name Kahar meaning Conqueror, is as fast as the wind and few horses dare race him.

His father spoke to him, "My son, without even knowing it, you have prepared Al Hadeer for such a race. You have ridden him long distances through the desert often, treated him right with good food and water, groomed him daily, but most of all you have shown your horse the love and respect that you have for him, and praised Allah for his being. This is what gives Al Hadeer his speed and strength, and it is this that will push him to win the race."

So every day Azeez continued to do as he always did. He will groom his horse, jump on his back bareback and gallop through the sand at long distances, always to return to the tribe exhausted and ready to collapse. Fifteen days before the big race the father told Azeez that the next day he will set a match race against the fastest horse that his uncle owned; her name being Al Riyah meaning The Wind. This mare, Azeez learned, was from the same sire as Al Hadeer.

The boy was very much excited for this match race, so that night he stayed under the tent with Al Hadeer carefully grooming him until he could no longer fight the sleepiness that was overcoming him. In the morning the announcement was made of the practice race. All the tribe members and those of the Bin Wathel tribe as well, gathered to form a corridor to witness this race.

Azeez approached the corridor then climbed upon

the back of Al Hadeer. The brilliant white stallion was radiant under the red, wool saddle that was imported from Damascus with its matching bridle and breastplate. The screaming and applause had started as soon as the two appeared from out of the tent. All this was followed by the arrival of Al Riyah, a glistening chestnut mare adorned with a black wool saddle, bridle and breastplate. Prancing at the starting line Al Hadeer started to move forward, but Azeez quickly took hold of him and waited for the signal to be given.

The father stated the rules clearly. Upon the cue, the two would go straight one half mile, then turn around and return to where they began. The first to cross the line would be the winner. Al Hadeer was snorting and not at ease. He did not want to wait. The signal was given and the two horses shot like an arrow with the crowds encouraging along the way.

Al Riyah was two lengths ahead of Al Hadeer and every time the boy got close to his uncle's horse the uncle will scream "hatt! hatt!" and the mare will find another gear and go faster. Al Riyah, ahead of Al Hadeer, had just made the turn when she passed the white steed, and as on cue she whinnied at Al Hadeer.

The boy made the turn and on the straight line back Azeez realized that he is behind and he might lose the race. As he pushed Al Hadeer to gallop faster, Azeez brought up memories of his riding in the desert, free and against the wind, and he remembered how Al Hadeer always responded to his encouragement, so he dropped the reins, patted Al Hadeer twice on each side of his neck, then he shouted, "Allah Akhbar! Allah Akhbar! Allah is great! Allah is great! ".

Upon hearing this divine call Al Hadeer gathered all his remaining energy, and then just nearing the finish line, he galloped past Al Riyah finishing the race only a few feet ahead of the mare. Azeez knew in his heart that this magnificent steed had been guided by the hand of Allah the Almighty!

Hearing the jubilation of the crowd and the cheers, many tears of joy began to stream down the cheek of

Azeez, tears of pride as he realized that he owned a true race horse. After being congratulated by his father and his uncle, and the many people in the crowd, Azeez led Al Hadeer to walk a bit, and then to give him his well deserved treat of dates and milk.

While leading his beloved Al Hadeer, a voice from the crowd following him was heard.

"Mabrouk yah Azeez. Mashallah, Mashallah, may Allah keep you both safe."

It was the young boy that he fought with from the Bin Wathel tribe. Once he heard about the trial race the boy wanted to see by his own eyes how fast was the horse of his competitor.

The boy said to Azeez, "There is no need to have the race in fifteen days. After witnessing the speed of Al Hadeer, I am humbled to say that I do not believe that Kahar will ever beat Al Hadeer and for now, with the blessing of the Bin Wathel tribe leaders, all our conditions are met. I do hope with the permission of Allah that we can become friends and enjoy our horses together peacefully."

Azeez embraced his new friend, and then fell to his knees in praises to Allah for all his good fortune and many blessings.

Hikayat al Mahrousseh

The Story of the Protected One

"Appreciate what you have.

Respect your horse.

Treat each one kindly,

and you will receive

in return

an inner satisfaction

that cannot be

bought or described."

– Bachir Bserani

Every Muslim dreams of one day to make the pilgrimage to the holy city of Mecca, called the Hajj. Thus he will be closer to heaven. It is a long and difficult journey for most. When an old man from Hamah, Syria went to the Hajj, he had finally realized his lifelong dream. At peace with himself and Allah, he returned to his tribe.

Upon his return he learned that his beloved mare Mahrousseh, meaning The Protected One, was sold to the Pasha of Egypt. The Pasha had been travelling through when his eyes touched upon the beauty of this mare. During the absence of the old man, the son was lured by the large sum of money that was offered for Mahrousseh. The old man told his son that he did a great wrong, and that he will reclaim Mahrousseh if it be the will of Allah.

The old man travelled for months on foot from Damascus to Cairo stopping at every village or tribe to rest, and for food and water. He travelled as he could through the desert heat in the day time, and even at times during the cold of night. He was in general treated well along the way, but at his arrival to Cairo he was very tired, hungry, and sick.

Upon approaching the palace of Barjah, he was denied entrance. He pleaded with the guard that he must see the Pasha. It was of great importance. Looking like a beggar he was denied again. The old man asked to see the stables of the Pasha and when given the direction he went and slept outside at the horses' compound to rest, and then a time later went to look for his beloved Mahrousseh.

Every time the Pasha came to the stable to admire his horses or ride them he could see from a distance the old man with a cane wandering about, as if a lost soul.

On one of the visits by the Pasha, he asked to the guard, "This old man with the cane, why is he always at the stables. Is he perhaps one of the workers who take care of my horses? Why does he seem so sad? "

The guard replied to the Pasha, "This old man come from the land of Syria to see the Pasha of Egypt, and he refused to go back until he speak with you, my Sire."

The Pasha who was a fair man was very disturbed that an old man is treated this way. He ordered for the guard to bring the old man before him. When he was in front of the Pasha he was asked what were his wishes.

The Pasha said, "Why, my guest, is it so important to talk to the Pasha? "

The old man answered in a very weak voice, "I am here to buy back my mare Mahrousseh. She was sold by my son to you, my Sire, without my blessing while I was at the Holy City."

The Pasha apologized to him knowing what this man went through, knowing the suffering he has endured. Then the Pasha gently told him, "But my friend, your mare is with my other mares and if you come with me and look at my horses you will see that I have two hundred of them in the pasture. How will you recognize your mare to get her back? What if you pick the wrong mare? Would it be fair to both of us?"

The old man answered, "Sire you are correct, I will not recognize my mare as her colors and markings are similar to many of your mares that are in the pasture."

And with a voice choked with tears he told the kind Pasha, "Sire if I do not know my mare, it is my mare that will know me. And if she does not I will yet return your money and Mahrousseh will remain here for you. And I will never claim her again.

The Pasha was moved by the devotion of this gentle man. He went on foot with him to the pasture, and then the old man shouted with his weak voice, "Ya Mahrousseh, Ya Mahrousseh, Oh Protected one, Oh Protected One!"

Only one beautiful pure white mare called back to him while trotting swiftly toward him. The old man put his arms out towards the mare. She came to him, and then slowly walked up between his outstretched arms, then placed her head gently against his chest.

The old man cried, "Pasha, this is my Mahrousseh." The old man lovingly patted her neck, and then he reached to the side of the mare, gently stroking her. He could see that her belly had grown since he last saw her. Suddenly a soft kick could be felt from within. He took a step back a bit startled, and then said with a smile, "My sire, she has come back to me indeed, but with a most cherished gift, she is with foal!"

The Pasha shouted, "Mabrouk! Mabrouk! Mashallah! Congratulations! Congratulations! May Allah be with you!"

The old man handed to the Pasha the money in the leather pouch he was to return. The Pasha reached out to the old man and put his hands around the hands of the old man and the pouch.

The Pasha then said, "I thank you for your devotion to this divine creature. Please take your beloved Mahrousseh and return to your home, and take this pouch with you as well. Please take this as a gift from me so it will help you to return safely with your beloved Mahrousseh."

And so the old man returned to Damascus with Mahrousseh, his loyal friend and companion, guided by Allah the most gracious, the most merciful.

Hikayat Al Inteesar

The Story of the Conquest

Written pedigrees at the time of the Prophet Mohammed were non-existing. Every Bedouin, of course, knew their horses and their pedigree by heart. But with the increasing abundance and movement of the desert Arabian horse, whether by sale, gift or conquest throughout the Arabian Peninsula and beyond, beginning approximately in the year 1200 Hijri (1785 A.D.) written pedigrees to the Bedouin became important.

ritten pedigrees at the time of the Prophet Mohammed were non-existing. Every Bedouin, of course, knew their horses and their pedigree by heart. But with the increasing abundance and movement of the desert Arabian horse whether by sale, gift, or conquest throughout the Arabian Peninsula and beyond, beginning approximately in the year 1200 Hijri (1785 A.D.), written pedigrees to the Bedouin became important.

This story to follow has been carried down from this time period. It was first told to me by my grandfather when I was a young boy. We used to sit every night in the tent, and the elders would sip some teas, and my grandfather would ask to the young boys if a story should be told.

The memory brings a smile to my face as I was always the first to jump up with excitement. I so very much enjoyed to hear about the legends of our ancestors and their Arabian horses. And the story began ...

At one time the Shomar tribes roaming in the areas of Syria and Iraq, and traveling between these two countries as well as Lebanon, were in a vicious battle with another neighboring Bedouin tribe. This battle lasted for seven days and seven nights, with the Shomar tribe being victorious. As a reward for their victory, the Shomar tribe took sixty of the purest and most cherished Arabian horses from their enemy.

Many days passed and the defeated tribesmen had been repairing their tents, and mourning from all their casualties, and speaking of those they had buried, when one day they saw suddenly from the distance three horsemen. One sat upon a beautiful chestnut Arabian mare, another upon an exquisite bluish grey stallion, and the other rode an exotic dark bay mare.

The men of the tribe were always on alert and quickly realized that the horsemen were from the Shomar tribe, their enemy that just defeated them. Quickly they all prepared their weapons and mounted their steeds, ready to defend their tribe again. As the Shomar warriors approached, the tribesmen could see a white banner being carried by the man on the chestnut horse. This banner was a symbol from the Shomar warriors meaning, "We come in peace!"

One of the elder tribesmen, a Sheik, shouted to his men to lower their weapons. He said, "This is not the hospitality of the desert. Even though we were defeated by the Shomar, we must show them our respect. We must hear what they have come to say".

So the tribesmen lowered their weapons and they all made a circle around the Sheik who was being shaded under a large tent. An opening was left in the circle of men for the three warriors to enter. The riders cautiously entered into the circle, dismounted their horses and stood before the Sheik.

And the Sheik of the tribe asked them, "What is the occasion that we are having that you come to visit us?

Is it not enough that you have defeated us in battle and stolen our most prized Arabian stallions and mares."

One of the warriors shouted, "We are here to request the pedigree of those horses; their name, their origin, their breeding. "

Well, of course, the young men surrounding the Sheik

jumped forward with their hand on their daggers, ready to fight. The Sheik raised his hand and then lowered it, motioning the men to be at ease and he then said, "These warriors are coming here for a reason".

He then ordered to be retrieved the written pedigrees of the sixty horses. And so the papers were brought to the Sheik who took them, then held them up above his head, to Allah. One by one the Sheik gave the paper to the enemy.

When all the sixty papers were given the Sheik turned and shouted to his tribesmen, "These horses were won by conquest and are now the property of the Shomar tribe. The Shomar will honor these creatures as we have honored them and their sacred bloodlines will endure."

He then turned back to the enemy warriors and said, "Now go in peace". The three warriors mounted their steeds, retreated from the circle and rode off into the desert. Now the young warriors were shouting to their leader asking how this could be, and how unfair this was to just give to the enemy the pedigrees of the Arabians.

The Sheik responded, "If the Shomar took our

horses without the paper with the bloodlines, and without the beautiful names we bestowed to our beloved Arabian horses, our prized mares and stallions would be lost, and all that we worked our life to maintain, that our ancestors have handed to us, the purity of the Arab horse will be lost. With the Shomar having the pedigrees, the bloodlines can continue on. If another tribe were to defeat the Shomar and claim those Arabian horses, then as by the law of the desert, the papers will be passed on again. In time, maybe you here will see these horses come back to us."

And the tribesmen understood the Sheik's wisdom and that this wisdom that the elders possess is how the tribes have maintained the bloodlines and purity of the desert Arabian horse through the centuries.

There is a great respect for the wisdom of the elders and the customs of the desert.

And I am sure till now when you go to a stable, or you go to a tent in the Arabian desert, and somebody shows to you a beautiful Arabian ... you will be given the paper with the name of the horse and the bloodlines.

A Pure and True Translation of an Authentic Bedouin Pedigree

*Arabian horses in the desert are
cherished possessions and while a human
baby may not have a record of birth nor
a celebration, a Bedouin
will always record the birth of a
foal and have festivities.
When a foal is born all the witnesses
to the foaling will gather to
record every mark or distinction
the foal possesses
as well as the name of the sire and
of the dam. All this are kept in a
leather pouch that the foal will
carry around his neck from the
time he is weaned until the time
he reaches a year old.*

– Bachir Bserani

Name and Family Tree

In the name of Allah, most compassionate, most merciful. Praise and peace be on our Prophet Mohammed and His followers until judgment day, and peace be with whoever reads this testimony.

The foal from the ARMAD tribe, with four white socks and a white star on the forehead, from the SEGLAWEE strain, was given the name OBAYAN. His skin, like milk, is soft to the touch, he looks like the horses that the Prophet described in his Hadith and that Allah mentioned in his Holy Book.

This SEGLAWEE foal was bought by KASHROUN, the son of MOUHEET from the ANZAH tribe.

The sire of this foal is the pure KUHAYLAN stallion named MERJAN and his dam is the famous SEGLAWEYAH white mare called JARWAT.

We are witnesses to the above and that the purity of this foal surpasses his sire and dam. This is what we say, what we witnessed, and what we swear to regarding the above testimony and thanks to the Almighty.

Written on the 16th of January of the year 1220 Hijri

Witnesses:
Ahmad Al Arabi   Ameer Ibn Mahmood

The Arabian Dancing Horse

The art of training the Arabian Dancing Horse is a complicated and very skillful art that is not widely shared with the outside world.

The Arabian Desert played a fighting field to many Arabian tribes. To capture your imagination you must close your eyes and go back many centuries and imagine two powerful tribes declaring war on each other. Be it to recapture a lost honor or a payback for an unfortunate bad blood between them. Imagine a long line drawn in the sand and on either side a few feet away from each other were hundreds upon hundreds of horsemen riding the finest steeds in the land, all dressed with beautiful and colorful saddles, bridles and breastplates, all facing each other and ready for battle.

Visualize with me the many strains that formed these beautiful Bedouin armies. The Seglawi strain horses with their breathtaking beauty, the Obeyan with their stocky and strong frame, the Kuhaylan with their beautiful and shiny mane and tail. Visualize with me and listen to the sound of battle, the cry of the riders, the zalgouta (shouting loudly with the rolling of the tongue) of the woman from a distance encouraging her fighter to be strong, and fight with courage and determination. At the end of one line are several men with tablat (large drums) and mazzameer (flutes). On the other end of the line is the same set up of drums and flutes belonging to the opposite tribe. These musicians are beating the tablat and playing the mazzameer, creating music that is lively and along with the gentle urging of their riders start prancing in place, swaying with the music, shaking their head up and down, collecting their body, and telling their rider they are ready to go. *This* is the Arabian dancing horse.

After the battle, the winning tribe would celebrate. They showed off the many horses they acquired as a result of winning the battle and the festivity and the dances would begin. Into the crowd came those beautiful horses to perform their dance. The crowd exalted, the applaud was constant, the drums would beat steadily, and the flutes from a distance urged everybody, horses and human, to enjoy the moment, for what they accomplished was beyond description.

This is the history of the Arabian dancing horse. It originated from the Gazou (*raids*) or Harb (*battles*). Following from this history there continues to be shown off the Arabian dancing horse in happy occasions like important guest appearances, competitions, weddings, or any festive celebration. The dancing horse could be from any strain. What is most important is that some horses will show from their early age a very keen ear to music. And

Arab men playing their tablat (large drums) and mazzameer (flutes) at a wedding celebration in Egypt. Photo is taken from actual video footage.

the Bedouin who are good horsemen, and who have a keen knowledge of the horse and its structure will decide which horse will be trained from a tender age to be a dancing horse to perform in many happy occasions.

The outside world has admired, raised, and bred the Arabian horse. They have trained these horses to do almost anything from showing in a ring to endurance riding, to racing, to driving, to cutting, to dressage, to jumping and to every equitation or riding discipline that there is. The only thing that has not been successfully accomplished in this country and Europe and by those not from the Middle East is having trained an Arabian horse to dance. And this I believe, is because the art of training the Arabian dancing horse is a complicated and very skillful art that is not widely shared with the outside world. The delicate and masterful training of the dancing horse starts at the age of three and it takes one year plus for this talented young horse to learn the basic fundamentals of the movement. Much patience is needed during this process. And it should be noted that those horses, when they are selected to be a dancing horse, will be trained solely for that purpose.

We first teach those horses to salute by raising their front leg and bowing. Then we start teaching them to move in place to the beat of the drums. The horse must have an elastic back, be able to take instructions, and remember them day in and day out. The slightest sound, the slightest drum beat, the slightest noise, will make the Arabian dancing horse react. From a young age in Syria, I was fascinated with the dancing horse. My first encounter with these magnificent performers was in a town called Hama which is approximately 150 kilometers north of Damascus. I was invited with my family to a big wedding. The father of the bride was an old acquaintance to my family.

When we arrived a few minutes late the tents were erected, the guests were all seated, the music was playing. The beat of the drums, coordinated with the flutes, was exalting the crowd to clap their hands and stomp their feet to the rhythm. We were received with *zagaleet* (many women making loud sound with their voice and tongue). And our places were secured near the bride's family. The bride and the groom all dressed up, were seated at the center at the other end of the tent. The belly dancers were encouraging the crowd to get involved with the music and festivity. The atmosphere was electrifying. Suddenly, the announcer asked the crowd to keep their eyes on the entrance of the big tent.

As the music raised its pitch, a beautiful pure white Arabian horse all dressed up in the finest Bedouins headset, breastplate, and a blue Arabian handmade saddle entered the tent prancing to the beat of the music. Not one person in the crowd was seated. All eyes were on this beautiful Arabian horse with his simply dressed rider making an entrance of a King with a steed that God gave beauty and arrogance beyond description. My heart stopped. My eyes were mesmerized on this Divine combination. My feet were moving to the rhythm that the horse and the music created. It was then I decided that I will seek knowledge from the best horsemen to learn the art of teaching Arabian horses how to dance.

After studying under a few Bedouin masters, watching them, listening to their instruction, I was able to train successfully my own Arabian. I trained my dancing Arabian horse in Damascus where I had my horses stabled. We participated in competitive performances that were held annually at *Nadee al Feroussiah*, the riding club. The dancing horses came from all over the Middle East. We performed under tents with many spectators enjoying the festivities.

The photos above and below are from video footage of a traditional wedding held in a small town north of Alexandria, Egypt, in 2004. This beautiful dancing horse was presented by the groom's family at the celebration to honor the bride, her family and guests.

Bachir Bserani with his horse, Don Diablo (Dee), in the early stages of training to be an Arabian Dancing Horse.

In the United States I was lucky to own an Arabian horse that was sensitive to music. And from the time I purchased him when he was three years old I worked with him teaching him the fundamentals. And his intelligence, obedience and his natural head carriage made my job so much easier. He was a delight of the neighbors, and many who knew my Arabian horse, endearingly called "Dee", could not have enough of watching him perform to the music. Dee was featured in 1988 on a local television show as *The Dancing Horse* from Pompey, a suburb of Syracuse, New York.

The training of the Arabian Dancing Horse must be done by a Master. This is very important as the young horse could learn many bad habits that might be extremely difficult to correct later on. The training starts with the horse being at a tender age of three to four years old. For one year we teach him with patience how to carry himself with the utmost supple back, proper balance, and many, many hours under the saddle with suppling exercises. When the time arrives we start playing Arabic music with lively rhythm. We will watch our horse's ears and eyes. They will tell us the scope of his desire to move with the music.

Then after a year we take him in the box. This is set up with ground poles placed 24 feet apart, closed at all the corners, except one whereby to enter or exit. We will work him first on the ground. We settle our pupil, play the Arabic music and with a light stick or whip start tapping his front legs one at a time following the rhythm of the music. Once we get a positive result we stop, take him to his stall and reward him. We follow this procedure for a month with daily work, or as long as necessary. Usually before very long, we suddenly realize that this most talented horse is picking up his diagonal feet almost together. During the training we must hold him with the reins, keep his head set, and do not let the horse move forward or back to avoid work. With my late horse, *Don Diablo*, I reached a point that his head was set almost vertical to the ground and I could tap with my stick on the ground when I am beside him while moving my feet and he will follow his movement with the rhythm of the music being played. After a month or two depending on the horse, we then proceed to mounted exercises.

As I mentioned, the process of teaching an Arabian horse to dance is difficult and demanding. It must be done only by a Master horseman. I am taking the liberty to share my own experience and knowledge about this fine art of riding and presenting your beautiful Arabian. Once you have witnessed the beauty and the elegance of a dancing horse not only will you be taken to a different level of performance, but you will realize, of course, why the Arabian horse is considered by many around the world as the most beautiful gift that *Allah* bestowed upon humankind.

Authentic Arabian Horse Names

Volume II

Special Note

El or Al, meaning *The*, could be used preceding
most names to give the horse more *Admiration*, *Dignity* and *Power*.
El is used in Egypt and North Africa.
Al is used in the Middle East.
For example:
El Marees (colt): The South Wind
Al Bahieh (filly): The Shining One

Ibn (Son of) and Bint (Daughter of) could precede
the name to *Honor* or *Give Closeness* to a founding mare or stallion.
For Example:
Ibn Al Moubarak: Son of the Blessed One
Bint El Salam: Daughter of the Peace

Bint Bint Shams: Granddaughter of the Sun
Ibn Ibn Wahm: Grandson of the Illusion

Some words can be used in combination
for a more descriptive name.
For Example:
Amir Al Zeel: Prince of the Shadow

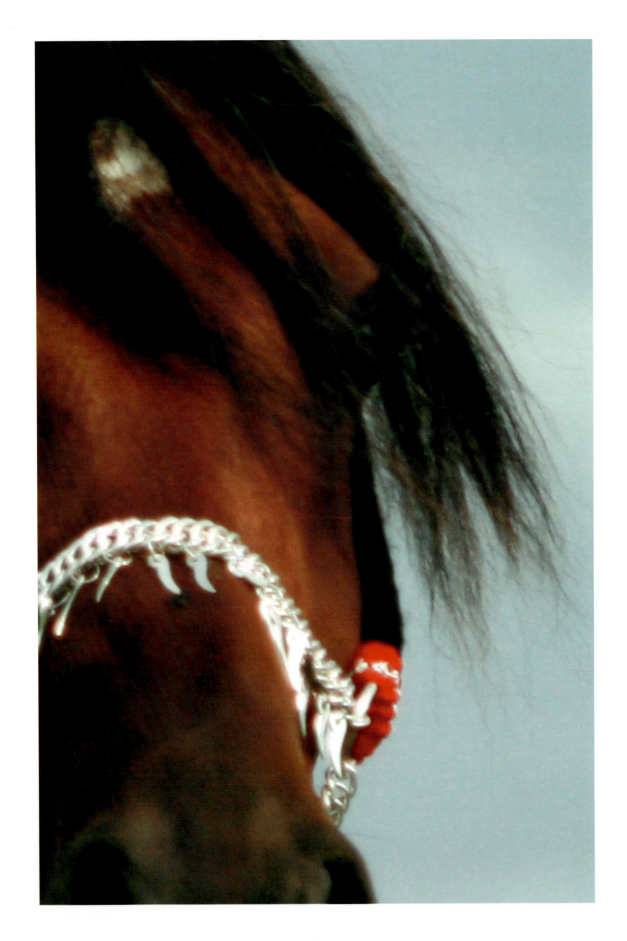

Using the Dictionary

This dictionary is divided into two sections:
Arabic – English and *English – Arabic*.

In observing the headings at the top of each page
you will note that all of the pages on the left are
"*Mouher*" or names for the colt, in the masculine form.
Likewise all of the right hand pages are
"*Mouhra*" or names for the filly in the feminine form.
Words are listed alphabetically with each letter of the
alphabet having its own heading for easy use.

If we are to honor the Arabian horses of today in the
same way they have been honored for centuries past,
please carefully consider your name selection.
When choosing an authentic Arabic name,
I would encourage you to please keep in mind the
guidelines that I have outlined over
the next few pages.

Guidelines to Follow When Choosing an Arabic Name

1- Give your foal a name only after its birth.
To name a foal before its birth in the desert, for the Bedouins, it is bad luck. The characteristics, markings, colors, etc. of the foal are favorable to consider when selecting the name.

2- Choose a name unique to your foal. Never choose to name a foal the same name as a famous person, or a person well known to you. This will not be honorable, and may cause confusion.
For Example:
I am known to you. My name is Bachir meaning, *One Who Brings Good News*. If this meaning is desirable the following names will be appropriate for your foal:
MOUBASHER pronounced *MOO-BAH-SHER* or
AL BACHIR pronounced *AHL-BAH-SHEER*.
Both of these names maintain the meaning of *One Who Brings Good News*, yet are a different form of my name Bachir.

3- Be cautious when combining two Arabic names when naming your foal. When possible seek the advice of a native Arabic speaker or scholar.
For Example:
These names, when used with another Arabic word that starts with a vowel, will change slightly.
NEGMAH – STAR
NEGMAT AL HAYAT – THE STAR OF LIFE
AROUSSAH – BRIDE
AROUSSAT AL SAHRAH – THE DESERT BRIDE

4- Never gather letters from the Sire's name and Dam's name and try to form a name that could have no meaning or be comical, or embarrassing. This practice is widely used in the United States and abroad, and in my opinion, for the sake of your Arabian horses, should be completely abandoned.

5- Never give a foal a combination of an Arabic and a Romantic language (English, Spanish, etc.) name.
For Example:
BEAUTY AL SAHRAH – THE DESERT BEAUTY

6- Never choose a name for a foal what was given in the past to a famous stallion of or mare, even if such a stallion or mare has passed away.

**7- Never assume that the name you have chosen cannot be duplicated. Keep in mind that the name that you have chosen may have different forms as the Arabic language is rich in dialect and varies from country to country (ex. Egypt, Syria, Iraq, Iran, and United Arab Emirates).

For Example:
HILAL – MOON *(literary)* pronounced *HEE-LAHL*
KAMAR – MOON *(dialect)* pronounced *KAH-MAHR*
AJOUZ – OLD *(literary)* pronounced *AH-JOOZ*
KEITYARAH – OLD *(dialect)* pronounced *KEY-TEE-YAH-RAH*

8- Never give a colt a filly's name and vice versa. Always check with a knowledgeable person or source before finalizing your choice.

9-Avoid giving your foal an Arabic name with lettering that is difficult to pronounce.

For Example:
MESAOUD or *MASSOOD*
If not pronounced correctly the meaning will be changed. In my books Authentic Arabian Horse Names Volume I and II, most of the names chosen are easy to pronounce for a non-Arabic speaking person.

10- Never hesitate to ask help from Arabic scholars, but make sure they also have the knowledge of your language so they can understand the meaning of what you are trying to say when naming your foal. The BIG question is "Where to go for help?"

Author's Note :

— There are many sources on the internet, both good and bad. I advise checking with an Arabic speaking person or scholar about the correct use of the name.
I do provide this service through our website.
Please visit www.al-moussami.com for more information.

— Many horse discussion forums have members from around the world who speak Arabic and may answer your questions regarding the use of the Arabic language.

— Try to find publications that list Arabic names for horses. I am aware that there are not many. One such true Arabian horse names book, titled *Names of Arabian Horses and Their Riders*, was written by Ibn Al Eiraby Mohamad Ibn Ziad who passed away in 231 Hajri. This book was later translated and printed by an Italian scholar, Giorgio Louis Dalawida, from the University of Rome in the town of Lidden in 1928. And of course, there is my first publication, *Authentic Arabian Horse Names*, by Bachir Bserani with Kellie Kolodziejczyk.

— I strongly suggest that you stay away from an Arabic dictionary due to the difficulty of sounds for certain letters in the Arabic alphabet. It took two years to complete my first book due to the difficulty with working with only 17 letters out of more than 30 letters that exist in the Arabic alphabet. My goal was to find easy to prounounce words for a non-Arabic speaking person. Do not make it complicated. Keep it simple and poetic.

Arabic ~ English

In the Arabic language there are words for the male and female horse which describe the horse at various ages from birth to adult.

THE FEMALE HORSE:
At birth she is called
MUHRAH or *MOUHRA* meaning *FOAL*
At weaning she is called *HAWLI*
A one year old is *JADE*
A two and three year old is called *THANI*
Upon the fourth year *RIB'I*
And at five years old and beyond
she is called *QUAREHAH*

THE MALE HORSE:
At birth he is called
MUHR or *MOUHER* meaning *FOAL*
At weaning he is called *HAWLI*
A one year old is *JADE*
A two and three year old is called *THANI*
Upon the fourth year *RIB'I*
And at five years old and beyond
he is called *QUAREH*

Mouher (Colt)

ARABIC	PRONUNCIATION	TRANSLATION
~ A ~		
AATSHAN	AAT-SHAN	THIRSTY
ABADEE	AH-BAH-DEE	EVERLASTING
ABADI	AH-BAH-DEE	ETERNAL
ABAHWEE	AH-BAH-WEE	PATERNAL
ABOUNAH	AH-BU-NAH	REVERAND FATHER
ABSAHRAH	AHB-SAH-RAH	TO SEE, TO LOOK AT
ABSHARAH	AHB-SHAH-RAH	TO REJOICE AT
ADAHBEE	AH-DAH-BEE	MORAL, ETHICAL
ADEEB	AH-DEEB	EDUCATED
ADEED	AH-DEED	MANY
ADHAM	AD-HAM	DARK COLOR
ADNAH	AHD-NAH	NEAR TO SOMEONE
AHAD	AH-HAD	ONE
AHDEB	AH-DEB	WRITER, AUTHOR
AHKBAR	AHK-BAR	GREATER, BIGGER
AHRDEE	AHR-DEE	MY LAND, TERRESTIAL
AHREEJ	AH-REEJ	FRAGRANCE, SCENT
AHSEE	AH-SEE	TOUGH
AHSEL	AH-SEL	ORIGIN
AHSSAHSS	AH-SSAHSS	BASIS, FOUNDATION
AHZGAHR	AHZ-GAHR	SMALLER, YOUNGER
AJAHD	AH-JAHD	TO EXCEL
AJAJ	AH-JAJ	POWERFUL
AKALIYAH	AH-KAH-LEE-YAH	MINORITY
AKEED	AH-KEED	CERTAIN, FOR SURE
AKHAL	AHK-HAL	BLACK EYED
AKHAWEE	AH-KHA-WEE	BROTHERLY
AKHEE	AH-KEE	MY BROTHER
AKHEER	AH-KHEER	LAST, FINAL
AKRAB	AHK-RAHB	CLOSE TO SOMEONE
AKRASH	AHK-RASH	LARGE BELLY
AKSAH	AHK-SAH	EXTREME, UMOST

Mouhra (Filly)

ARABIC	PRONUNCIATION	TRANSLATION
\~ A \~		
ABADIYAH	AH-BAH-DEE-YAH	ETERNAL EXISTENCE
ADAHMIYAH	AH-DAH-MEE-YAH	HUMAN LIKE
ADEEBAH	AH-DEE-BAH	EDUCATED
AHLAM AL OUMR	AH-LAM-AL-OOMR	THE DREAM OF A LIFETIME
AHLAN WASAHLAN	AH-LAN-WA-SAH-LAN	WELCOME
AHSLEEYAH	AHS-LEE-YAH	AUTHENTIC
AHYAT	AH-YAHT	MIRACLE, WONDER
AJEERAH	AH-JEE-RAH	EMPLOYEE, WORKER
AJNAHBIYAH	AHJ-NAH-BEE YAH	FOREIGN
AKAHLIYAH	AH-KAH-LEE-YAH	MINORITY
AKSOUSSAH	AHK-SOO-SAH	SHORT STORY
AKTHARIYAH	AHK-THA-REE-YAH	MAJORITY
AL AKRAB	AL-AHK-RAB	THE CLOSER ONE
AL AMEERA AL RAQUASSA	AL-AH-MEE-RAH-AL-RAH-QUAH-SSAH	THE DANCING PRINCESS
AL AMS	AL-AHMS	YESTERDAY
AL AROUSS	AL-AH-ROOS	THE BRIDE
AL ARZAH	AL-AHR-ZAH	CEDAR TREE
AL AWSAT	AL-AW-SAT	THE MIDDLE
AL BADEEYAH	AL-BAH-DEE-YAH	THE DESERT
AL BADOU	AL-BAH-DOO	THE BEDOUINS
AL BEEDAYAH	AL-BEE-DAH-YAH	THE BEGINNING
AL HELWAH	AL-HEL-WAH	THE BEAUTIFUL ONE
AL IHTEEZAZ	AL-IH-TEE-ZAZ	THE SHAKE, THE SWING
AL IHTEEMAM	AL-IH-TEE-MAM	THE CONCERN
AL JABBARAH	AL-JAH-BAH-RAH	POWERFUL
AL JAZIRAH	AL-JAH-ZEE-RAH	THE ISLAND
AL KHAJOULEH	AL-KAH-JOO-LEH	THE TIMID ONE
AL MAJEEDAH	AL-MAH-JEE-DAH	THE GLORIOUS ONE
AL MOUNTAZARAH	AL-MOON-TAH ZAH-RAH	THE LONG AWAITED ONE
AL MOUTAKABIRAH	AL-MOO-TAH-KAH-BEE-RAH	THE PROUD ONE
AL NEEMRAH JAMEELA	AL-NEEM-RAH-JAH-MEE-LAH	THE BEAUTIFUL TIGRESS
AL OUGNEEYAH	AL-OUG-NEE-YAH	THE SONG

Mouher (Colt)

ARABIC	PRONUNCIATION	TRANSLATION
AKSAHR	AHK-SAR	SHORTER
AKSOUSSAH	AHK-SOO-SAH	SHORT STORY
AKTAR	AHK-TAHR	MORE THAN
AKTARIYAH	AHK-TAH-REE-YAH	MAJORITY
AL AHWAHL	AL-AH-WAHL	THE FIRST ONE
AL ANEED	AL-AH-NEED	THE STUBBORN ONE
AL BATTAL	AL-BAH-TAL	THE HERO, THE FEARLESS ONE
ALEEF	AH-LEEF	DOMESTIC, TAMED
ALF	AHLF	A THOUSAND
AL FARASS AL HARBI	AL-FAH-RAHS-AL-HAR-BEE	THE WAR HORSE
ALF BARAKAH	AHLF-BAH-RAH-KAH	A THOUSAND BLESSINGS
ALF SADEEK	AHLF-SAH-DEEK	A THOUSAND FRIENDS
AL GHARB	AL-GARB	THE WEST
ALI	AH-LEE	HIGH ONE, ELEVATED
ALI JAMEEL	AH-LEE-JAH-MEEL	BEAUTIFUL AND ELEVATED
AL JANOUBEE	AL-JAH-NOO-BEE	THE SOUTH WIND
AL KAMEL	AL-KAH-MEL	THE PERFECT ONE
AL LAHAB	AL-LAH-HAB	THE ONE WHO LIGHTS THE FLAME
AL MAHAB	AL-MAH-HAB	THE SURGE
AL MALHOUZ	AL-MAL-HOOZ	THE MARKED ONE
ALMAZ	AHL-MAZ	DIAMOND
AL MOUBAKKER	AL-MOO-BAH-KER	THE EARLY ONE
AL MOUHAREB AL ASIL	AL-MOO-HAH-REB-AL-AH-SEEL	THE PURE WARRIOR
AL MOUNTASSER	AL-MOON-TAH-SER	THE VICTORIOUS, THE CONQUEROR
AL NAR	AL-NAR	THE FIRE
AL RASSOUL	AL-RAH-SOOL	THE PROPHET
AL SAMED	AL-SAH-MED	THE ONE WHO STANDS WITH PRIDE
AL SHARQ	AL-SHARK	THE EAST
AL WAHAB	AL-WAH-HAB	THE GIVER
AMAHMEE	AH-MAH-MEE	FIRST (IN FRONT)
AMAM	AH-MAM	IN FRONT
AMAN	AH-MAN	SAFETY, SECURITY
AMANAH	AH-MAH-NAH	FAITHFULNESS, LOYALTY

Mouhra (Filly)

ARABIC	PRONUNCIATION	TRANSLATION
AL OUMTHOULAH	AL-OUM-THOO-LAH	THE LESSON, THE EXAMPLE
AL SHARK	AL-SHARK	THE EAST
ALEEFAH	AH-LEE-FAH	TAMED, DOMESTICATED
ALF BARAKAH	ALF-BAH-RAH-KAH	A THOUSAND BLESSINGS
ALF HOUB	ALF-HOOB	A THOUSAND LOVE'S
ALF SHOUKRAN	ALF-SHOO-KRAHN	A THOUSAND THANK YOU'S
ALMASAH JASSIRAH	AL-MAH-SAH-JAH-SEE-RAH	RARE JEWEL
ALMAZAH	AL-MAH-ZAH	DIAMOND
ALMAZAT AL OYOUN	AL-MAH-ZAT-AHL-OU-YOON	THE DIAMOND OF THE EYE
AMAL	AH-MAL	HOPE
AMANAT	AH-MAH-NAT	TRUST
AMANAT AL SOUR	AH-MAH-NAT-AHL-SOOR	CONFIDENT
AMEENAH	AH-ME-NAH	SECURE, TRUSTED, FAITHFUL
AMEENAT AL ALB	AH-ME-NAT-AHL-ALB	THE TRUST OF THE HEART
AMEERAH	AH-ME-RAH	PRINCESS
AMEERATI	AH-MEE-RAH-TEE	MY PRINCESS
AMERIKIYAH	AH-MEH-REE-KEY-YAH	AMERICAN (GIRL)
AMINAT HAYATEE	AH-MEE-NAT-HAH-YAH-TEE	THE ONE TRUSTED WITH MY LIFE
AMIRAT AL AYLOUL	AH-MEE-RAT-AL-AY-LOOL	THE QUEEN OF SEPTEMBER
AMIRAT AL JABAL	AH-MEE-RAT-AL-JAH-BAL	PRINCESS OF THE MOUNTAIN
AMLAHSIYAH	AHM-LAH-SEE-YAH	SMOOTH, SLEEK
ANEEKAH	AH-NEE-KAH	ELEGANT
ANEESAH	AH-NEES-AH	FRIENDLY, TAMED
ANMASH	AHN-MASH	FRECKLED
ANOUF	AH-NOOF	PROUD, DISDAINFUL
ARISTOCRATEEYAH	AH-RIS-TOE-CRAH-TEE-YAH	ARISTOCRAT
ASEERAT AL ALB	AH-SEE-RAT-AL-ALB	THE PRISONER OF THE HEART
ASFOURAH	AHS-FOO-RAH	BIRDIE
ASIRAH	AH-SEE-RAH	CAPTURED, TAKEN
ASIRAH	AH-SEE-RAH	PRISONER, CAPTIVE
ASSAHSSIYAH	AH-SSAH-SSEE-YAH	ORIGINAL, FIRST
ASSILAH	AH-SEE-LAH	OF NOBLE ORIGIN
AWLAHWIYAH	AW-LAH-WEE-YAH	PRIORITY

Mouher (Colt)

ARABIC	PRONUNCIATION	TRANSLATION
AMEEN	AH-MEEN	TRUSTWORTHY
AMEEN-SEYREE	AH-MEEN-SAY-REE	THE GUARDIAN OF MY SECRET
AMEER AL GHARB	AH-MEER-AL-GHARB	THE PRIDE OF THE WEST
AMER	AH-MER	COMMANDER, CHIEF
AMIR AL FERAR	AH-MEER-AL-FEE-RAR	PRINCE OF ESCAPE
AMIRI	AH-MEE-REE	MY PRINCE
ANTAR AL MAJEED	AN-TAR-AL-MAH-JEED	WARRIOR OF THE NOBLE ONE
ARISTOCRATI	AH-RIS-TOE-CRAH-TEE	ARISTOCRATIC
ASAHLAH	AH-SAH-LAH	ORIGINALITY
ASASSEE	AH-SAH-SSEE	FUNDAMENTAL, BASIC
ASEER	AH-SEER	PRISONER, CAPTIVE
ASEER	AH-SEER	CAPTURED, ARRESTED
ASFAL	AS-FAL	LOWER
ASHKAR	AHSH-KAHR	BLOND, FAIR
ASHYAB	AHSH-YAHB	GRAY HAIRED
ASLAMAH	AHS-LAH-MAH	TO EMBRACE ISLAM
ASLEE	AHS-LEE	AUTHENTIC
ASMAR	AHS-MAHR	BROWN, DARK
ASWAD AL OUYOUN	AS-WAD-AL-OO-YOON	THE BLACK EYED ONE
ATRASH	AT-RASH	DEAF
ATWAHL	AT-WALL	LONGER
AZAH	AH-ZAH	HARM, DAMAGE
AZAHL	AH-ZAHL	ETERNITY
AZAHLEE	AH-ZAH-LEE	AGELESS, ETERNAL
AZAN	AH-ZAN	CALL TO PRAYER
AZAR	AH-ZAR	MARCH (MONTH)
AZMAH	AHZ-MAH	CRISIS
AZRAK	AHZ-RAK	BLUE

~ B ~

BADAN	BAH-DAN	BODY, PHYSIQUE
BADANEE	BAH-DAH-NEE	PHYSICAL
BADAWI	BAH-DAH-WEE	NOMAD, BEDOUIN
BADEE	BAH-DEE	APPARENT, VISIBLE

Mouhra (Filly)

ARABIC	PRONUNCIATION	TRANSLATION
AYAT	AH-YAT	SIGN, TOKEN, SYMBOL
AYKOUNAH	AYE-KOO-NAH	ICON
AYLOOL	AYE-LOOL	SEPTEMBER (MONTH)
AZAHLEE	AH-ZAH-LEE	AGELESS, ETERNAL
AZAHLEEYAT AL WOUJOOD	AH-ZAH-LEE-YAHT-AL-WOO-JOOD	THE ETERNAL EXISTENCE
AZALIYAH	AH-ZAH-LEE-YAH	ETERNITY
AZAMAH	AH-ZAH-MAH	GREATNESS

~ B ~

ARABIC	PRONUNCIATION	TRANSLATION
BADAHAH	BAH-DAH-HAH	SELF CONSCIOUS, SHY
BADAWIYAH	BAH-DAH-WEE-YAH	FEMALE BEDOUIN
BADIHIYAH	BAH-DEE-HEE-YAH	SELF EVIDENT
BADILAH	BAH-DEE-LAH	SUBSTITUTE
BADILAT AL MAHBOOB	BAH-DEE-LAT-AL-MAH-BOOB	THE SUBSTITUTE OF THE SWEET ONE
BADILAT AL OYOUN	BAH-DEE-LAT-AL-OYOUN	THE SUBSTITUTE OF THE EYES
BADIRAH	BAH-DEE-RAH	SIGN, INDICATION
BADIYAH	BAH-DEE-YAH	DESERT
BADR AL HAYAT	BADR-AL-HAH-YAT	THE MOON OF LIFE
BADR HAYATI	BADR-HAH-YAH-TEE	THE MOON OF MY LIFE
BAHEEJAH	BAH-HEE-JAH	HAPPY, PLEASANT
BAHILA	BAH-HEE-LAH	BRILLIANT
BAHIRAH	BAH-HEE-RAH	DAZZLING
BAHIYAH	BAH-HEE-YAH	BEAUTIFUL, GORGEOUS
BAHIZAH	BAH-HEE-ZAH	EXCESSIVE
BAHLAWANIYAH	BAH-LAH-WAH-NEE-YAH	ACROBATIC
BAHRAJAT	BAH-RAH-JAT	SHEER SPLENDOR
BALA BADEEL	BAH-LAH-BAH-DEEL	NO SUBSTITUTE
BALAT	BAH-LAT	BUNDLE
BANAFSAJIYAH	BAH-NAF-SAH-JEE-YAH	VIOLET COLOR
BARIDAH	BAH-REE-DAH	COLD, ICED
BAROONAH	BAH-ROO-NAH	BARONESS
BARRAKAH	BAHR-RAH-KAH	SPARKLING, SHINY
BARRIYAH	BAH-REE-YAH	TERRESTRIAL
BASHANA	BAH-SHAH-NAH	PRINCESS, LEADER OF THE TRIBE

Mouher (Colt)

ARABIC	PRONUNCIATION	TRANSLATION
BADEEHI	BAH-DEE-HEE	SELF-EVIDENT, OBVIOUS
BADEEL	BAH-DEEL	SUBSTITUTE, REPLACEMENT
BADR	BAH-DER	FULL MOON
BAHEET	BAH-HEET	PALE, NOT COLORFUL
BAHER	BAH-HER	DAZZLING, BRILLIANT
BAHEZ	BAH-HIZ	EXCESSIVE
BAHHAR	BAH-HAR	SAILOR, SEAMAN
BAHIJ	BAH-HEEJ	JOYFUL
BAHJAT	BAH-JAT	JOY, DELIGHT
BAHKR	BAHKR	FIRST BORN
BAHKSHISH	BAHK-SHEESH	TIP
BAHKTI	BAHK-TEE	GOOD LUCK, GOOD FORTUNE
BAHLASH	BAH-LAHSH	FREE
BAHSEK	BAH-SEK	HIGH, TALL
BAHSSAH	BAH-SAH	TO KISS
BAHZ	BAHZ	HAWK, FALCON
BAKHEEL	BAHK-KHEEL	STINGY, SPARING
BAKHOOR	BAH-KHOOR	INCENSE
BAKKAR	BAH-KAHR	TO RISE EARLY
BAKSHEESH	BAHK-SHEESH	GRATUITY
BAL	BAHL	ATTENTION
BALADI	BAH-LAH-DEE	NATIVE
BALAWANI	BAH-LAH-WAH-NEE	ACROBATIC
BALOOL	BAH-LOOL	JESTER, CLOWN
BALOOR	BAH-LOOR	CRYSTAL
BALOOT	BAH-LOOT	OAK
BANAFSAJ	BAH-NAF-SAJ	VIOLET
BARAAT	BAR-AAT	FIREFLY
BARAKAH	BAH-RAH-KAH	TO BLESS
BARBAREE	BAR-BAH-REE	BARBARIAN
BARED	BAH-RED	COLD
BARED AL ALWAN	BAH-RED-AL-AL-WAN	THE CLEAR COLORS
BAREEJAH	BAH-REE-JAH	WAR SHIP, BATTLE SHIP

Mouhra (Filly)

ARABIC	PRONUNCIATION	TRANSLATION
BASHARIYAH	BAH-SHAH-REE-YAH	MANKIND, PEOPLE
BASHASHAH	BAH-SHAH-SHAH	CHEERFULNESS
BASHOOSHAH	BAH-SHOO-SHAH	CHEERFUL
BASIKAH	BAH-SEE-KAH	HIGH TAIL
BASSALAH	BAH-SAH-LAH	COURAGE, BRAVERY
BASSARAH	BAH-SAH-RAH	FORTUNE TELLER
BASSIRAH	BAH-SEE-RAH	ENDOWED WITH EYESIGHT
BASSISSAT AL AMAL	BAH-SEE-SAT-AL-AH-MAL	THE GLIMPSE OF HOPE
BASSMAH	BAHS-MAH	SMILE
BASSMAH ILAHIYAH	BAS-MAH-EE-LAH-HEE-YAH	DIVINE SMILE
BASSMAT AL NEFOUS	BAS-MAT-AL-NEH-FOOS	THE IMPRINT OF THE SOUL
BATALA	BAH-TAH-LAH	HERO
BATALAH	BAH-TAH-LAH	HEROINE, CHAMPION
BATALAT AL DAR	BAH-TAH-LAT-AL-DAHR	THE DAUGHTER OF THE HOME
BATTASHAH	BAH-TAH-SHAH	DESTRUCTIVE
BAWSAT	BAW-SAT	KISS
BAYAHD AL NAHAR	BAH-YAD-AL-NAH-HAR	THE LIGHT OF THE DAY
BAYNANAH	BAY-NAH-NAH	BETWEEN US
BEIT MOUBARAK	BEIT--MOO-BAH-RAK	BLESSED HOUSE
BEITAWIYAH	BEY-TAH-WEE-YAH	HOMEBODY (LIKES TO STAY HOME)
BERWAHZAT ALBEE	BER-WAH-ZAHT-AL-BEE	THE FRAME OF MY HEART
BIKRAH	BIK-RAH	MAIDEN, UNSPOILED
BINT	BEENT	DAUGHTER (OF)
BINT AL AJOUZ	BEENT-AL-AH-JOOZ	THE DAUGHTER OF THE OLD WISE ONE
BINT AL BADIYAH	BEENT-AL-BAH-DEE-YAH	THE DAUGHTER OF THE DESERT
BINT AL GHARB	BEENT-AL-GHARB	DAUGHTER OF THE WEST
BINT AL HAWAH	BEENT-AL-HAH-WAH	DAUGHTER OF THE WIND
BINT AL JENOUB	BEENT-AL-JEH-NOOB	DAUGHTER OF THE SOUTH
BINT AL KABIR	BEENT-AL-KAH-BEER	THE DAUGHTER OF THE GREAT ONE
BINT AL MALIK	BEENT-AL-MAH-LEEK	THE DAUGHTER OF THE KING
BINT AL NEFOUS	BEENT-AL-NEH-FOOS	THE DAUGHTER OF THE SOUL
BINT AL SHAMAL	BEENT-AL-SHAH-MAL	DAUGHTER OF THE NORTH
BINT AL SHARQ	BEENT-AL-SHARK	DAUGHTER OF THE EAST

Mouher (Colt)

ARABIC	PRONUNCIATION	TRANSLATION
BARMIL	BAR-MEEL	BARREL
BARR	BARR	LAND
BARRAD	BAH-RAD	ICE BOX
BARRAK	BAH-RAK	SHINING, SPARKLING
BARTEEL	BAR-TEEL	BRIBE
BASEL	BAH-SEL	BRAVE, BOLD
BASEM	BAH-SEM	SMILING
BASHA	BAH-SHAH	WELL RESPECTED
BASHAYER	BAA-SHAH-YER	GOOD OMENS
BASHBASH	BASH-BASH	A CHEERFUL SMILE
BASHEK	BAH-SHEK	SPARROW
BASHOOSH	BAH-SHOOSH	SMILING, BRIGHT FACE
BASSAR	BAH-SAR	FORTUNE TELLER
BASSAREF	BAH-SAH-REF	VISUAL, OPTICAL
BASSIR	BAH-SEER	ENDOWED WITH GOOD EYESIGHT
BASSISS	BAH-SEESS	SLOW GLITTER OR SPARKLE
BASSMAT	BASS-MAHT	IMPASSIONED
BATAL	BAH-TAL	HERO
BATAL ASIL	BAH-TAL-AL-AH-SEEL	THE PURE HERO
BATATAN	BAH-TAH-TAN	ABSOLUTE, DEFINITVE
BATOOL	BAH-TOOL	VIRGIN, PURE
BATTEL	BAH-TEL	VOID
BAYAN	BAH-YAN	SHOWN, COME TO VIEW
BEDOUN	BEE-DOON	BEYOND
BEDOUN THAMAN	BEE-DOON-THAH-MAN	BEYOND PRICE, PRICELESS
BEEKAR	BEE-KAHR	COMPASS
BERSHANAH	BER-SHAH-NAH	CAPSULE
BERWAHZ	BER-WAHZ	FRAME
BIL	BIL	DURING
BIRJEEM	BEER-JEEM	CLOVER, TREFOIL
BIZREH	BIZ-REH	SEED
BOOHAYRAH	BOO-HAY-RAH	LAKE, BODY OF WATER
BOOKHAR	BOO-KHAR	VAPOR, STEAM

Mouhra (Filly)

ARABIC	PRONUNCIATION	TRANSLATION
BOAHBOOHAH	BOAH-BOO-HAH	AFFLUENCE
BOODRAH	BOO-DRAH	POWDER
BOOHAYRAH	BOO-HAY-RAH	LAKE, BODY OF WATER
BOUMAH	BOO-MAH	OWL
BOUSHRAH	BOOSH-RAH	GOOD NEWS
BOUSTAN	BOOS-TAN	GARDEN
BOUSTANIYAH	BOOS-TAH-NEE-YAH	GARDENER
BRONZIYAH	BRON-ZEE-YAH	MADE OF BRONZE
BULBULAH	BOOL-BOO-LAH	NIGHTINGALE

~ D ~

ARABIC	PRONUNCIATION	TRANSLATION
DABAHBAH	DAH-BAH-BAH	TANK
DABBOURAH	DAH-BOO-RAH	HORNET, WASP
DABBOUSS ZAINEE	DAH-BOOSS-ZAI-NEE	SAFETY PIN
DABKA	DAB-KAH	MIDDLE EASTERN DANCE
DAHEEMAN	DAH-EE-MAN	ALL THE TIME
DAHFFAT	DAH-FAT	HELM
DAHFIRAT	DAH-FEE-RAT	PIGTAIL
DAHINAH	DAH-HEE-NAH	TO TALK SWEETLY
DAHIYAT	DAH-HEE-YAHT	MISFORTUNE, DISASTER
DAHLIAH	DAH-LEE-YAH	GRAPEVINE
DAHMA	DAH-MAH	DARK COLOR
DAHMAR	DAH-MAR	DESTRUCTION
DAHMISSAH	DAH-MEE-SAH	DARK, DEEP BLACK
DAHRAT	DAH-RAT	VILLA
DAHROURAT	DAH-ROO-RAT	NECESSITY, NEED
DAHSHAT	DAH-SHAT	ASTONISHMENT
DAHWARAH	DAH-WAH-RAH	TUMBLE DOWN
DAJAHJAH	DAH-JAH-JAH	HEN
DAJAHLAH	DAH-JAH-LAH	SWINDLER
DAJJINAH	DAH-JEE-NAH	TAME, DOMESTICATED
DALAHLAT	DAH-LAH-LAT	SIGNIFICANCE
DALAL	DAH-LAL	COQUETRY, FLIRT
DALEELAH	DAH-LEE-LAH	SYMBOL

Mouher (Colt)

ARABIC	PRONUNCIATION	TRANSLATION
BOORHAN	BOOR-HAN	PROOF, EVIDENCE
BOORJ	BOORJ	TOWER
BOORJ FALAKI	BOORJ-FAH-LAH-KEE	SIGN (OF THE ZODIAC)
BOOSHRAH	BOOSH-RAH	GOOD NEWS
BOUM	BOOM	OWL
BOURKAN	BOOR-KAHN	VOLCANO
BOURTHON	BOOR-THON	CLAW, TALON
BOURTOOKAL	BOOR-TOO-KAL	ORANGE (FRUIT)
BOURTOOKALEE	BOOR-TOO-KAH-LEE	ORANGE (COLOR)
BOUTOOLAT	BOO-TOO-LAT	CHAMPIONSHIP
BOUTOOLEH	BOO-TOO-LEH	HEROIC
BULBUL	BOOL-BOOL	NIGHTINGALE

~ D ~

ARABIC	PRONUNCIATION	TRANSLATION
DABBOUR	DAH-BOOR	WASP
DABBOUSS	DAH-BOOSS	PIN
DAHBAHB	DAH-BAHB	FOG, MIST
DAHFTAR	DAHF-TAR	NOTEBOOK
DAHHAN	DAH-HAN	PAINTER
DAHHEN	DAH-HEN	TO FLATTER
DAHIMAN	DAH-EE-MAN	ALWAYS, FOREVER
DAHJJAL	DAH-JAL	CHARLATAN, IMPOSTER
DAHLEEZ	DAH-LEEZ	CORRIDOR
DAHLIL	DAH-LEEL	GUIDE, LEADER
DAHMESS	DAH-MESS	DARK, DEEP BLACK
DAHOUB	DAH-OOB	PERSISTANT, DILIGENT
DAHR	DAHR	AGE, ERA
DAHRAKEE	DAH-RAH-KEE	POLICEMAN
DAJJEN	DAH-JEN	PARTIAL DARKNESS, GLOOMY
DALEEL	DAH-LEEL	SIGN, INDICATION
DALLAH	DAH-LAH	TO SHOW
DALLAL	DAHLAL	BROKER, AGENT
DALLALAH	DAH-LAH-LAH	TO PAMPER, TO SPOIL
DAMEER	DAH-MEER	CONSCIENCE

Mouhra (Filly)

ARABIC	PRONUNCIATION	TRANSLATION
DALLALAH	DAH-LAH-LAH	FEMALE AGENT, GUIDE
DAMDAMAH	DAM-DAH-MAH	TO MURMER
DAMEER AL WEJDAN	DAH-MEER-AL-WEJ-DAN	THE CONSCIENCE OF THE HEART
DANDANAH	DAN-DAH-NAH	TO CHANT
DAREEJAH	DAH-REE-JAH	POPULAR
DAREESSAH	DAH-REE-SSAH	SCHOLAR
DARFEEL	DAR-FEEL	DOLPHIN
DARWISHAH	DAHR-WEE-SHAH	SIMPLY HONEST
DASSISSAH	DAH-SEE-SAH	INTRIGUE
DAWAHMAH	DAH-WAH-MAH	SPINNING TOP
DAWAH	DAH-WAH	MEDICINE
DAWAHR	DAH-WAHR	WANDERING, AMBULENT
DAWAHR AL SHAMS	DAH-WAHR-AL-SHAMS	SUNFLOWER
DAWAHRAN	DAH-WAH-RAN	SPINNING, TURNING
DAWALEE	DAH-WAH-LEE	GRAPE LEAF
DAWASSAT	DAH-WAH-SSAT	ACCELERATOR
DAWRAT	DAW-RAT	ROUND
DAWREE	DAW-REE	PERIODIC, REGULAR
DAWREEYAT	DAW-REE-YAT	PATROL
DAYDAN	DAY-DAN	HABIT, CUSTOM
DAYEEMAH	DAH-YEE-MAH	ETERNAL
DAYNOONAT	DAY-NOO-NAT	LAST JUDGEMENT
DEEBAJ	DEE-BAJ	SILK BROCADE
DEEBAJAT	DEE-BAH-JAT	PREFACE
DEECOR	DEE-COR	DECORATION
DEELALAT	DEE-LAH-LAT	AUCTION, BROKERAGE
DEEMAD	DEE-MAHD	BANDAGE
DEEYAHNAT	DEE-YAH-NAT	RELIGION
DEIFAH	DEY-FAH	GUEST, VISITOR
DEIFALLAH	DEYF-AL-LAH	GOD'S VISITOR
DEWAHN	DEE-WAHN	COUNCIL, ASSEMBLY
DEYJOUR	DEY-JOOR	DARKNESS
DICTATORIAT	DIC-TAH-TOR-EE-AT	DICTATORSHIP

Mouher (Colt)

ARABIC	PRONUNCIATION	TRANSLATION
DAMMAR	DAH-MAR	DESTROYER
DAR	DAHR	HOME
DARDAR	DAR-DAR	ELM TREE
DAREE	DAH-REE	MY HOME
DAREJ	DAH-REJ	CURRENT
DARESS	DAH-RESS	STUDENT
DASTOUR	DAS-TOOR	CONSTITUTION
DAWAH	DAH-WAH	MEDICINE
DAWAHM	DAH-WAHM	CONTINUANCE
DAWAHMAH	DAW-WAH-MAH	TO TURN
DAWAHR	DAH-WAHR	ROTATING, REVOLVING
DAWAHR AL SHAMS	DAH-WAHR-AL-SHAMS	SUNFLOWER
DAWAHRAN	DAH-WAH-RAN	ROTATION
DAWRAK	DAW-RACK	FLASK
DAYEM	DAH-YEM	LASTING, PERMANENT
DAYNOONAT	DAY-NOON-NAT	LAST JUDGEMENT
DEEBAJ	DEE-BAJ	SILK GARMENT
DEENI	DEE-NEE	HOLY
DEERHAM	DEER-HAM	MONEY
DEEYAT	DEE-YAHT	BLOOD MONEY
DEIF	DEIF	GUEST
DEIF ALLAH	DEIF-AL-LAH	VISITOR FROM ALLAH
DEIF AL OYOUN	DEIF-AL-OYOON	EYES OF THE GUEST
DEIR	DEIR	MONASTERY
DEWANN	DEE-WANN	COLLECTION
DIBSS	DIBSS	MOLASSES
DIPLOMACEE	DEE-PLO-MAH-SEE	POLITICIAN
DOUB	DOOB	BEAR
DOUKHAN	DOO-KHAN	SMOKE
DOULAB	DOO-LAB	WHEEL
DOULDOUL	DOOL-DOOL	PORCUPINE
DOURDOUR	DOER-DOER	WHIRLPOOL
DOUWAHR	DOO-WAHR	VERTIGO

Mouhra (Filly)

ARABIC	PRONUNCIATION	TRANSLATION
DIPLOMASIYAH	DEE-PLO-MAH-SEE-YAH	DIPLOMATIC
DORDOUR	DOUR-DOUR	WHIRLPOOL
DOURRAT	DOO-RAT	PEARL
DOUMYAT	DOOM-YAT	DOLL, TOY
DOUNIA	DOO-NEE-YAH	THE WORLD, LIFE
DOURI	DOO-REE	SPARROW
DOURRA	DOO-RAH	PEARL
DUNYAHWIYAH	DUN-YAH-WEE-YAH	EARTHLY, MUNDANE
~ E ~		
EJABIYAH	EE-JAH-BEE-YAH	POSITIVE
EJAZAH	EE-JAH-ZAH	VACATION
ELA AL ABAD	ELA-AL-AH-BAD	ETERNAL
ERADAH	EE-RAH-DAH	GAIN
EYAB	EE-YAB	RETURN
~ F ~		
FADEEHAT	FA-DEE-HAT	SCANDAL
FADEELAT	FA-DEE-LAT	MERIT, VIRTUE
FADEEYAT	FAH-DEE-YAT	RANSOM
FADILAH	FAH-DEE-LAH	RIGHTEOUS
FADIYAH	FAH-DEE-YAH	TO SACRIFICE
FADL	FADL	FAVOR, GRACE
FADOULEH	FAH-DOO-LEH	CURIOUS, FOLLOWER
FADOULIYA	FA-DOO-LEE-YAH	INQUISITIVE
FAEDAT	FAH-EE-DAT	ADVANTAGE
FAHKHAMAT	FAH-KAH-MAT	MAGNIFICENCE
FAJR	FAJR	BEGINNING, START
FAKEERAH	FAH-KEE-RAH	DESTITUTE, POOR
FAKHOURAH	FAH-KOO-RAH	PROUD
FALAKEE	FAH-LAH-KEE	ASTRONOMIC
FALLAHAH	FAH-LAH-HAH	PEASANT LADY
FALSAFAT	FAL-SAH-FAT	PHILOSOPHY
FANNANAH	FAH-NAH-NAH	ARTIST
FARAH	FAH-RAH	HAPPINESS

Mouher (Colt)

ARABIC	PRONUNCIATION	TRANSLATION
DUNYAHWEE	DUN-YAH-WEE	WORLDLY
~ E ~		
EDAH	EE-DAH	CLARIFICATION
EJAB	EE-JAB	AFFIRMATIVE
EJABEE	EE-JAH-BEE	POSITIVE
EJAR	EE-JAR	LEASE, RENT
ELA AL ABAD	ELA-AL-AH-BAD	ETERNAL
EL GRECO	EL-GREY-CO	THE GREEK
ELMASS	ELL-MASS	DIAMOND
EL SOURRI	EL-SOO-REE	THE MYSTIC
EMAN	EE-MAN	BELIEF, FAITH
EWAN	EE-WAN	PALACE
EYAB	EE-YAB	RETURN
~ F ~		
FADEL	FAH-DELL	HONEST, GOOD
FADI	FAH-DEE	TO SARIFICE
FADL	FADL	MERIT
FADOULEE	FAH-DOO-LEE	CURIOUS
FAEK	FAH-EK	EXCESSIVE
FAEZ	FAH-EZ	CHAMPION
FAHD	FAHD	CHEETAH, LEOPARD
FAHEEM	FAH-HEEM	SMART, INTELLIGENT
FAHTRI	FAHT-REE	NATURAL, NATIVE
FAISAL	FAY-SAL	ARBITRATOR
FAJR	FAJR	DAWN
FAKEER	FAH-KEER	NEEDY
FAKHAMAT	FAH-KAH-MAT	GREATNESS
FALAK	FAH-LAK	ORBIT
FALSAFAT	FAL-SAH-FAT	PHILOSOPHY
FANNAN	FAH-NAN	ARTIST
FAQUED	FAH-KED	WITHOUT, DEPRIVED OF
FAQUEM	FAH-KEM	TO AGGRAVATE
FARAH	FAH-RAH	HAPPINESS

Mouhra (Filly)

ARABIC	PRONUNCIATION	TRANSLATION
FARANJIYAH	FAH-RUN-JEE-YEH	EUROPEAN WOMAN
FARAS	FAH-RAS	MARE
FARASHAH	FAH-RAH-SHAH	BUTTERFLY
FARDAT	FAR-DAT	ONE OF A PAIR
FARDIYAH	FAR-DEE-YAH	ASSUMPTION
FAREEDAH	FAH-REE-DAH	UNEQUALED, ONE OF A KIND
FAREESAT	FAH-REE-SAT	VICTIM, PREY
FARHANAH	FAR-HAH-NAH	HAPPY, GLAD
FARIDAH	FAH-REE-DAH	ONE OF A KIND
FARISSAH	FAH-REE-SAH	HORSEWOMAN
FARISSEE	FAH-REE-SEE	PERSIAN
FASSAHAT	FAH-SAH-HAT	ELOQUENCE
FASSEELAT	FAH-SEE-LOT	FAMILY, GROUP
FASSIDAH	FAH-SEE-DAH	SPOILED, CORRUPTED
FATIHAH	FAH-TEE-HAH	LIGHT, BRIGHT
FATINAH	FAH-TEE-NAH	THRILLING, BEAUTIFUL
FATIRAH	FAH-TEE-RAH	LUKEWARM
FAWARAT	FAH-WAH-RAT	BUBBLING FOUNTAIN
FAWRAT	FAW-RAT	SURGE, BOOM
FAYEEZAH	FAH-YEE-ZAH	WINNER
FAYROUZ	FAY-ROOS	TURQUOISE, PRECIOUS STONE
FEENJAN	FEEN-JAN	CUP
FEERAQ	FEE-RAK	SEPARATION
FERAR	FEE-RAR	ESCAPE
FERDOUS	FER-DOWS	PARADISE
FERQUAT	FER-KAT	GROUP, BAND
FIDAHIYAH	FEE-DAH-EE-YAH	COMMANDO
FIDAT	FEE-DAT	SILVER
FIDFAD	FEED-FAD	FLOWING
FIKRAT	FIK-RAT	IDEA, OPINION
FISSFISSAT	FISS-FEE-SSAT	ALFALFA
FITNAT	FEET-NAT	INTELLIGENCE
FITRAT	FEET-RAT	DISPOSITION, CHARACTER

Mouher (Colt)

ARABIC	PRONUNCIATION	TRANSLATION
FARAJ	FAH-RAJ	TO RELIEVE
FARANJ	FAH-RANGE	EUROPEAN
FARDIYAH	FAR-DEE-YAH	ALONE
FAREED	FAH-REED	UNIQUE
FAREEQ	FAH-REEK	SIDE TEAM
FAREESAT	FAH-REE-SAT	PREY
FAREK	FAH-REK	SEPARATE, TO PART WITH
FARESS	FAH-RESS	HORSEMAN
FARISSI	FAH-REE-SEE	PERSIAN
FARRAN	FAH-RAN	BAKER
FARWAT	FAR-WHAT	FUR (S)
FASHELL	FAH-SHELL	UNSUCCESSFUL
FASSAHAT	FAH-SAH-HAT	ELOQUENCE
FASSED	FAH-SSED	CORRUPT, SPOILED
FASSEEH	FAH-SEEH	FLUENT
FATEH	FAH-TEH	LIGHT, BRIGHT
FATEH AL BELAD	FAH-TEH-AL-BEE-LAD	THE CONQUEROR, THE VICTOR
FATEN	FAH-TEN	CAPTIVATING, CHARMING
FATER	FAH-TER	LUKEWARM
FATN	FATN	TO CHARM
FATTAH	FAH-TAH	YOUNG MAN
FATTRAT	FAH-TRAT	PERIOD, TIME
FAWAR	FAH-WAR	WATER FOUNTAIN
FAWDAH	FAW-DAH	ANARCHY, CHAOS
FAWDAWEE	FAW-DAH-WEE	DISORDERED
FAWREE	FAW-REE	INSTANT
FAWZ	FAWZ	VICTORY
FAYAD	FAH-YAD	TORRENTIAL
FAYEZ	FAH-YEZ	WINNER
FEDAEE	FEE-DAH-EE	MARTYR
FEEDAT	FEE-DAT	SILVER
FEEFAD	FEED-FAD	WIDE, LOOSE
FEEL	FEEL	ELEPHANT

Mouhra (Filly)

ARABIC	PRONUNCIATION	TRANSLATION
FOOLAZ	FOO-LAZ	STEEL
FOOTAH	FOO-TAH	TOWEL
FOOTNAT	FOOT-NAT	SEDUCTION, APPEAL
FOUKAHAT	FOO-KAH-HAT	HUMOR, JOKE
FOULAYFOULAH	FOO-LAY-FOO-LAH	RED PEPPER
FOURJAT	FOOR-JAT	SHOW, SPECTACLE
FOUSHAR	FOO-SHAR	POPCORN

~ H ~

ARABIC	PRONUNCIATION	TRANSLATION
HABAYEB	HAH-BAH-YEB	FRIENDS
HABBIBAT	HAH-BEE-BAT	DEAR
HABIBA	HAH-BEE-BAH	FRIEND
HABIBATI AL JAMEELAH	HAH-BEE-BAH-TEE-AL-JAH-MEE-LAH	BEAUTIFUL SWEETHEART
HABITAH	HAH-BEE-TAH	DESCENDING
HADALAH	HAH-DAH-LAH	TO COO (DOVES)
HADARAH	HAH-DAH-RAH	TO GROWL
HADBAT	HAD-BAT	HILL, MOUND
HADDAF	HAH-DAF	GOAL, AIM
HADDAMAH	HAH-DAH-MAH	TO TEAR, DESTRUCTIVE
HADEER	HAH-DEER	ROAR OF A WATERFALL
HADER	HAH-DER	ROARING, LOUD
HADIYA	HAH-DEE-YAH	PRESENT, GIFT
HADIYAH MIN ALLAH	HAH-DEE-YAH-MIN-AL-LAH	GIFT FROM GOD
HADIYAT AL JANOUB	HAH-DEE-YAT-AL-JAH-NOOB	GIFT OF THE SOUTH
HADIYAT AL RAML	HAH-DEE-YAT-AL-RAML	THE GIFT OF THE SAND
HADIYAT HAYATI	HAY-DEE-YAT-HAH-YAH-TEE	THE GIFT OF MY LIFE
HAEEJJAH	HAH-EE-JAH	ROUSED, EXCITED
HAJEENAH	HAH-JEE-NAH	CROSSBREED
HAJEERAH	HAH-JEE-RAH	MIDDAY, NOON
HAJJARAH	HAH-JAH-RAH	NOMADS, WANDERERS
HALAT	HAH-LAT	HALO
HALAWAH	HAH-LAH-WAH	BEAUTY
HALLOUSAT	HAH-LOO-SAT	HALLUCINATION
HAMAT	HAH-MATT	SUMMIT

Mouher (Colt)

ARABIC	PRONUNCIATION	TRANSLATION
FEERAQ	FEE-RAK	SEPARATION
FENJAN	FEN-JAN	CUP
FERAR	FEE-RAR	ESCAPE
FERDOUS	FER-DOWS	PARADISE
FERHAN	FIR-HAN	DELIGHTED
FOOLAZ	FOO-LAZ	STEEL
FOOTAH	FOO-TAH	TOWEL
FOUAD	FOO-AD	HEART
FOUKAHI	FOO-KAH-HEE	COMICAL
FOURSAN	FOOR-SAN	HORSEMEN
FOUSHAR	FOO-SHAR	POPCORN
FOUSTOK	FOOS-TOC	PISTACHIO
FOUTOUWAHT	FOO-TOO-WHAT	YOUTHFULNESS
FOUTTAT	FOO-TAT	MORSELS

~ H ~

ARABIC	PRONUNCIATION	TRANSLATION
HAALIK	HAH-LIK	HIGH
HABAHEB	HAH-BAH-HEB	FIREFLY
HABAYEB	HAH-BAH-YEB	FRIENDS
HABET	HAH-BET	FALLING
HABIBI	HAH-BEE-BEE	DARLING, FRIEND
HADAH	HAH-DAH	TO GUIDE
HADARAH	HAH-DAH-RAH	ROAR
HADBAN	HAD-BAN	HADBAN TRIBE, HADBAN STRAIN
HADDAF	HAH-DAF	PURPOSE
HADDAM	HAH-DAM	DESTRUCTIVE
HADEE	HAH-DEE	GUIDE, LEADER
HADEER	HAH-DEER	ROAR OR RUMBLE OF A WATERFALL
HADER	HAH-DER	THUNDEROUS
HADIYAT	HAH-DEE-YAT	GIFT
HAEJJ	HAH-EJJ	EXCITED, AGITATED
HAELL	HAH-EL	FRIGHTFUL, TERRIFYING
HAFEED AL RAML	HAH-FEED-AL-RAML	RELATIVE OF THE SAND
HAJAH	HAH-JAH	SATIRIZE

Mouhra (Filly)

ARABIC	PRONUNCIATION	TRANSLATION
HAMIDAH	HAH-MEE-DAH	QUIET
HAMRAH	HAM-RAH	REDDISH
HAMSAT	HAM-SAT	WHISPER
HANA	HAH-NAH	BLISS, HAPPINESS
HARABAT	HAH-RAH-BAT	RUNAWAY
HARAMI	HAH-RAH-MEE	PYRAMIDICAL
HAREEBAH	HAH-REE-BAH	RUNAWAY
HARWALAH	HAR-WAH-LAH	TO JOG
HASIBAH	HAH-SEE-BAH	OF NOBLE BIRTH
HAWADAT	HAH-WAH-DAT	LENIENCY
HAWAH	HAH-WAH	PASSION
HAWAH AL SAHRAH	HAH-WAH-AL-SAH-RAH	THE WIND OF THE DESERT
HAWAHEE	HAH-WAH-EE	AERIAL
HAWALAT	HAH-WAH-LAT	TO TERRIFY
HAWANAT	HAH-WAH-NAT	TO FACILITATE
HAWIYAH	HAH-WEE-YAH	AMATEUR
HAWIYAT	HAH-WEE-YAT	IDENTITY
HAYAT	HAY-AT	SHAPE, APPEARANCE
HAYBAT	HAY-BAT	DIGNITY, SOLEMNITY
HAYINAH	HAH-YEE-NAH	FACILE, EASILY ACCOMPLISHED
HAYKAL	HAY-KAL	TEMPLE
HAYMANAH	HAY-MAH-NAH	TO CONTROL
HAZEELAH	HAH-ZEE-LAH	SKINNY, THIN, POOR
HAZEEMAH	HAH-ZEE-MAH	DEFEAT
HAZLEE	HAZ-LEE	COMICAL
HAZZAR	HAH-ZAR	NIGHTINGALE
HAZZAZ	HAH-ZAZ	ROCKING
HEBAH ILAHIYAH	HEE-BAH-EE-LAH-HEE-YAH	DIVINE GIFT
HEBAT	HEE-BAT	PRESENT, DONATION
HEJIRAH	HEE-JEE-RAH	HEGIRA
HELWEH	HEL-WEH	SWEETLY BEAUTIFUL
HILAL	HEE-LAHL	CRESCENT MOON
HILAL LATIFA	HEE-LAL-LAH-TEE-FAH	A GENTLE MOON

Mouher (Colt)

ARABIC	PRONUNCIATION	TRANSLATION
HAJAR	HAH-JAR	ABANDON
HAJEEN	HAH-JEEN	CROSSBREED
HAJEM	HAH-JEM	TO ATTACK
HAJER	HAH-JER	TO EMIGRATE
HAJESS	HAH-JESS	OBSESSION
HAL	HAL	CARDAMOM
HALAH	HAH-LAH	HELLO
HAMAJEE	HAH-MAH-JEE	SAVAGE
HAMASAH	HAH-MAH-SAH	WHISPER
HAMED	HAH-MED	STILL, CALM
HAMESH	HAH-MESH	FOOTNOTE
HARABAH	HAH-RAH-BAH	FLEE
HARAM	HAH-RAM	PYRAMID
HAREB	HAH-REB	FUGITIVE
HARRAB	HAH-RAB	SMUGGLE
HARRAJAH	HAH-RAH-JAH	CLOWN, JESTER
HARWALAH	HAR-WAH-LAH	TROT, JOG
HAWAH	HAH-WAH	LOVE
HAWAH AL SAHRA	HA-WAH-AL-SAH-RAH	THE WIND OF THE DESERT
HAWAHEE	HAH-WAH-EE	AERIAL
HAWEE	HAH-WEE	HOBBYIST
HAYAT	HAY-AT	FORM
HAYBAT	HAY-BAT	FEAR
HAYEN	HAH-YEN	EASILY ATTAINED
HAYKAL	HAY-KAL	TEMPLE
HAYMANAH	HAY-MAH-NAH	TO DOMINATE
HAZAL	HAH-ZAL	PLAY
HAZAM	HAH-ZAM	DEFEAT
HAZEEL	HAH-ZEEL	LEAN
HAZZAR	HAH-ZAR	NIGHTINGALE
HEBAT	HEE-BAT	GIFT
HEGIRAH	HEH-JEER-AH	HEGIRA (FLIGHT OF MOHAMMAD FROM MECCA)
HEMMAT	HEE-MATT	DETERMINATION

Mouhra (Filly)

ARABIC	PRONUNCIATION	TRANSLATION
HILAL MAHROUSSEH	HEE-LAL-MAH-ROO-SSEH	A PROTECTED MOON
HIMMAT	HEE-MATT	RESOLUTION
HINDAM	HIN-DAM	TIDINESS
HIRAT	HEE-RAT	CAT (FEMALE)
HIWAYAT	HEE-WAH-YAT	HOBBY
HIYAJJ	HEE-YAJJ	AGITATION
HIYAM	HEE-YAM	FALLING IN LOVE
HOODAH	HOO-DAH	RIGHT GUIDANCE
HOODEB	HOO-DEB	EYELASHES
HOOTAF	HOO-TAF	SHOUTING
HOUDNAT	HOOD-NAT	TRUCE
HOUGREE	HOOJ-REE	OF THE HEGIRA
HOUJOUM	HOO-JOOM	ATTACK, ASSAULT
HOUJRAT	HOOJ-RAT	EXODUS, EMMIGRATION
HOULIYAT	HOO-LEE-YAT	JEWEL
HOULIYAT AL NIL	HOO-LEE-YAT-AL-NEEL	THE JEWEL OF THE NILE
HOUNAYHAT	HOO-NYE-HAT	MOMENT

~ I ~

ARABIC	PRONUNCIATION	TRANSLATION
IBADAT	EE-BAH-DAT	ANNIHILATION
IBDAL	IB-DAHL	SUBSTITUTION
IBRAT	IB-RAT	NEEDLE
IBTASSEM	IB-TAH-SEM	SMILE
IBTIHAJ	IB-TEE-HAJ	JUBILATION
IBTIHAJAH	IB-TEE-HA-JAH	TO REJOICE
IBTISSAMAH	IB-TEE-SAH-MAH	A SMILE
IBTISSAMAH ANISA	IB-TEE-SAH-MAH-AH-NEE-SAH	GENTLE SMILE, KIND SMILE
IBTISSAN	IB-TEE-SAN	SMILING
IDAHFAT	EE-DAH-FAT	ADDICTION
IDRAK	EE-DRAHK	REALIZATION
IHTAJAZAH	IH-TAH-JAH-ZAH	DISAPPEAR
IHTAMAH	IH-TAH-MAH	TO SEEK PROTECTION
IHTEEFAL	IH-TEE-FAL	CELEBRATION
IHTEELAL	IH-TEE-LAL	OCCUPATION FORCES

Mouher (Colt)

ARABIC	PRONUNCIATION	TRANSLATION
HEWAYAT	HEE-WAH-YAT	FAVORITE PASTURE
HEYAJJ	HEE-YAJJ	EXCITEMENT
HEYAM	HEE-YAM	PASSIVE
HILAL	HEE-LAL	MOON
HILAL AL SAHRAH	HEE-LAL-AL-SAH-RAH	THE DESERT MOON
HILAL LATIF	HEE-LAL-LAH-TEEF	A GENTLE MOON
HILAL MABROUK	HEE-LAL-MAHB-ROOK	A BLESSED MOON
HINDAM	HIN-DAM	NEATNESS
HOODNAT	HOOD-NAT	ARMISTICE
HOONAYHAT	HOO-NYE-HAT	LITTLE WHILE
HOOWAH	HOO-WAH	HE
HOOWAHT	HOO-WHAT	ABYSS
HOUBOUB	HOO-BOOB	BLOWING WIND
HOUGREE	HOOJ-REE	OF THE HEGIRA
HOUJOUM	HOO-JOOM	OFFENSIVE

~ I ~

ARABIC	PRONUNCIATION	TRANSLATION
IBBAN	IB-BAN	DURING
IBDAL	IB-DAHL	EXCHANGE
IBHAM	IB-HAM	OBSCURITY
IBL	IBL	CAMELS
IBN	IBN	SON OF
IBREEK	IB-REEK	PITCHER, JUG
IBTASSEM	IB-TAH-SEM	SMILE
IBTIHAL	IB-TEE-HAL	PRAYER
IBTIKAR	IB-TEE-KAR	INVENTION
IDAHRI	EE-DAH-REE	EXECUTIVE
IDMAN	ED-MAN	ADDICTION
IHTAKAMAH	IH-TAH-KAH-MAH	TO SEEK DECISION
IHTEEJAJ	IH-TEE-JAJ	PROTEST, OBJECTION
IHTEEKAK	IH-TEE-KAK	FRICTION
IHTEEKAR	IH-TEE-KAR	CONTEMPT
IHTEELAL	IH-TEE-LAL	OCCUPATION
IHTEEYAT	IH-TEE-YAT	CAUTION, CARE

Mouhra (Filly)

ARABIC	PRONUNCIATION	TRANSLATION
IHTEEMAL	IH-TEE-MAL	POSSIBILITY
IHTEESHAM	IH-TEE-SHAM	MODESTY
IJAHBAT	EE-JAH-BAT	ANSWER
IJAHDAT	EE-JAH-DAT	EXCELLENCE
IJMAHLEE	IJ-MAH-LEE	TOTAL, ENTIRE
IJTAZABAH	EEJ-TAH-ZAH-BAH	TO ATTRACT
IKHLASS	IKH-LASS	SINCERITY, HONESTY
IKHTALAFAH	IKH-TAH-LAH-FAH	TO DISAGREE
IKHTEELAF	IKH-TEE-LAF	DISSIMILARITY
IKHTEESAR	IKH-TEE-SAR	ABBREVIATION
IKHTEEYAR	IKH-TEE-YAR	CHOICE
IKHTEEYAREE	IKH-TEE-YAH-REE	OPTIMAL
INSHALLAH	IN-SHAH-LAH	GOD'S WILLING
IRTAB	IR-TAB	DOUBT, SUSPECT
IRTAKABAH	IR-TAH-KAH-BAH	TO COMMIT
IRTAKAHZAH	IR-TAH-KAH-ZAH	TO LEAN ON
IRTEEBAT	IR-TEE-BAT	LIAISON
IRTEEYAH	IR-TEE-YAH	SATISFACTION
ISBANIAH	ISS-BAH-NEE-YAH	SPANISH
ISHARAT	EE-SHAH-RAT	SIGN, MARK, SYMBOL
ISHARAT AL JAMAL	EE-SHAH-RAT-AL-JAH-MAL	SIGN OF BEAUTY
ISLAME	ISS-LAH-MEE	ISLAMIC
ISTAFADAH	ISS-TAH-FAH-DAH	TO CONCLUDE
ISTAHSANAH	ISS-TAH-SAH-NAH	TO FAVOR, LIKE
ISTEEHAL	ISS-TEE-HAL	TO BE IMPOSSIBLE
ISTEEJAB	ISS-TEE-JAB	TO RESPOND TO
ISTEEKALAT	ISS-TEE-KAH-LAT	RESIGNATION
ISTIFSAR	ISS-TIF-SAR	INQUIRY
ISTISLAM	ISS-TIS-LAM	SURRENDER
ITHARAT	EE-THAH-RAT	EXCITEMENT
ITHBAT	ITH-BAT	VERIFICATION
ITTEEKAL	IT-TEE-KAL	DEPENDENCE
ITTEEZAN	IT-TEE-ZAN	COMPOSURE

Mouher (Colt)

ARABIC	PRONUNCIATION	TRANSLATION
IJAHZAT	EE-JAH-ZAT	HOLIDAY, VACATION
IJBAR	IJ-BAR	COMPULSION
IJBAREE	IJ-BAH-REE	COMPULSORY
IJMAHL	IJ-MAHL	SUMMED UP
IJMAHLEE	IJ-MAH-LEE	OVERALL
IJTAZ	IJ-TAZ	TO CROSS
IKHRAJ	IKH-RAJ	TAKING OUT
IKHTALAKAH	IKH-TAH-LAH-KAH	TO INVENT
IKHTEELAF	IKH-TEE-LAF	DIFFERENCE
IKHTEELAT	IKH-TEE-LAT	CONFUSION
IKHTEESAS	IKH-TEE-SAS	SPECIALIZATION
INSHALLAH	IN-SHAH-LAH	GOD'S WILLING
INTEESAR	IN-TEE-SAR	CONQUEST
IRHAB	IR-HAB	TERROR
IRHABE	IR-HAH-BEE	TERRORIST
IRSAL	IR-SAL	DISPATCH
IRSHAD	IR-SHAD	GUIDANCE
IRTEEBAT	IR-TEE-BAT	RELATION, LIASON
IRTEEJAL	IR-TEE-JAL	IMPROVISATION
ISHTEERAK	ISH-TEE-RAK	PARTICIPATION
ISTABEL AL HILAL	IS-TAH-BEL-AL-HEE-LAL	THE FARM OF THE MOON
ISTIBDAL	ISS-TIB-DAL	SUBSTITUTION
ISTIFHAM	ISS-TIF-HAM	QUESTION
ISTIFZAZ	ISS-TIF-ZAZ	PROVOCATION
ISTIJMAM	ISS-TIJ-MAM	RECREATION, FUN
ISTIKBAL	ISS-TIK-BAL	RECEPTION
ISTIKLAL	ISS-TIK-LAL	INDEPENDENCE
ITTAR	EE-TAR	FRAMEWORK
ITTEEHAM	IT-TEE-HAM	ACCUSATION
ITTEEKAL	IT-TEE-KAL	RELIANCE
ITTEESAL	IT-TEE-SAL	CONNECTION
IZDEEHAR	IZ-DEE-HAR	PROSPERITY
IZDEEWAJ	IZ-DEE-WAJ	DUALISM, A DOUBLE CHARACTER

Mouhra (Filly)

ARABIC	PRONUNCIATION	TRANSLATION
IZDAHARAH	IZ-DAH-HAH-RAH	TO FLOURISH
IZDEEYAD	IZ-DEE-YAD	INCREASE, GROWTH

~ J ~

NOTE: The letter "J" or "G" is to be used as a soft "J" like in the word "JUMP".

For Example: JAMEELAH or GAMEELAH–BEAUTIFUL

The Soft "J" sound will be used in the Literary Arabic, but of course it is up to the individual to use the sound preferred from his or her Arabic speaking region.

ARABIC	PRONUNCIATION	TRANSLATION
JABALEE	JAH-BAH-LEE	MOUNTAINOUS
JABANAH	JAH-BAH-NAH	GRAVEYARD
JABBAL	JAH-BAL	MOUNTAIN
JABBARAH	JAH-BAH-RAH	STRONG
JABHAT	JAB-HAT	FOREHEAD
JABLAT	JAB-LAT	NATURAL DISPOSITION
JADARAT	JAH-DAH-RAT	WORTH, MERIT
JADEEDAH	JAH-DEE-DAH	NEW, MODERN
JADEELAH	JAH-DEE-LAH	BRAID
JADEERAH	JAH-DEE-RAH	RELIABLE
JADWAL	JAD-WAHL	TIME TABLE, SCHEDULE
JAFAF	JAH-FAF	ARID
JAHADAH	JAH-HAH-DAH	TO FIGHT
JAHILAH	JAH-HEE-LAH	MEDICATED
JAHIZAH	JAH-HEE-ZAH	PREPARED
JAHWAHREB	JAH-WAH-REB	STOCKINGS
JAIRAT	JAH-EE-RAT	OPPRESSIVE
JAIZAT	JAH-EE-ZAT	PRIZE, REWARD
JALABIAH	JAH-LAH-BEE-YAH	DESERT DRESS
JALALAH	JAH-LAH-LAH	GRANDEUR
JALBAT	JAL-BAT	NOISE
JALEED	JAH-LEED	ICE
JALEELAH	JAH-LEE-LAH	SOLEMN
JALIAT	JAH-LEE-YAT	COMMUNITY
JALSSAT	JAL-SAT	GATHERING, SESSION
JAMEEDAH	JAH-MEE-DAH	RIGID

Mouher (Colt)

ARABIC	PRONUNCIATION	TRANSLATION
IZMEEL	IZ-MEEL	CHISEL
IZN	IZN	PERMISSION

~ J ~

NOTE: *The letter "J" or "G" is to be used as a soft "J" like in the word "JUMP".*
For Example: JAMEELAH *or* GAMEELAH–BEAUTIFUL
The Soft "J" sound will be used in the Literary Arabic, but of course it is up to the individual to use the sound preferred from his or her Arabic speaking region.

ARABIC	PRONUNCIATION	TRANSLATION
JABAL	JAH-BAL	MOUNTAIN
JABAN	JAH-BAN	LACKS COURAGE, COWARD
JABBAR	JAH-BAR	STRONG, MIGHTY
JABHAT	JAB-HAT	THE BATTLE FRONT
JABROOT	JAB-ROOT	DICTATORSHIP
JADEED	JAH-DEED	NEW, MODERN
JADEER	JAH-DEER	WORTHY
JADWAL	JAD-WAHL	CREEK, BROOK
JAERR	JAH-ERR	UNJUST, UNFAIR
JAEZ	JAH-EZ	PERMISSIBLE
JAFAF	JAH-FAF	DRYNESS
JAHADAH	JAH-HAH-DAH	TO STRIKE
JAHD	JAHD	EFFORT
JAHEZ	JAH-HEZ	READY
JAHF	JAHF	DRY
JALAB	JAH-LAB	JULEP
JALAL	JAH-LAL	MAGNIFICENCE
JALEEL	JAH-LEEL	HONORABLE, SUBLIME
JALEEL AL ASHKAR	JAH-LEEL-AL-ASH-KAR	THE MAGNIFICENT CHESTNUT
JALIAT	JAH-LEE-YAT	COLONY
JALLAD	JAH-LAD	EXECUTIONER
JAMAHEER	JAH-MAH-HEER	GATHERING
JAMAL GALEEL	JAH-MAL-JAH-LEEL	GREAT BEAUTY
JAMED	JAH-MED	SOLID, HARD
JAMIL	JAH-MEEL	GRACEFUL, LOVELY
JAMR	JAMR	COAL

Mouhra (Filly)

ARABIC	PRONUNCIATION	TRANSLATION
JAMEELAH	JAH-MEE-LAH	PRETTY, BEAUTIFUL
JAMEELAT AL ALWAN	JAH-MEE-LAT-AL AL-WAN	COLORFUL BEAUTY
JAMHOURIAT	JAM-HOO-REE-YAT	REPUBLIC
JAMILAH	JAH-MEE-LAH	GORGEOUS
JAMRAH	JAM-RAH	COAL
JANNAT	JAH-NAT	PARADISE
JASSOURAH	JAH-SOO-RAH	BRAVE
JASSOUSSAH	JAH-SOO-SAH	SPY
JASSOUSSIAT	JAH-SOO-SEE-YAT	SPYING
JAWAHER	JAH-WAH-HER	JEWELRY
JAWDAT	JAW-DAT	GOODNESS
JAWHARAH	JOUW-HAH-RAH	JEWEL, PRECIOUS STONE
JAWHARAH NADIRAH	JOUW-HAH-RAH-NAH-DEE-RAH	RARE JEWEL
JAWLAT	JAW-LAT	JOURNEY
JAWWADAH	JAH-WAH-DAH	GENEROUS
JAWZAT	JAW-ZAT	WALNUT
JAYIDDAH	JAH-YEE-DAH	WELL REFINED
JAZABAH	JAH-ZAH-BAH	CHARMING, CUTE
JAZEERAH	JAH-ZEE-RAH	ISLAND
JAZIBIYAH	JAH-ZEE-BEE-YAH	ATTRACTION
JAZMAT	JAZ-MATT	BOOTS
JEEDAL	JEE-DAL	ARGUMENT
JEEL	JEEL	AGE, ERA
JEHAT	JEH-HAT	DIRECTION
JEHAZ	JEH-HAZ	SYSTEM
JENAYAT	JEH-NAH-YAT	FELONY
JENOON	JEH-NOON	MADNESS, FOOLISHNESS
JENOUBEE	JEH-NOO-BEE	SOUTHERN WIND
JENSIYAT	JEN-SEE-YAT	NATIONALITY
JIDDAH	JEE-DAH	GRANDMOTHER
JINSS	JINSS	KIND SOUL
JOUDJOUD	JOOD-JOOD	CRICKET
JOUMJOUMAH	JOOM-JOO-MAH	SKULL

Mouher (Colt)

ARABIC	PRONUNCIATION	TRANSLATION
JANNAT	JAH-NAT	PARADISE
JANOUB	JAH-NOOB	SOUTH
JANOUBEE	JAH-NOO-BEE	SOUTHERN
JANZEER	JAN-ZEER	CHAIN
JAR	JAR	NEIGHBOR (MALE)
JARASS	JAH-RASS	BELL, SONG
JAREE	JAH-REE	FLOWING
JARRAH	JAH-RAH	BUCKET
JASSOUR	JAH-SOOR	BOLD, COURAGEOUS
JASSOUSS	JAH-SOOS	SPY
JASSOUSSIAT	JAH-SOO-SEE-YAT	SPYING
JAWAB	JAH-WAB	ANSWER, REPLY
JAWAD	JAH-WAD	HORSE, STEED
JAWHARAH	JAW-HA-RAH	JEWEL
JAWWAD	JAH-WWAD	GENEROUS
JAYED	JAH-YED	FINE, VERY GOOD
JAZAB	JAH-ZAB	ATTRACTIVE
JAZEEL	JAH-ZEEL	ABUNDANT, AMPLE
JAZZAR	JAH-ZAR	BUTCHER
JEEDAR	JEE-DAR	WALL
JEEL	JEEL	GENERATION
JEELD	JEELD	THE SKIN
JEHAZ	JEE-HAZ	SYSTEM
JIDD	JIDD	GRANDFATHER
JIHAD	JEE-HAD	HOLY WAR
JINN	JINN	DEMON
JISR	JISR	BRIDGE
JIZR	JIZR	ROOT
JOOD	JOOD	GENEROSITY
JOUB	JOOBB	WELL
JOUDJOUD	JOOD-JOOD	CRICKET
JOULOUSS	JOO-LOOS	SITTING DOWN
JOUNDEE	JOON-DEE	SOLDIER

Mouhra (Filly)

ARABIC	PRONUNCIATION	TRANSLATION
JOUMLAT	JOOM-LAT	SEVERAL, MANY
JOUNAZ	JOO-NAZ	REQUIEM
JOUNDIYAT	JOON-DEE-YAT	ARMY MEMBER (FEMALE)
JOURN	JOORN	BASIN

~ K ~

ARABIC	PRONUNCIATION	TRANSLATION
KABEERAH	KAH-BEE-RAH	THE OLDEST ONE, LARGE
KAFEELAH	KAH-FEE-LAH	SPONSOR
KAFEELAT OUMRI	KAH-FEE-LAT-OOM-REE	THE SPONSOR OF MY LIFE
KAFIAH	KA-FEE-YAH	HEAD DRESS
KAFIFAH	KAH-FEE-FAH	BLIND
KAFIRAH	KAH-FEE-RAH	INFIDEL
KAHLEDIAH	KAH-LEH-DEE-YAH	FROM THE KAHLEDIAH
KAHRAMAN	KAH-RAH-MAN	AMBER
KAJLANEH	KAJ-LAH-NEH	SHY
KALAHM HANOON	KAH-LAHM-HAH-NOON	TENDER TALK
KALALAT	KAH-LAH-LAT	FATIGUE, EXHAUSTION
KAMAHLEE	KAH-MAH-LEE	LUXURIOUS
KAMAHLIYAT	KAH-MAH-LEE-YAT	ARTICLES OF LUXURY
KAMANJAT	KAH-MAN-JAT	FIDDLE
KAMEELA	KAH-MEE-LAH	PERFECT
KAMEELAT-AL-AWSAF	KAH-MEE-LAT-AL-AW-SAF	THE ONE WITH PERFECT FEATURES
KAMILAH	KAH-MEE-LAH	PERFECT
KANNAT	KAH-NAT	DAUGHTER IN LAW
KANZ-AL-OUYOUN	KANZ-AL-OU-YOON	THE TREASURE OF THE EYES
KANZAT	KAHN-ZAT	SWEATER
KANZEE	KAHN-ZEE	MY TREASURE
KARAMAH	KAH-RAH-MAH	GENEROSITY
KARAMAT	KAH-RAH-MAT	RESPECT
KARAZ	KAH-RAHZ	CHERRY
KAREEMA	KAH-REE-MAH	GIVING, GENEROUS
KAREEMAT AL SHARAF	KAH-REE-MAT-AL-SHAH-RAF	NOBLE AND KIND
KARIMA	KAH-REE-MAH	GENEROUS, GIVING
KARMAT	KAHR-MAT	GRAPEVINE

Mouher (Colt)

ARABIC	PRONUNCIATION	TRANSLATION
\~ K \~		
KABEER	KAH-BEER	GREAT, LARGE
KABOUSS	KAH-BOOSS	NIGHTMARE, FRIGHTENING DREAM
KABOUSS ASWAD	KAH-BOOSS-AHS-WAD	BLACK NIGHTMARE
KAFEEF	KAH-FEEF	BLIND
KAFEEL	KAH-FEEL	BAILSMAN, ONE WHO GUARANTEES
KAFEEL OUMRI	KAH-FEEL-OUM-REE	THE SPONSOR OF MY LIFE
KAFER	KAH-FER	INFIDEL
KAFIYAH	KA-FEE-YAH	ARAB HEAD DRESS
KAHAR AL JABAL	KAH-HAR-AL-JAH-BAL	THE CONQUEROR OF THE MOUNTAIN
KAHFALAT	KAH-FAH-LAT	GUARANTY
KAHLED	KAH-LED	FOR EVER
KAHRAMAN	KAH-RAH-MAN	AMBER
KAKOUL	KAH-KOOL	AS A WHOLE, ALL TOGETHER
KALAHM	KAH-LAHM	SPEECH
KALAHM LAZIZ	KAH-LAHM-LAH-ZEEZ	BEAUTIFUL SPEECH
KAMAL	KAH-MAL	PERFECTION
KAMAL AL KAMAL	KAH-MAL-AL-KAH-MAL	THE PERFECTION OF PERFECTION
KAMAM	KAH-MAM	VIOLIN
KAMEEN	KAH-MEEN	AMBUSH, TRAP
KAMEL	KAH-MEL	PERFECT, COMPLETE
KAMEL AL AWSAF	KAH-MEL-AL-AW-SAF	THE ONE WITH PERFECT FEATURES
KAMIYAT	KAH-MEE-YAT	QUANTITY, AMOUNT
KARAM	KAH-RAM	GENEROSITY
KARAMAT	KAH-RAH-MAT	DIGNITY
KARAZ	KAH-RAHZ	CHERRY
KAREEM	KAH-REEM	GENEROUS, GIVING
KAREEM AL SHARAF	KAH-REEM-AL-SHAH-RAF	THE HONORABLE GIVING ONE
KARIM	KAH-REEM	GIVING, GENEROUS
KARM	KAHRM	GARDEN
KARMAT	KAHR-MAT	GRAPEVINE
KARRAM	KAH-RRAM	TO HONOR
KASB	KAHSB	GAIN, PROFIT

Mouhra (Filly)

ARABIC	PRONUNCIATION	TRANSLATION
KASHEEFAH	KAH-SHEE-FAH	SEARCHER
KASHEEFAT AL NOOR	KAH-SHEE-FAT-AL-NOOR	LIGHT SEARCHER
KASLAHNAH	KAHS-LAH-NAH	LAZY, INACTIVE
KASSARAH	KAH-SAH-RAH	THE ONE WHO BREAKS THINGS
KASSIBAH	KAH-SEE-BAH	WINNER
KASSRAT	KAHS-RAT	FRAGMENT, FRACTION
KATHEEFAH	KAH-THEE-FAH	INTENSE
KATIBAH	KAH-TEE-BAH	WRITER
KATKOOT	KAHT-KOOT	CHICK
KAYISSAH	KAH-YEE-SAH	CHARMING
KAYNOUNAT AMALEE	KAY-NOON-NAT-AH-MAH-LEE	THE HOPE OF MY EXISTANCE
KAZOOZAH	KAH-ZOO-ZAH	REFRESHMENT
KEELMAH HANOONAH	KEEL-MAH-HAH-NOO-NAH	A TENDER WORD
KEELMAH HELWAH	KEL-MAH-HEL-WAH	A BEAUTIFUL WORD
KEELMAT	KEEL-MAT	A WORD
KEELMAT AL HAYAT	KEEL-MAT-AL-HAH-YAT	THE WORD OF LIFE
KEELMAT AL SIR	KEEL-MAT-AL-SIR	PASSWORD
KEYASAT	KEY-YAH-SAT	COURTESY, POLITENESS
KHAFALAT	KAH-FAH-LAT	GUARANTY, SECURITY
KHAMILAH	KAH-MEE-LAH	PERFECT
KIFAYAT	KEE-FAH-YAT	SUFFICIENT
KIZBAT NEESAN	KEEZ-BAT-NEE-SAN	APRIL FOOLS
KOMIDIAH	KO-MEE-DEE-YAH	COMEDY
KOTCHINAH	KO-TCHEE-NAH	PLAYING CARDS
KOUHOULAT	KOO-HOO-LAT	MIDDLE AGE
KOULFAT AL AHLAM	KOOL-FAT-AL-AH-LAM	THE EXPENSE OF THE DREAMS
KOULOUHOUM	KOO-LOO-HOOM	ALL OF THEM
KOUNOOZ	KOO-NOOZ	MANY TREASURES
KOURAT THALJ	KOO-RAT-THALJ	SNOW BALL
KOURAT AL ARD	KOO-RAT-AL-ARD	GLOBE, SPHERE
KOUSOUF	KOO-SOOF	ECLIPSE
KOUSOUF AL HILAL	KOO-SOOF-AL-HEE-LAL	ECLIPSE OF THE MOON
KOUWAHRAT	KOO-WAH-RAT	BEE HIVE

Mouher (Colt)

ARABIC	PRONUNCIATION	TRANSLATION
KASHEF	KAH-SHEF	SEARCHER
KASHEF AL NOOR	KAH-SHEF-AL-NOOR	THE LIGHT SEARCHER
KASHKOOL	KASH-KOOL	PATCHWORK
KASSAR	KAH-SAR	TO BREAK, FRACTURE
KASSEB	KAH-SEB	WINNER, CHAMPION
KASSER	KAH-SER	BIRD OF PREY
KATEB	KAH-TEB	WRITER
KATEER	KAH-TEER	MUCH, MANY
KATEERAN	KAH-TEER-RAN	VERY MUCH
KATHEEF	KAH-THEEF	DENSE, THICK
KAYESS	KAH-YES	COURTEOUS, POLITE
KAYNOONAT	KAY-NOON-NAT	BEING, EXISTANCE
KELMAT	KEEL-MAT	EXPRESS OPINION
KENZ	KENZ	TREASURE
KENZ GAHLEE	KENZ-GAH-LEE	VALUABLE TREASURE
KEYANN	KEY-YAN	ENTITY, BEING
KEZBAH BAYDAH	KEEZ-BAH-BAY-DAH	WHITE LIE
KIRSH	KIRSH	BIG BELLIED
KOLONEL	CO-LO-NEL	COLONEL
KOOHLEE	KOOH-LEE	NAVY BLUE
KOOLAB	KOO-LAB	HOOK, CLAMP
KOOTAYAB	KOO-TAH-YEB	BOOKLET
KORNISH	KOR-NEESH	COASTAL ROAD
KOUBR	KOUBR	GREATNESS IN SIZE
KOUFR	KOUFR	INFIDELITY
KOUFRAN	KOOF-RAN	DISBELIEF (IN RELIGION)
KOUKABAT	KOW-KAH-BAT	TROOP, GROUP
KOURAT	KOO-RAT	BALL, GLOBE
KOURAT THALJ	KOO-RAT-THALJ	SNOWBALL
KOUSHOUF	KOO-SHOOF	DISCOVERIES
KOUSOUF	KOO-SOOF	ECLIPSE
KOWKAB	KOW-CAB	STAR
KOWKAB SAMAHWEE	KOW-CAB-SAH-MAH-WEE	A HEAVENLY STAR

Mouhra (Filly)

ARABIC	PRONUNCIATION	TRANSLATION
KOWKABAH	KOW-KAH-BAH	A STAR
KOWKABAH SAMAHWIYAH	KOW-KAH-BAH-SAH-MAH-WEE-YAH	HEAVENLY STAR
KOWKABAT NOJOUN	KOW-KAH-BAT-NOO-JOON	CONSTELLATION
KUWAITIYAH	KOO-WAY-TEE-YAH	FROM KUWAIT

~ L ~

ARABIC	PRONUNCIATION	TRANSLATION
LABAKAT	LAH-BAH-KAT	DECORUM
LABAN	LAH-BAN	YOGURT
LABEEBAH	LAH-BEE-BAH	WISE, JUDICIOUS
LABOUAT	LAH-BOO-AT	LIONESS
LADOODAH	LAH-DOO-DAH	BITTER ENEMY
LAEEMAH	LAH-EE-MAH	WICKED, SORDID
LAFITAH	LAH-FEE-TAH	STRIKING
LAFLAF	LAF-LAF	COVER UP
LAHEEMAT	LAH-EE-MAT	CRITIC
LAHFITAT	LAH-FEE-TAT	BILLBOARD
LAHJAT	LAH-JAT	DIALECT
LAHNAT	LAH-NAT	CURSE
LAHOUTEE	LAH-HOO-TEE	THEOLOGICAL
LAHZAT	LAH-ZAT	MOMENT
LAJNAT	LAJ-NAT	COMMITTEE
LAKMAT	LAK-MATT	PUNCH, A QUICK STRIKE
LAKTAT	LAHK-TAT	SNAPSHOT
LAMHAT	LAM-HAT	GLANCE
LANIHAYAT	LAH-NEE-HAH-YAT	INFINITY
LASMAT	LAS-MAT	KISS
LATAFAT	LAH-TAH-FAT	GENTLENESS, KINDNESS
LATEEFAH	LAH-TEE-FAH	GENTLE, KIND
LATEEMAT	LAH-TEE-MAT	PARENTLESS
LAWLAB	LAW-LAB	SPIRAL
LAYLA	LAY-LAH	NIGHT, EVENING
LAYLIYAH	LAY-LEE-YAH	NOCTURNAL
LAZAT	LAH-ZAT	DELIGHT
LAZAWARDI	LAH-ZAH-WAR-DEE	BLUE SKY

Mouher (Colt)

ARABIC	PRONUNCIATION	TRANSLATION
KOWN	KOWN	COSMOS, WORLD
KUWAITI	KOO-WAY-TEE	FROM KUWAIT

~ L ~

ARABIC	PRONUNCIATION	TRANSLATION
LABAN	LAH-BAN	MILK
LABEEB	LAH-BEEB	INTELLIGENT
LABEYK	LAH-BEYK	AT YOUR SERVICE
LADOOD	LAH-DOOD	MORTAL ENEMY
LAEIM	LAH-EIM	EVIL
LAFAZ	LAH-FAZ	EXPRESSION
LAFEETAT	LAH-FEE-TAT	BILLBOARD
LAFET	LAH-FET	EYE CATCHING
LAHED	LAH-HED	TOMB
LAHEEB	LAH-HEEB	FLAME, BLAZE
LAHMEH	LAH-MEH	THE SHINING ONE
LAHN	LAHN	MELODY
LAHOO	LAH-HOO	AMUSEMENT
LAHOOT	LAH-HOOT	THEOLOGY
LAKAT	LAH-KAT	CATCHER
LAMABAL	LAH-MAH-BAL	INDIFFERENT
LAMARKAZEE	LAH-MAR-KAH-ZEE	DECENTRALIZED
LAMESS	LAH-MESS	TO BE IN TOUCH WITH
LAMESS EL AMAR	LAH-MESS-EL-AH-MAR	TO TOUCH THE MOON
LAMSAT AL NAR	LAM-SAT-AL-NAR	THE TOUCH OF FIRE
LANIHAYAT	LAH-NEE-HAH-YAT	INFINITY
LASHART	LAH-SHART	NO CONDITION
LATAFAH	LAH-TAH-FAH	TO TREAT WITH KINDNESS
LATEEF	LAH-TEEF	GENTLE, KIND
LAWAH	LAH-WAH	TO TWIST
LAWZ	LAWZ	ALMOND
LAYEN	LAH-YEN	TENDERNESS, GENTLENESS
LAYLEE	LAY-LEE	NOCTURNAL
LAYTH	LAYTH	LION
LAZAT	LAH-ZAT	PLEASURE

Mouhra (Filly)

ARABIC	PRONUNCIATION	TRANSLATION
LAZEEMAT	LAH-ZEE-MAT	INDISPENSIBLE
LAZEEZ	LAH-ZEEZ	DELICIOUS
LEEBIYAT	LEE-BEE-YAT	FROM LIBYA
LEEJAM	LEE-JAM	BRIDLE
LEESANI	LEE-SAN-EE	LINGUISTIC
LEILA	LAY-LAH	NIGHT, EVENING
LEKMAT	LEK-MATT	MORSEL
LEYLAH	LEY-LAH	NIGHT, EVENING
LEYMOON	LEY-MOON	LEMON
LOUKNAT	LOOK-NAT	ACCENT
LOULOUIYAT	LOO-LOO-EE-YAT	PEARLS
LOUTFEEYAH	LOOT-FEE-YAH	GENTLE ONE
LOUYOUNAT	LOO-YOU-NAT	SOFTNESS
LOUZOUM	LOO-ZOOM	NECESSITY

~ M ~

ARABIC	PRONUNCIATION	TRANSLATION
MAAROUFA	MAH-ROO-FAH	FAMOUS, WELL KNOWN
MABHOURAH	MAB-HOO-RAH	OVERWHELMED
MABLOULAH	MAB-LOO-LAH	MOISTENED, SLIGHTLY WET
MABROOKA	MAB-ROO-KAH	CONGRATULATIONS
MABSOUTAH	MAB-SOO-TAH	HAPPY, PLEASED
MADDAT	MAH-DAT	INGREDIENT
MADINA	MAH-DEE-NAH	CITY
MAEELAH	MAH-EE-LAH	BENT
MAEEWAH	MAH-EE-WAH	SHELTER
MAEEZOUNAH	MAH-EE-ZOO-NAH	PERMITTED
MAGIDAA	MAH-JEE-DAH	GLORIOUS, HIGHLY RESPECTED
MAHASSEN	MAH-HAH-SEN	CHARMS
MAHBOUB	MAH-BOOB	SWEETHEART
MAHBOUBA	MAH-BOO-BAH	LOVED ONE, DARLING
MAHBOUSSAH	MAH-BOO-SAH	IMPRISONED
MAHDOUMEH	MAH-DOO-MEH	IRRISTIBLE, CLOSE TO THE HEART
MAHFOUZAH	MAH-FOO-ZAH	PROTECTED ONE
MAHILAH	MAH-HEE-LAH	BARREN

Mouher (Colt)

ARABIC	PRONUNCIATION	TRANSLATION
LAZAWARDI	LAH-ZAH-WAR-DEE	AZURE, BLUE OF THE CLEAR SKY
LAZEEZ	LAH-ZEEZ	DELICIOUS
LAZEM	LAH-ZEM	NECESSARY
LEBNANE	LEB-NAH-NEE	FROM LEBANON
LEE	LEE	MINE
LEEFT	LEEFT	TURNIP
LEEKLAK	LEEK-LAK	STORK
LIBEE	LEE-BEE	FROM LIBYA
LIBLAB	LIB-LAB	IVY
LIL	LIL	TO
LISS	LEESS	THIEF
LOOB	LOOB	CORE
LOOBAN	LOO-BAN	FRANKINCENSE
LOOBDAT	LOOB-DAT	MANE OF A LION
LOULOU	LOO-LOO	PEARLS
LOUN	LOWN	COLOR, TINT
LOUTF	LOUTF	TO BE KIND TO
LOUTFAN	LOOT-FAN	KINDLY, PLEASE
LOUTFEE	LOOT-FEE	GRACIOUS ONE

~ M ~

ARABIC	PRONUNCIATION	TRANSLATION
MAAROUF LIL ABAD	MAA-ROOF-LIL-AH-BAD	KNOWN FOREVER
MABHOUR	MAB-HOOR	DAZZLED
MABROUK	MAH-BROOK	CONGRATULATIONS
MABSOOT	MAB-SOOT	HAPPY
MADEE	MAH-DEE	PAST
MADKHAL	MAH-KHAL	ACCESS
MAEJJ	MAH-EJJ	SURGING
MAEL	MAH-EL	INCLINED
MAESSAT	MAH-EE-SAT	TRAGEDY
MAEZOUN	MAH-EE-ZOON	AUTHORIZED
MAGEED	MAH-JEED	GLORIOUS, HIGHLY RESPECTED
MAHAB AL LAHEEB	MAH-HAB-AL-LAH-HEEB	SURGE OF THE FLAME
MAHAB AL REIH	MAH-HAB-AL-REEH	SURGE OF THE STORM

Mouhra (Filly)

ARABIC	PRONUNCIATION	TRANSLATION
MAHIRAH	MAH-HEE-RAH	CLEVER, SMART
MAHKKAR	MAH-KAR	WITY, FOXY
MAHROUSSEH	MAH-ROO-SSEH	PROTECTED
MAHZEEHAH	MAH-ZEE-HAH	TO HAVE FUN
MAISSAT	MAH-EE-SAT	TRAGEDY
MAIZAH	MAH-EE-ZAH	GOAT (FEMALE)
MAJDOULAH	MAJ-DOO-LAH	TWISTED
MAJEEDAH	MAH-JEE-DAH	GLORIOUS, HIGHLY RESPECTED
MAJHOULAH	MAJ-HOO-LAH	ANONYMOUS
MAJNOUNAH	MAJ-NOON-AH	CRAZY
MAKHOUZAH	MAH-KHOO-ZAH	TAKEN
MAKHTOUFAH	MAKH-TOO-FAH	ABDUCTED
MALAKEH SAMAWIYAH	MAH-LAH-KAY-SAH-MAH-WEE-YAH	ANGEL FROM HEAVEN
MALIKAT AL BOUSTAN	MAH-LEE-KAT-AL BOOS-TAN	QUEEN OF THE FIELD
MAMZOUJAH	MAM-ZOO-JAH	MIXED
MARAH	MAH-RAH	JOVIAL, HAPPY
MARARAH	MAH-RAH-RAH	BITTERNESS
MARGHOUBAH	MAR-GHOO-BAH	DESIRED
MARHABAH	MAR-HAH-BAH	HELLO, WELCOME
MARRAT	MAH-RAT	ONCE
MARZOUKAH	MAR-ZOO-KAH	SHE IS BLESSED
MASHEETAT	MAH-SHEE-TAT	HAIRDRESSER
MASHOORA	MAHSH-HOO-RAH	FAMOUS
MASR	MASR	EGYPT
MASRIAH	MASS-REE-YAH	EGYPTIAN
MASSAT	MAH-SAT	DIAMOND
MASSDAR	MASS-DAR	ORIGIN
MASSIRAT	MAH-SEE-RAT	LONG WALK
MASSTOURAH	MASS-TOO-RAH	CONCEALED
MATLOUBAH	MAT-LOO-BAH	DESIRED
MATROUKA	MAT-ROO-KAH	ABANDONED
MAWJOUDAH	MAW-JOO-DAH	AVAILABLE
MEETHAL	MEE-THAL	IMAGE

Mouher (Colt)

ARABIC	PRONUNCIATION	TRANSLATION
MAHBOUB	MAH-BOOB	BELOVED
MAHDEE	MAH-DEE	MATERIAL
MAHEK	MAH-HEK	TO BICKER WITH
MAHER	MAH-HER	SKILLED
MAHKER	MAH-KER	SLY, CUNNING
MAHMOOD	MAH-MOOD	PRAISED
MAJD	MAJD	GLORY, HONOR
MAJEED	MAH-JEED	HIGHLY RESPECTED, GLORIOUS
MAJHOUL	MAJ-HOOL	UNKNOWN
MAJID	MAH-JEED	GLORIFIED, EXHALTED
MAJLIS	MAJLIS	COUNCIL
MAJNOON	MAJ-NOON	INSANE, CRAZY
MAKHTOUF	MAKH-TOOF	KIDNAPPED
MAKSAD	MAK-SAD	DESTINATION
MALEH	MAH-LEH	SALTY
MALEK	MAH-LEK	PROPRIETOR
MAR	MAR	SAINT
MARAH	MAH-RAH	JOYFUL
MARAJAN	MAH-RAH-JAN	PARTY
MARGHOUB	MAR-GHOOB	DESIREABLE
MARHABAH	MAR-HAH-BAH	HELLO, WELCOME
MARJ	MARJ	PASTURE
MASEEL	MAH-SEEL	IDENTICAL
MASHEE	MAH-SHEE	WALKING
MASS	MASS	DIAMOND
MASSAR	MAH-SAR	PATH, ROUTE
MASSARAT HADBAN	MAH-SAH-RAT-HAD-BAN	THE JOY OF THE HADBAN TRIBE
MATANAT	MAH-TAH-NAT	STRENGTH
MATLOUB	MAT-LOOB	WANTED
MATROUK	MAT-ROOK	ABANDONED
MATTAR	MAH-TAR	LIGHT RAIN, SHOWER
MATTER	MAH-TER	RAINY
MAULOOD BIL RAAD	MAW-LOOD-BIL-RAAD	BORN DURING THUNDER

Mouhra (Filly)

ARABIC	PRONUNCIATION	TRANSLATION
MEKKAWIYEH	MEE-KAH-WEE-YEH	FROM THE TOWN OF MECCA
MERJAN	MER-JAN	CORAL
MIYAH AL AMTAR	MEE-YAH-AL-AM-TAR	RAIN WATERS
MIZMAR	MIZ-MAR	FLUTE
MOUABADAH	MOO-AH-BAH-DAH	EVERLASTING
MOUAJAHRAH	MOO-AH-JAH-RAH	LEASED
MOUAJALLAH	MOO-AH-JAH-LAH	DELAYED
MOUAMARAT	MOO-AH-MAH-RAT	INTRIGUE
MOUANASS	MOO-AH-NASS	FEMININE
MOUASSASSAT	MOO-AH-SAH-SAT	FOUNDATION
MOUASSAT	MOO-AH-SAT	COMFORT
MOUAYIDAH	MOO-AH-YEE-DAH	SUPPORTER
MOUBADALAT	MOO-BAH-DAH-LAT	EXCHANGE
MOUBADARAT	MOO-BAH-DAH-RAT	INITIATIVE
MOUBAHAH	MOO-BAH-HAH	ALLOWED
MOUBAHATHAT	MOO-BAH-HAH-THAT	DISCUSSION
MOUBALAT	MOO-BAH-LAT	ATTENTION
MOUBARADAH	MOO-BAH-RAH-DAH	CHILLED
MOUBARAKAT	MOO-BAH-RAH-KAT	BLESSED
MOUBARAZAT	MOO-BAH-RAH-ZAT	DUELING
MOUBASHARAT	MOO-BAH-SHAH-RAT	DIRECTOR
MOUBASSIRAH	MOO-BAH-SEE-RAH	FORTUNE TELLER
MOUBAWAB	MOO-BAH-WAB	CLARIFIED, BECOME PURE
MOUBAZIRRAH	MOO-BAH-ZEE-RAH	SQUANDERER
MOUBHAMAH	MOOB-HAH-MAH	VAGUE
MOUBHIJAH	MOOB-HEE-JAH	JOYFUL
MOUBKIRAH	MOOB-KEE-RAH	PREMATURE
MOUBTASSIMAH	MOOB-TAH-SEE-MAH	SMILING
MOUBYADAH	MOOB-YAH-DAH	WHITISH
MOUDALALAH	MOO-DAH-LAH-LAH	PAMPERED
MOUDAMIRAH	MOO-DAH-MEE-RAH	DEMOLISHER
MOUDARIBAH	MOO-DAH-REE-BAH	TRAINER
MOUDARISSAH	MOO-DAH-REE-SAH	SCHOOL TEACHER

Mouher (Colt)

ARABIC	PRONUNCIATION	TRANSLATION
MAULOOD LIL LAMS	MAW-LOOD-LIL-LAMS	BORN TO TOUCH
MAWHOOB	MAO-HOOB	GIFTED
MAZEED	MAH-ZEED	TO BECOME GREATER
MAZHAB	MAZ-HAB	FAITH
MEDRAR	MED-RAR	TORRENTIAL
MELK	MELK	PROPERTY
METHAL	MEE-THAL	IMAGE
MEYAH	MEE-YAH	WATERS
MIRWI	MEER-WEE	WATERED
MIRWI AL AATSHAN	MEER-WEE-AL-AAT-SHAN	SATISFYING THE THIRSTY ONE
MOOJREM	MOOJ-REM	OUTLAW
MOOSHAWASH	MOO-SHAH-WAHSH	MURKY
MOUABBAD	MOO-AH-BAD	ETERNAL
MOUAHSESS	MOO-AH-SESS	FOUNDER
MOUAKHAR	MOO-AH-KHAR	REAR
MOUAMARAT	MOO-AH-MAH-RAT	PLOT
MOUAYED	MOO-AH-YED	SUPPORTER
MOUAZAR	MOO-AH-ZAR	FORGIVEN
MOUBAL	MOO-BAL	MINDFUL
MOUBARAD	MOO-BAH-RAD	COOLED
MOUBARAK	MOO-BAH-RAK	BLESSED
MOUBARAR	MOO-BAH-RAR	JUSTIFIED
MOUBAREZ	MO-BAH-REZ	DUELIST
MOUBASHER	MOO-BAH-SHER	ONE WHO BRINGS GOOD NEWS
MOUBASSER	MOO-BAH-SER	FORTUNE TELLER
MOUBHAM	MOOB-HAM	OBSCURE
MOUBHEJ	MOOB-HEJ	DELIGHTFUL
MOUBKER	MOOB-KER	PREMATURE
MOUBTAHEJ	MOOB-TAH-HEJ	REJOICING
MOUBTASSEM	MOOB-TAH-SEM	SMILING
MOUBYAD	MOOB-YAD	WHITISH
MOUDAMER	MOO-DAH-MER	DESTROYER
MOUDAREB	MOO-DAH-REB	TRAINER

Mouhra (Filly)

ARABIC	PRONUNCIATION	TRANSLATION
MOUDIRAH	MOO-DEE-RAH	ADMINISTRATOR
MOUEELIMAH	MOO-EE-LEE-MAH	FAITHFUL
MOUFADALEH	MOO-FAH-DAH-LEH	FAVORED BY ALL
MOUFADALLAH	MOO-FAH-DAH-LAH	MY FAVORITE
MOUHABABAH	MOO-HAH-BAH-BAH	LOVEABLE
MOUHARIBAH	MOO-HAH-REE-BAH	FIGHTER
MOUHRA SAWDAH	MOOH-RAH-SAW-DAH	BLACK FILLY
MOUHSEENAH	MOOH-SEE-NAH	CHARITABLE
MOUHTARAMAH	MOOH-TAH-RAH-MAH	RESPECTED
MOUJABAHAH	MOO-JAH-BAH-HAH	CONFRONTATION
MOUJAHIDAH	MOO-JAH-HEE-DAH	STRUGGLE
MOUJIDAH	MOO-JEE-DAH	SKILLED
MOUJIZAH	MOO-JEE-ZAH	MIRACLE
MOUKADASSAH	MOO-KAH-DAH-SSAH	HOLY
MOUMIRAH	MOO-MEE-RAH	FRUITFUL
MOUMTAZAH	MOOM-TAH-ZAH	EXCEPTIONAL
MOUNDAHISHAH	MOON-DAH-HEE-SHAH	SURPRISED
MOURABEEYAH	MOO-RAH-BEE-YAH	EDUCATOR
MOURAFEEKAH	MOO-RAH-FEE-KAH	COMPANION
MOURAHIKAH	MOO-RAH-HEE-KAH	TEENAGER
MOURASILAH	MOO-RAH-SEE-LAH	CORRESPONDENT
MOUSILAH	MOO-SEE-LAH	SENDER
MOUSSAFIRAH	MOO-SAH-FEE-RAH	TRAVELER
MOUTAAHIBAH	MOO-TAH-AH-HEE-BAH	READY
MOUTAAKIDAH	MOO-TAH-AH-KEE-DAH	CERTAIN, FOR SURE
MOUTAALIMAH	MOO-TAH-AH-LEE-MAH	IN PAIN
MOUTABADILAH	MOO-TAH-BAH-DEE-LAH	ALTERNATE
MOUTAFAHILAH	MOO-TAH-FAH-EE-LAH	OPTIMISTIC
MOUTAFARIJAH	MOO-TAH-FAH-REE-JAH	SPECTATOR
MOUTAHALIFAH	MOO-TAH-HAH-LEE-FAH	ALLIED
MOUTAHARIBAH	MOO-TAH-HAH-REE-BAH	MILITANT
MOUTAHARIRAH	MOO-TAH-HAH-REE-RAH	LIBERATED
MOUTAHAZIBAH	MOO-TAH-HAH-ZEE-BAH	PREJUDICED

Mouher (Colt)

ARABIC	PRONUNCIATION	TRANSLATION
MOUDARESS	MOO-DAH-RESS	TEACHER
MOUDEER	MOO-DEER	DIRECTOR
MOUFADAHL	MOO-FAH-DAHL	FAVORED BY ALL
MOUFATESH	MOO-FAH-TESH	INSPECTOR
MOUHABAB	MOO-HAH-BAB	CHARMING
MOUHAREB	MOO-HAH-REB	WARRIOR, FIGHTER
MOUHEB	MOO-HEB	LOVER
MOUHIB	MOO-HEEB	LOVING
MOUHSEN	MOOH-SEN	CHARITABLE
MOUIMEN	MOO-EE-MEN	BELIEVER
MOUJAHED	MOO-JAH-HED	STRUGGLER
MOUKHTAR	MOOK-TAR	SELECTED
MOULOUKI	MOO-LOO-KEE	MAJESTIC
MOUMTAZ	MOOM-TAZ	DISTINGUISHED
MOUNDAHESH	MOON-DAH-HESH	SURPRISED
MOURABI	MOO-RAH-BEE	EDUCATOR
MOURAFEK	MOO-RAH-FEK	BODYGUARD
MOURASEL	MOO-RAH-SELL	CORRESPONDENT
MOUROD	MOO-ROD	WANTED
MOUROUR	MOO-ROOR	PASSAGE (ACT OF PASSING THROUGH)
MOUSABAKAT	MOO-SAH-BAH-KAT	RACE (WITH HORSES)
MOUSAYTAR	MOO-SAY-TAR	DOMINATING
MOUSSAHEB	MOO-SAH-HEB	COMPANION
MOUTAAHKED	MOO-TAH-AH-KED	CERTAIN
MOUTAFAEL	MOO-TAH-FAH-EL	OPTIMISTIC
MOUTAFAREJ	MOO-TAH-FAH-REJ	SPECTATOR
MOUTAGHASSEB	MOO-TAH-GHA-SSEB	OLD FASHIONED
MOUTAHAHEB	MOO-TAH-AH-HEB	READY
MOUTAHAREB	MOO-TAH-HAH-REB	EVASIVE
MOUTAHARER	MOO-TAH-HAH-RER	LIBERAL
MOUTAJADED	MOO-TAH-JAH-DED	RENEWED
MOUTAJAWAL	MOO-TAH-JAH-WAL	WANDERER
MOUTAJAWEB	MOO-TAH-JAH-WEB	RESPONSIVE

Mouhra (Filly)

ARABIC	PRONUNCIATION	TRANSLATION
MOUTAJADIDAH	MOO-TAH-JAH-DEE-DAH	RENEWED
MOUTAJALIDAH	MOO-TAH-JAH-LEE-DAH	FROZEN
MOUTAJAWALAH	MOO-TAH-JAH-WAH-LAH	TRAVELLING
MOUTAJAWIBAH	MOO-TAH-JAH-WEE-BAH	RESPONSIVE
MOUTAJIRAH	MOO-TAH-JEE-RAH	TRADER
MOUTAKABIRAH	MOO-TAH-KAH-BEE-RAH	CONCEITED
MOUTAKALIMAH	MOO-TAH-KAH-LEE-MAH	SPEAKER
MOUTALAWINAH	MOO-TAH-LAH-WEE-NAH	WITH DIFFERENT COLORS
MOUTAMALMILAH	MOO-TAH-MAL-MEE-LAH	RESTLESS
MOUTAMARIDAH	MOO-TAH-MAH-REE-DAH	REBEL
MOUTAMAYIZA	MOO-TAH-MAH-YEE-ZAH	SPECIAL
MOUTAMAYIZAH	MOO-TAH-MAH-YEE-ZAH	DISTINCT
MOUTAMINAH	MOO-TAH-MEE-NAH	TRUSTWORTHY
MOUTARABITAH	MOO-TAH-RAH-BEE-TAH	CONNECTED
MOUTASHADIDAH	MOO-TAH-SHAH-DEE-DAH	INFLEXIBLE, UNYIELDING
MOUTASSALIMAH	MOO-TAH-SAH-LEE-MAH	RECEIVER
MOUTASSALITAH	MOO-TAH-SAH-LEE-TAH	DOMINEERING
MOUTASSATIRAH	MOO-TAH-SAH-TEE-RAH	VEILED
MOUTATALIBAH	MOO-TAH-TAH-LEE-BAH	DEMANDING
MOUTATARIFAH	MOO-TAH-TAH-REE-FAH	EXTREME
MOUTATAWIRAH	MOO-TAH-TAH-WEE-RAH	ADVANCED
MOUTAWAJAH	MOO-TAH-WAH-JAH	CROWNED
MOUTAYASSIRAH	MOO-TAH-YAH-SEE-RAH	FEASIBLE
MOUTAZAYIDAH	MOO-TAH-ZAH-YEE-DAH	GROWING
MOUTAZINAH	MOO-TAH-ZEE-NAH	PRUDENT, CAUTIOUS
MOUTRIBAH	MOO-TREE-BAH	SONGSTRESS

~ N ~

ARABIC	PRONUNCIATION	TRANSLATION
NAAJAT	NAH-JAT	SHEEP (FEMALE)
NABAHAT	NAH-BAH-HAT	INTELLIGENCE
NABIGHAH	NAH-BEE-GHAH	GENIUS
NABILAH	NAH-BEE-LAH	NOBLE WOMAN
NABLAT	NAB-LAT	ARROW
NABRAT	NAB-RAT	ACCENT

Mouher (Colt)

ARABIC	PRONUNCIATION	TRANSLATION
MOUTAJER	MOO-TAH-JER	MERCHANT
MOUTAKABER	MOO-TAH-KAH-BER	PROUD, ARROGANT
MOUTAKADEM	MOO-TAH-KAH-DEM	ADVANCED
MOUTAKALEM	MOO-TAH-KAH-LEM	SPEAKER
MOUTALAWEM	MOO-TAH-LAH-WEM	COLORFUL
MOUTAMALMEL	MOO-TAH-MAHL-MEL	FIDGETY
MOUTAMARED	MOO-TAH-MAH-RED	REBELLIOUS
MOUTAMAYEZ	MOO-TAH-MAH-YEZ	DISTINGUISHED
MOUTAMAYEZ	MOO-TAH-MAH-YEZ	SPECIAL
MOUTANAKER	MOO-TAH-NAH-KER	DISGUISED
MOUTASSALET	MOO-TAH-SAH-LET	MASTERFUL
MOUTASSATER	MOO-TAH-SAH-TER	DISGUISED
MOUTATALEB	MOO-TAH-TAH-LEB	DEMANDING
MOUTATAREF	MOO-TAH-TAH-REF	RADICAL
MOUTATAWIAR	MOO-TAH-TAH-WEE-AR	SOPHISTICATED
MOUTAYAM	MOO-TAH-YAM	MADLY IN LOVE WITH
MOUTAZEN	MOO-TAH-ZEN	WISE, USES CAUTION
MOUZDAHER	MOOZ-DAH-HER	FLOURISHING
~ N ~		
NABAD	NAH-BAD	PULSE
NABAWI	NAH-BAH-WEE	PROPHETIC
NABEE	NAH-BEE	PROPHET
NABIL	NAH-BEEL	NOBLEMAN
NADEEM	NAH-DEEM	COMPANION, FRIEND
NADEM	NAH-DEM	REPENTANT
NADIR	NAH-DEER	RARE
NADIR AL SHAMALEE	NAH-DEER-AL-SHAL-MAH-LEE	THE RARE NORTH WND
NAEB	NAH-EB	DEPUTY
NAFAK	NAH-FAK	TUNNEL
NAFAR	NAH-FAR	PERSON, INDIVIDUAL
NAFASS	NAH-FASS	BREATH
NAFEER	NAH-FEER	TRUMPET
NAFS	NAFS	SOUL, SPIRIT

Mouhra (Filly)

ARABIC	PRONUNCIATION	TRANSLATION
NABTAT	NAB-TAT	SPROUTING PLANT
NADARAT	NAH-DAH-RAT	FRESHNESS
NADBAT	NAD-BAT	MARK, SCAR
NADEERAN	NAH-DEE-RAN	RARELY, SELDOM
NAFDAT	NAF-DAT	ESCAPE
NAFEESAT	NAH-FEE-SAT	VALUABLE
NAFISSAH	NAH-FEE-SAH	PRICELESS, BEYOND VALUE
NAFKAT	NAF-KAT	EXPENSE
NAFOURAH	NAH-FOO-RAH	FOUNTAIN
NAFSANI	NAF-SAH-NEE	PSYCHOLOGICAL
NAHDAT	NAH-DAT	AWAKENING
NAHIFAT	NAH-HEE-FAT	THIN, SLIM
NAHIYAT	NAH-HEE-YAT	DIRECTION
NAHLAT	NAH-LAT	BEE
NAHLAT HAYATEE	NAH-LAT-HAH-YAH-TEE	THE BEE OF MY LIFE
NAIMAH	NAH-EE-MAH	BLISS
NAJAT	NAH-JAT	RESCUE
NAJEEBAH	NAH-JEE-BAH	SUPERIOR
NAKEELAH	NAH-KEE-LAH	CARRIER
NAKHAT	NAK-HAT	FLAVOR
NAKHWAT	NAKH-WHAT	CHIVALRY
NAQUAT	NAH-KAT	CAMEL (FEMALE)
NAQUOUD	NAH-KOOD	BELL
NAR	NAR	FIRE, WARMTH
NARGHILEH	NAR-JEE-LEH	WATER PIPE FOR TOBACCO
NASHALAT	NAH-SHAH-LAT	PICK POCKET, THIEF
NASHEEAT	NAH-SHEE-AT	YOUNGSTER
NASHEETA-EL-ZARKA	NAH-SHEE-TAH-EL-ZAR-KAH	THE PLAYFUL GRAY
NASHEETAH	NAH-SHEE-TAH	ACTIVE
NASHRAT	NASH-RAT	PUBLICATION, A PUBLISHED WORK
NASHWAT	NASH-WHAT	ECSTASY
NASSABAH	NAH-SAH-BAH	IMPOSTER
NASSEEB	NAH-SEEB	FATE, DESTINY

Mouher (Colt)

ARABIC	PRONUNCIATION	TRANSLATION
NAFS AL NIL	NAFS-AL-NEEL	SPIRIT OF THE NILE
NAGHAM	NAH-GHAM	MELODY
NAGHEM	NAH-GHEM	HARMONIZER
NAHAR	NAH-HAR	DAYTIME
NAHEM	NAH-HEM	GREEDY
NAHHAL	NAH-HAL	BEEKEEPER
NAHKI	NAH-KEE	PURE, CLEAR
NAHR	NAHR	RIVER
NAIM	NAH-EEM	COMFORT, CONTENT
NAJAH	NAH-JAH	SUCCESS
NAJEEB	NAH-JEEB	HIGHBORN, EXCELLENT
NAJJAR	NAH-JAR	CARPENTER, BUILDER
NAKEEB	NAH-KEEB	CAPTAIN
NAKHL	NAKHL	PALM TREE
NAMASH	NAH-MASH	FRECKLES
NAMOUSS	NAH-MOOS	LAW, CODE
NAQUED	NAH-QUED	CRITIC
NAR	NAR	FIRE
NAR AL ABAD	NAR-AL-AH-BAD	ETERNAL FLAME
NAR AL HILAL	NAR-AL-HEE-LAL	THE FIRE OF THE MOON
NAR AL SHAMS	NAR-AL-SHAMS	THE FIRE OF THE SUN, THE SUN FIRE
NAR AZAR	NAR-AH-ZAR	THE FIRE OF MARCH
NAREE	NAH-REE	FIERY
NASEEM	NAH-SEEM	DISTINGUISHED, ELEGANT
NASEK	NAH-SEK	LONER
NASHAL	NAH-SHALL	PICKPOCKET
NASHEED	NAH-SHEED	SONG OF PRAISE, ANTHEM
NASHEET	NAH-SHEET	ENERGETIC
NASR	NASR	VICTORY
NASSAB	NAH-SAB	SWINDLER
NASSAJ	NAH-SAJ	WEAVER
NASSEEB	NAH-SEEB	DESTINY
NASSEEB ELAHI	NAH-SEEB-EE-LAH-HEE	DIVINE DESTINY

Mouhra (Filly)

ARABIC	PRONUNCIATION	TRANSLATION
NASSEEBAH	NAH-SEE-BAH	RELATIVE
NASSIHAT	NAH-SEE-HAT	ADVICE
NASSIYAT	NAH-SEE-YAT	FORELOCK
NASSMAT	NASS-MAT	FRESH BREATH OF AIR
NATEEJAT	NAH-TEE-JAT	RESULT, OUTCOME
NAWAT	NAH-WHAT	SEED
NAYEEQUAH	NAH-YEE-KAH	CHOOSY, PARTICULAR
NAZAFAT	NAH-ZAH-FAT	CLEANLINESS
NAZAHAT	NAH-ZAH-HAT	INTEGRITY, FAIRNESS
NAZARAT	NAH-ZAH-RAT	PRISON
NAZEEFAH	NAH-ZEE-FAH	PURE
NAZEERAH	NAH-ZEE-RAH	EQUIVALENT, COUNTERPART
NAZHAT	NAZ-HAT	PROMENADE
NAZLAT	NAZ-LAT	DESCENT, ANCESTRY
NAZRAT	NAZ-RAT	GLANCE, A QUICK LOOK
NEEKAYAT	NEE-KAH-YAT	SPITE, ANNOYANCE
NEELEE	NEE-LEE	INDIGO COLOR
NEEYAT	NEE-YAT	PURPOSE
NEEZAMIYAH	NEE-ZAH-MEE-YAH	DISCIPLINED
NEHAYAT	NEE-HAH-YAT	THE END
NEJJARAT	NEH-JAH-RAT	WOOD SHAVINGS
NEJMAT	NEJ-MATT	STAR
NIKKAB	NEE-KAB	VEIL
NISF AL LEIL	NISF-AL-LAY-IL	MIDNIGHT
NISF AL NAHR	NISF-AL-NAHR	MIDDAY
NOOKTAT	NOOK-TAT	SPECKLE
NOOR AL HAMRA	NOOR-AL-HAM-RAH	THE LIGHT OF THE CHESTNUT MARE
NOOR AL SHAGRA	NOOR-AL-SHAG-RAH	THE LIGHT OF THE CHESTNUT ONE
NOUBOUAT	NOO-BOO-AT	DIVINE PREDICTION
NOUBOUWAT	NOO-BOO-WHAT	PROPHECY
NOUBZAT	NOOB-ZAT	BIOGRAPHY
NOUFOUS	NOO-FOOS	SOULS, SPIRITS
NOUFOUS AL NIL	NOO-FOOS-AL-NEEL	SPIRITS OF THE NILE

Mouher (Colt)

ARABIC	PRONUNCIATION	TRANSLATION
NASSEEM	NAH-SEEM	BREEZE
NASSER	NAH-SER	CHAMPION, CONQUEROR
NASSER AL SHAMAL	NAH-SER-AL-SHAH-MAL	THE CONQUEROR OF THE NORTH
NATEK	NAH-TEK	ARTICULATE
NATOUR	NAH-TOOR	DOORMAN, DOORKEEPER
NAWAR	NAH-WAR	MAY
NAWM	NAWM	SLEEP
NAZAR	NAH-ZAR	SIGHT
NAZEEF	NAH-ZEEF	PURE, CLEAN
NAZEER	NAH-ZEER	COUNTERPART, EQUAL
NAZER	NAH-ZER	SUPERINTENDANT, DIRECTOR
NAZR	NAZR	VOW
NEEDAL	NEE-DAL	STRUGGLE
NEESAN	NEE-SAN	APRIL
NEETAK	NEE-TAK	RANGE
NIJM	NIJM	BIG STAR, PLANET
NIMR	NIMR	TIGER
NISR	NISR	EAGLE
NOOR	NOOR	LIGHT, GLEAM
NOOR AL SHAGRA	NOOR-AL-SHAG-RAH	THE LIGHT OF THE CHESTNUT ONE
NOORI	NOO-REE	MY LIGHT
NOUBL	NOOBL	NOBILITY
NOUR AL RAML	NOOR-AL-RAML	THE LIGHT OF THE SAND

~ R ~

ARABIC	PRONUNCIATION	TRANSLATION
RABANI	RAH-BAH-NEE	DIVINE, FROM HEAVEN
RABBEH	RAH-BEH	WINNER
RADEE	RAH-DEE	PLEASED, CONTENT
RADEEF	RAH-DEEF	RESERVE
RAED	RAH-ED	THUNDER
RAEJ	RAH-EJ	WIDESPREAD
RAFASS	RAH-FASS	KICKER
RAFEEK	RAH-FEEK	COMPANION
RAFEEQ	RAH-FEEK	COMPANION

Mouhra (Filly)

ARABIC	PRONUNCIATION	TRANSLATION
NOUFOUZ	NOO-FOOZ	INFLUENCE
NOUKHBAT	NOOKH-BAT	CHOICE
NOUKTAT	NOOK-TAT	JOKE
NOUSHABAT	NOO-SHAH-BAT	ARROW
NOUZRAT	NOOZ-RAT	RARITY

~ R ~

ARABIC	PRONUNCIATION	TRANSLATION
RAAHFAT	RAH-AH-FAT	MERCY
RABANIYAH	RAH-BAH-NEE-YAH	FROM GOD
RABBAT	RAH-BAT	GODDESS
RABEEBAH	RAH-BEE-BAH	STEPDAUGHTER
RABEETAT	RAH-BEE-TAT	CONNECTION, LINK
RADADAH	RAH-DAH-DAH	REPEAT
RADEEFAT	RAH-DEE-FAT	SUBSTITUTE
RADEEYAH	RAH-DEE-YAH	SATISFIED, CONTENT
RADIYAT	RAH-DEE-YAT	CONTENT, SATISFIED
RAEEMAT	RAH-EE-MAT	TO CARESS
RAFAHAT	RAH-FAH-HAT	WELL BEING
RAFEEDAH	RAH-FEE-DAH	REJECTING
RAFEEDAT	RAH-FEE-DAT	SUPPORT
RAFEEKATI	RAH-FEE-KAH-TEE	MY COMPANION
RAFIAT	RAH-FEE-AT	RAISING
RAFSAT	RAF-SAT	A KICK
RAGHBAT	RAGH-BAT	DISIRE, WISH
RAGHIBAH	RAH-GHEE-BAH	WISHFUL
RAGHWAT	RAGH-WAT	FOAM, LATHER
RAHABAH	RAH-HAH-BAH	WELCOME, TO GREET
RAHABAT	RAH-HAH-BAT	VASTNESS
RAHALAT	RAH-HAH-LAT	NOMAD (FEMALE)
RAHEELAT	RAH-HEE-LAT	RIDING CAMEL
RAHIBAT	RAH-HEE-BAT	NUN
RAHINAT	RAH-HEE-NAT	PRISONER (OF)
RAHLAT	RAH-LAT	JOURNEY
RAHMAT	RAH-MAT	COMPASSION, MERCY

Mouher (Colt)

ARABIC	PRONUNCIATION	TRANSLATION
RAFRAF	RAF-RAF	KINGFISHER
RAGHAH	RAH-GHAH	EVADE
RAGHEB	RAH-GHEB	DESIRIOUS
RAHAFAT	RAH-AH-FAT	COMPASSION
RAHAL	RAH-HAL	TRAVELER
RAHEB	RAH-HEB	MONK
RAHEEL	RAH-HEEL	DEPARTURE
RAHEEM	RAH-HEEM	LENIENT
RAHOUM	RAH-HOOM	MERCIFUL
RAJAH	RAH-JAH	TO HOPE
RAKASS	RAH-KASS	DANCER
RAKEEB	RAH-KEEB	OBSERVER
RAKM	RAKM	NUMBER
RAMAD	RAH-MAD	ASHES
RAMAH	RAH-MAH	DESIRE
RAMEE	RAH-MEE	RIFLEMAN
RAMIK	RAH-MEEK	GRACEFUL, ELEGANT
RAML	RAML	SAND
RAML AL SAHRAH	RAML-AL-SAH-RAH	THE SAND OF THE DESERT
RAOUF	RAH-OOF	MERCIFUL
RAOUM	RAH-OOM	LOVING, TENDER
RAQUASS	RAH-KAHSS	DANCER
RASAN	RAH-SAN	HALTER
RASED	RAH-SED	OBSERVER
RASEED	RAH-SEED	BALANCE
RASHAD	RAH-SHAD	BRIBERY
RASHASH	RAH-SHASH	SPLASH
RASHED	RAH-SHED	COUNSELOR, MENTOR
RASHI	RAH-SHEE	BRIBER
RASMAHLI	RAS-MAH-LEE	CAPITALIST
RASSAM	RAH-SAM	PAINTER, ARTIST
RASSM	RASSM	OFFICIAL
RASSOUL	RAH-SOOL	MESSENGER

Mouhra (Filly)

ARABIC	PRONUNCIATION	TRANSLATION
RAJAH	RAH-JAH	WISH, HOPE
RAJFAT	RAHJ-FAT	TREMBLE
RAKASSAH	RAH-KAH-SAH	DANCER (FEMALE)
RAKEEBAH	RAH-KEE-BAH	OBSERVER (FEMALE)
RAKHMAT	RAKH-MAT	EGYPTIAN VULTURE
RAKSAT	RAK-SAT	A DANCE
RAKSAT AL HILAL	RAK-SAT-AL-HEE-LAL	DANCE OF THE MOON, MOON DANCE
RAML AL SAHRAH	RAML-AL-SAH-RAH	THE SAND OF THE DESERT
RAMLEE	RAM-LEE	SANDY
RAMZEE	RAM-ZEE	SYMBOLIC
RAOUFAH	RAH-OO-FAH	COMPASSIONATE
RAOUMAH	RAH-OO-MAH	AFFECTIONATE
RAQUASA	RAH-QUA-SAH	DANCER
RAQUESSAH	RAH-QUE-SAH	DANCER (FEMALE)
RASALAH	RAH-SAH-LAH	CORRESPOND, SUIT, MATCH
RASEEDAH	RAH-SEE-DAH	OBSERVER
RASHAKAT	RAH-SHAH-KAT	GRACEFULNESS
RASHASH	RAH-SHASH	SPLASH
RASHEEDAH	RAH-SHEE-DAH	GRACEFUL
RASHEEKAH	RAH-SHEE-KAH	AGILE
RASHEEYAT	RAH-SHEE-YAT	BRIBER
RASHIDAT	RAH-SHEE-DAT	MAJOR
RASHWAT	RASH-WHAT	HUSH MONEY
RASIDA	RAH-SEE-DAH	WATCHER
RASSAMAH	RAH-SAH-MAH	ARTIST, PAINTER (FEMALE)
RASSANAT	RAH-SAH-NAT	GRAVITY
RASSASSAT	RAH-SAH-SAT	BULLET
RASSOULAH	RAH-SOO-LAH	MESSENGER (FEMALE)
RAWADAH	RAH-WAH-DAH	SEDUCE
RAWIYAT	RAH-WEE-YAT	STORYTELLER (FEMALE)
RAYAT	RAH-YAT	FLAG
RAZANAT	RAH-ZAH-NAT	SOLEMNITY
RAZEENAT	RAH-ZEE-NAT	SOLEMN

Mouher (Colt)

ARABIC	PRONUNCIATION	TRANSLATION
RASSOUL ALLAH	RAH-SOOL-AL-LAH	GOD'S MESSENGER
RATEB	RAH-TEB	OFFICER (IN THE MILITARY)
RAWEE	RAH-WEE	STORYTELLER
RAYESS	RAH-YESS	LEADER, PRESIDENT
RAZAZ	RAH-ZAZ	DRIZZLE
RAZEEL	RAH-ZEEL	MISCHIEVOUS
RAZEEN	RAH-ZEEN	CALM
REBAT	REE-BAT	RIBBON
REIH	REEH	STORM
REJOULAT	REE-JOO-LAT	MANHOOD
ROOSHD	ROOSHD	REASON
ROUBAN	ROO-BAN	CAPTAIN
ROUHAYEM	ROO-HAH-YEM	THE KIND HEARTED ONE
ROUHMAN	ROOH-MAN	GRACIOUS (THE)
ROUKAD	ROO-KAD	SLEEP

~ S ~

ARABIC	PRONUNCIATION	TRANSLATION
SAAD	SAH-AD	GOOD LUCK
SABEK	SAH-BEK	PREVIOUS
SABIL	SAH-BEEL	DRINKING FOUNTAIN
SADEED	SAH-DEED	RELEVANT
SADIQUI	SAH-DEE-KEE	MY FRIEND
SAEB	SAH-EB	ABANDONED
SAED	SAH-ED	GOVERNING
SAEED	SAH-EED	BLESSED, HAPPY
SAEH	SAH-EH	TOURIST
SAEK	SAH-EK	DRIVER
SAER	SAH-ER	WALKER
SAESS	SAH-ESS	HORSE STABLE WORKER
SAFEER	SAH-FEER	AMBASSADOR
SAFI	SAH-FEE	PURE
SAFI-NOUR	SAH-FEE-NOOR	PURE LIGHT
SAFIR	SAH-FEER	AMBASSADDOR
SAHEB	SAH-HEB	COMPANION, PLAYFUL FRIEND

Mouhra (Filly)

ARABIC	PRONUNCIATION	TRANSLATION
SALMEE	SAL-MEE	PEACEFUL
SALUKI	SAH-LOO-KEE	SALUKI (DOG)
SAMAHAT	SAH-MAH-HAT	GENEROSITY
SAMAR	SAH-MAR	DARK SKIN
SAMAWIYAH	SAH-MAH-WEE-YAH	HEAVENLY, FROM HEAVEN
SAMIKAH	SAH-MEE-KAH	TOWERING
SAMIRAH	SAH-MEE-RAH	FRIEND
SAMRAH	SAHM-RAH	DARK ONE
SAMRAT	SAM-RAT	BROWN COLOR
SARIRAT	SAH-REE-RAT	INNER SELF
SARMADIYAH	SAR-MAH-DEE-YAH	ETERNAL
SATIHAT	SAH-TEE-HAT	TERRACE
SATTOU	SAH-TOO	ROBBERY
SATWAT	SAT-WHAT	INFLUENCE
SAWDAH	SAW-DAH	BLACK COLORED
SAYIDAT	SAH-YEE-DAT	LADY
SAYIDATEE	SAH-YEE-DAH-TEE	MY LADY
SAYYIDAH	SAH-YEE-DAH	BOSSY LADY
SEERAH	SEE-RAH	HER SECRET
SEERAT	SEE-RAT	CONDUCT
SEITARAT	SEY-TAH-RAT	AUTHORITY
SEMOU AL AMIRAH	SE-MOO-AL-AH-MEE-RAH	HER HIGHNESS
SER-DAB	SER-DAB	VAULT
SEROUR	SEE-ROOR	PLEASURE
SERRIYAT	SEH-REE-YAT	SECRECY
SHABABAT	SHAH-BAH-BAT	FLUTE
SHABAT	SHAH-BAT	YOUNG WOMAN
SHABHAT	SHAB-HAT	SUSPICION
SHABIHAT	SHAH-BEE-HAT	LOOK ALIKE
SHABKAT	SHAB-KAT	FISHNET
SHAFFAF	SHAH-FAF	TRANSPARENT
SHAFKAT	SHAF-KAT	COMPASSION, PITY
SHAGRAH	SHAG-RAH	CHESTNUT COLOR

Mouher (Colt)

ARABIC	PRONUNCIATION	TRANSLATION
SHAHAMAT	SHAH-HAH-MAT	GENEROSITY
SHAHEB	SHAH-HEB	PALE
SHAHED	SHAH-HED	WITNESS
SHAHEEK	SHAH-HEEK	INSPIRATION
SHAHEEN	SHAH-HEEN	FALCON
SHAHEM	SHAH-HEM	MAGNANIMOUS
SHAHIR	SHAH-HEER	FAMOUS
SHAHROUR	SHAH-ROOR	BLACKBIRD
SHAIB	SHAH-EB	WHITE HAIR
SHAKEEK	SHAH-KEEK	BROTHER
SHAKER	SHAH-KER	THANKFUL
SHAL	SHALL	SHAWL
SHALLAL	SHAH-LLAL	WATERFALL
SHAMAL	SHAH-MAL	NORTH
SHAMALEE	SHAH-MAH-LEE	NORTH WIND
SHAMAM	SHAH-MAM	MELON
SHAMEL	SHAH-MEL	COMPREHENSIVE
SHAMMAR	SHAH-MAR	TO TUCK
SHAR	SHAR	EVIL
SHARAB	SHAH--RAB	DRINK
SHARAF	SHAH-RAF	HONOR
SHAREB	SHAH-REB	DRINKER
SHARED	SHAH-RED	WANDERER
SHAREEK	SHAH-REEK	PARTNER
SHAREEK ANEES	SHAH-REEK-AH-NEES	TRUE FRIEND
SHAREEK MAJEED	SHAH-REEK-MAH-JEED	NOBLE PARTNER
SHAREEK TAWEEL	SHAH-REEK-TAH-WEEL	TALL PARTNER, TALL FRIEND
SHARESS	SHAH-RESS	AGGRESSIVE
SHARIF	SHAH-REEF	NOBLE
SHARKEE	SHAR-KEE	EASTERN
SHATAWI	SHAH-TAH-WEE	WINTERY
SHATER	SHAH-TER	SLY, CRAFTY
SHAWISH	SHAH-WISH	SERGEANT

Mouhra (Filly)

ARABIC	PRONUNCIATION	TRANSLATION
SHAHAMAT	SHAH-HAH-MAT	CHIVALRY
SHAHIDAT	SHAH-HEE-DAT	WITNESS
SHAHIRAH	SHAH-HEE-RAH	FAMOUS
SHAHIYAT	SHAH-HEE-YAT	APPETITE
SHAJRAT	SHAJ-RAT	TREE
SHAKHSIYAT	SHAKH-SEE-YAT	PERSONALITY
SHAKIRAH	SHAH-KEE-RAH	GRATEFUL
SHAKIRAT AL OMR	SHAH-KEE-RAT-AL-OMR	THE COMPANION FOR LIFE
SHAKIYKAT	SHAH-KEE-KAT	SISTER
SHAKLEE	SHAK-LEE	FORMAL
SHAKRAT	SHAK-RAT	BLONDNESS
SHAMALEE	SHAH-MAH-LEE	NORTHERLY
SHAMALIYAT	AHAH-MAH-LEE-YAT	FROM THE NORTH
SHAMAT	SHAH-MAT	BEAUTY MARK
SHAMAT	SHAM-AT	CANDLE
SHAMILAT	SHAH-MEE-LAT	GOOD QUALITY
SHAMS	SHAMS	THE SUN
SHAMS AL JANNAT	SHAMS-AL-JAH-NAT	THE SUN OF PARADISE
SHAMS AL SAHRAH	SHAMS-AL-SAH-RAH	THE DESERT SUN
SHAMSEE	SHAM-SEE	SOLAR
SHARARAT	SHAH-RAH-RAT	SPARKS
SHARBAT	SHAR-BAT	DRINKS
SHARESSAH	SHAH-REH-SAH	AGGRESSIVE
SHARIAH	SHAH-REE-AH	LAW
SHARIBAH	SHAH-REE-BAH	DRINKER
SHARIDAH	SHAH-REE-DAH	WANDERER
SHARIFAH	SHAH-REE-FAH	NOBLE
SHARIKAH	SHAH-REE-KAH	ASSOCIATE
SHARIKAT HAYATI	SHAH-REE-KAT-HAH-YAH-TEE	MY LIFE COMPANION
SHARKIYAH	SHAR-KEE-YAH	ORIENTAL
SHATIRAT	SHAH-TEE-RAT	SMART, EXPERIENCED
SHEEMAT	SHEE-MAT	CUSTOM
SHEERIRAH	SHEE-REE-RAH	WICKED

Mouher (Colt)

ARABIC	PRONUNCIATION	TRANSLATION
SHEEHAB	SHEE-HAB	SHOOTING STAR
SHETAN	SHEE-TAN	DEVIL
SHIBEL	SHI-BEL	LION CUB
SHOUHRAT	SHOO-RAT	FAME
SHOUROUK	SHOO-ROOK	SUNRISE
SHOURSHOUR	SHOOR-SHOOR	FINCH
SIHR	SIHR	MAGIC
SIJN	SIJN	PRISON
SILAH	SEE-LAH	WEAPON
SIMOU	SEE-MOO	HIGHNESS
SIMSAR	SIM-SAR	BROKER, MIDDLEMAN
SIRJ	SIRJ	SESAME OIL
SOUKN	SOUKN	HOT
SOUKOUN	SOO-KOON	CALM
SOUKOUT	SOO-KOOT	SILENCE
SOULOUM	SOO-LOOM	LADDER
SOULWAN	SOOL-WAN	CONSOLATION
SOUMSOUM	SOOM-SOOM	SESAME
SOUNDAN	SOON-SAN	ANVIL
SOUNOUNOU	SOO-NOO-NOO	SWALLOW
SOURJ	SOURJ	SADDLE
SOURRI	SOO-RREE	SECRETIVE
SOUSAN	SOO-SAN	LILY (FLOWER)
SOUWAR	SOO-WAR	BRACELET
SUBHAN-ALLAH	SUB-HAN-AL-LAH	GLORY TO GOD
SUKKAR	SOO-KAR	SWEET, SUGAR
SULTAN	SUL-TAN	SULTAN, SOVEREIGN
SUWAIDEE	SOO-WAY-DEE	FROM SUWAIDAH (MALE)

~ T ~

TABADOUL	TAH-BAH-DOOL	EXCHANGE
TABASSOUR	TAH-BAH-SOOR	TO SMILE
TABDIL	TAB-DEEL	TRADE
TABN	TABN	HAY

Mouhra (Filly)

ARABIC	PRONUNCIATION	TRANSLATION
SHEYTANEE	SHEY-TAH-NEE	DEVILISH
SHISHAH	SHEE-SHAH	NARGILEH (EGYPTIAN)
SHOUGHOUR	SHOO-GOOR	VACANCY
SHOUJAIRAT	SHOO-JAY-RAT	SHRUB
SHOURAT	SHOOH-RAT	RENOWN
SHOUROUK	SHOO-ROOK	SUNRISE
SIHREE	SIH-REE	MAGICAL
SIMAAH	SEE-MAH	FORGIVENESS
SIMSARAH	SIM-SAH-RAH	MIDDLE WOMAN, BROKER
SITR	SITR	SHIELD
SITT	SEETT	LADY
SITTAR	SEE-TAR	VEIL
SIYAHAT	SEE-YAH-HAT	TOURISM
SIYASSAT	SEE-YAH-SAT	POLITICS
SOUHOULAT	SOO-HOO-LAT	EASE
SOUKOUNAT	SOO-KOO-NAT	WARMTH, HEAT
SOUKRIYAT	SOOK-REE-YAT	SUGAR BOWL
SOULALAT	SOO-LAH-LAT	DYNASTY
SOUMSOUM	SOOM-SOOM	SESAME
SOURAT	SOO-RAT	IMAGE
SOURAT AL OUM	SOO-RAT-AL-OOM	IMAGE OF THE MOTHER
SOURAT OUMAHAH	SOO-RAT-OOM-MAH-HAH	IMAGE OF HER MOTHER
SOURIYAH	SOO-REE-YAH	SYRIAN (FEMALE)
SOUYOULAT	SOO-YOO-LAT	LIQUIDITY
SUBHAN ALLAH	SUB-HAN-AL-LAH	PRAISE THE LORD
SUKKARAH	SU-KAH-RAH	SWEET
SUKKARAH	SOO-KAH-RAH	SUGAR
SULTANAT	SUL-TAH-NAT	SULTANATE
SURA	SOO-RAH	CHAPTER OF THE HOLY KORAN
SUWADAWIYAH	SOO-WAY-DAH-WEE-YAH	WOMAN FROM SUWAIDAH
SUWAIDA	SOO-WAY-DEE-YAH	A TOWN IN SYRIA (BLACK CONNOTATION)

~ T ~

Mouher (Colt)

ARABIC	PRONUNCIATION	TRANSLATION
TABREED	TAB-REED	COOLING
TABRIR	TAB-REER	JUSTIFICATION
TABSHEER	TAB-SHEER	PREACHING
TABSIR	TAB-SEER	FORUNE TELLING
TAEETHEER	TAH-EE-THEER	INFLUENCE
TAFSEER	TAF-SEER	EXPLANATION
TAHAROUSH	TAH-HAH-ROOSH	TO PROVOKE
TAHDEED	TAH-DEED	THREAT
TAHEB	TAH-EB	REPENTANT
TAHKEEM	TAH-KEEM	ARBITRATION
TAHLEEL AL GAMAL	TAH-LEEL-AL-JAM-AL	DESCRIPTION OF BEAUTY
TAJAEID	TAH-JAH-EID	WRINKLES
TAJER	TAH-JER	MERCHANT, SHOP KEEPER
TAJLEED	TAJ-LEED	FREEZING
TAJMEEL	TAJ-MEEL	BEAUTIFICATION
TAJSEED	TAJ-SEED	INCORPORATION
TAKHREEB	TAKH-REEB	DESTRUCTION
TAM	TAM	COMPLETE
TAYYAR	TAH-YAR	CURRENT
TEEJARI	TEE-JAH-REE	COMMERCIAL
TEZKAR	TEZ-KAR	SOUVENIR
THAMAN	THAH-MAN	PRICE
TOURAB	TOO-RAB	EARTH
TOURJOUMAN	TOOR-JOO-MAN	TRANSLATOR

~ W ~

ARABIC	PRONUNCIATION	TRANSLATION
WADI	WAH-DEE	VALLEY
WAFD	WAFD	ENVOY
WAHAB	WAH-HAB	GIVER
WAHED	WAH-HED	ONE
WAHEED	WAH-HEED	ONLY SON
WAHM	WAHM	ILLUSION
WAJAHAT	WAH-JAH-HAT	HONOR, CONSIDERATION
WAJEB	WAH-JEB	DUTY

Mouhra (Filly)

ARABIC	PRONUNCIATION	TRANSLATION
TADBIR	TAD-BEER	ARRANGEMENT
TAHLIMAT	TAH-LEE-MAT	INSTRUCTIONS
TAHRIF	TAH-REEF	DISTORTION
TAHRIR	TAH-REER	LIBERATION
TAH-SEEL	TAH-SEEL	COLLECTION
TAHSEEN	TAH-SEEN	IMPROVEMENT
TAIBAT	TAH-EE-BAT	REPENTANT
TAJMEELEE	TAJ-MEE-LEE	BEAUTIFYING
TAJREEBAT	TAJ-REE-BAT	EXPERIMENT
TAKABOUR	TAH-KAH-BOOR	PRIDE, ARROGANCE
TAKDEEMAT	TAK-DEE-MAT	GIFT, PRESENT
TARBIYAT	TAR-BEE-YAT	EDUCATION
TARHEEB	TAR-HEEB	WELCOMING
TARNIMAT	TAR-NEE-MAT	HYMN, SONG
TARTILAT	TAR-TEE-LAT	CHANT, SONG
TATWEER	TAT-WEER	DEVELOPMENT
TAZAHOURAT	TAH-ZAH-HOO-RAT	DEMONSTRATION
TEEJARAT	TEE-JAH-RAT	COMMERCE
TEZKAR	TEZ-KAR	SOUVENIR
TOHFA	TOH-FAH	PRECIOUS
TOUHMAT	TOOH-MAT	ACCUSATION
TOURATH	TOO-RATH	HERITAGE
TOURJOUMANEH	TOOR-JOO-MAH-NEH	TRANSLATOR

~ W ~

ARABIC	PRONUNCIATION	TRANSLATION
WAHEEDAH	WAH-HEE-DAH	ONLY DAUGHTER
WAHIBAH	WAH-HEE-BAH	GIVER, GENEROUS
WAHJEEHAH	WAH-JEE-HAH	HONORABLE
WAJAHAT	WAH-JAH-HAT	PRESTIGE
WAJBAT	WAJ-BAT	SET OF SAME KIND
WAJNAT	WAJ-NAT	CHEEK
WAKEELAH	WAH-KEE-LAH	ONE WHO PLEADS A CAUSE
WAKEELAT	WAH-KEE-LAT	TRUSTED WITH A JOB
WALIYAH	WAH-LEE-YAH	RESPONSIBLE

Mouher (Colt)

ARABIC	PRONUNCIATION	TRANSLATION
WAJEEH	WAH-JEEH	WITH HONOR
WAKEEL	WAH-KEEL	ONE WHO PLEADS A CAUSE
WALI	WAH-LEE	CHIEF
WALEE AL BEIT	WAH-LEE-AL-BITE	HEAD OF THE HOUSE
WASIM	WAH-SEEM	GRACEFUL
WASSEET	WAH-SEET	MEDIATOR
WASSEK	WAH-SEK	RELIABLE
WASSIT	WAH-SEET	INTERMEDIARY
WATAN	WAH-TAN	COUNTRY
WATANI	WAH-TAH-NEE	MY COUNTRY
WATHEQ	WAH-THEK	CONFIDENT, SURE
WAZEER	WAH-ZEER	MINISTER
WAZWAZAH	WAZ-WAH-ZAH	HUMMING
WEEDAD	WEE-DAD	LOVE, AFFECTION
WEEDAH	WEE-DAH	FAREWELL
WEEQUAR	WEE-KAR	RESPECT
WEESAM	WEE-SAM	BADGE OF HONOR

~ Y ~

ARABIC	PRONUNCIATION	TRANSLATION
YABESS	YAH-BESS	DRY
YA-HAYATI	YAH-HAH-YAH-TEE	MY LIFE
YA-JAMEEL	YAH-JAH-MEEL	OH! BEAUTIFUL ONE
YAKOUT	YAH-KOOT	RUBY
YAMEEN	YAH-MEEN	OATH
YA-OUMEE	YAH-OO-MEE	OH! MOTHER
YAQEEN	YAH-KEEN	CONVICTION
YASERR	YAH-SERR	PROSPEROUS
YATAHALAK	YAH-TAH-AH-LAK	TO SHINE
YATIM	YAH-TEEM	ORPHAN
YOUNEES	YOO-NEES	JONAH

~ Z ~

ARABIC	PRONUNCIATION	TRANSLATION
ZABARDAJ	ZAH-BAR-DAJ	CRYSTALLITE
ZAFER	ZAH-FER	VICTORIOUS
ZAHAWAT	ZAH-HAH-WHAT	VIVIDNESS

Mouhra (Filly)

ARABIC	PRONUNCIATION	TRANSLATION
WARD AHMAR	WARD-AH-MAR	RED ROSES
WARDI	WAR-DEE	ROSE COLORED
WASEEMAH	WAH-SEE-MAH	FAIR
WASEETAH	WAH-SEE-TAH	MEDIATOR
WASSIKAH	WAH-SEE-KAH	RELIABLE
WASSIYAH	WAH-SEE-YAH	TESTAMENT
WATANIYAH	WAH-TAH-NEE-YAH	FAITHFUL TO ONE'S COUNTRY
WATHIQAH	WAH-THEE-KAH	CONFIDENT, SURE
WAZEERAH	WAH-ZEE-RAH	MINISTER
WEEDAD	WEE-DAD	LOVE, AFFECTION
WEEKAR	WEE-KAR	HIGH REGARD, PERFECT
WEESAK	WEE-SAK	BOND
WEHDAT	WEH-DAT	LONLINESS
WOUROUD	WOO-ROOD	ROSES

~ Y ~

ARABIC	PRONUNCIATION	TRANSLATION
YA HABIBTI	YAH-HAH-BEEB-TEE	OH! DARLING
YA HAWAH	YAH-HAH-WAH	OH! LOVE
YA HAYATI	YAH-HAH-YAH-TEE	MY LIFE
YA JAMEELA	YAH-JAH-MEE-LAH	OH! BEAUTIFUL
YAMAMAT	YAH-MAH-MAT	DOVE
YASIRAT	YAH-SEE-RAT	PROSPEROUS
YASMIN	YAH-MEEN	JASMINE
YASSARIAH	YAH-SAH-REE-YAH	LEFT HANDED
YATEEMAH	YAH-TEE-MAH	ORPHAN

~ Z ~

ARABIC	PRONUNCIATION	TRANSLATION
ZABIYAT	ZAH-BEE-YAT	GAZELLE (FEMALE)
ZAFEER	ZAH-FEER	SOUND OF WIND
ZAGLOULEH	ZAG-LOO-LEH	BIRD
ZAHABIYEH	ZAH-HAH-BEE-YEH	GOLDEN
ZAHAWAT	ZAH-HAH-WHAT	VIVIDNESS
ZAHRA	ZAH-RAH	FLOWER
ZAHRA AL MOUTAKAHBIRAH	ZAH-RAH-AL-MOO-TAH-KAH-BEE-RAH	THE PROUD AND GENTLE ONE
ZAHRAH	ZAH-RAH	FLOWER

Mouher (Colt)

ARABIC	PRONUNCIATION	TRANSLATION
ZAHER	ZAH-HER	EVIDENT, VISIBLE
ZAIM	ZAH-EEM	CHIEF, LEADER
ZAIR	ZAH-ERR	GUEST
ZAJAL	ZAH-JAL	UPROAR
ZAKEE	ZAH-KEE	SMART, INTELLIGENT
ZAKEE AL MOUHIB	ZAH-KEE-AL-MOO-HIB	THE SMART LOVED ONE
ZALAM	ZAH-LAM	DARKNESS
ZALEM	ZAH-LEM	DICTATOR
ZAMBOUR	ZAM-BOOR	HORNET
ZAMEEL	ZAH-MEEL	FRIEND
ZAMMAR	ZAH-MAR	PIPER
ZARIF	ZAH-REEF	EXQUISITE
ZAYED	ZAY-YED	ABUNDANT
ZEEJAJ	ZEE-JAJ	GLASS
ZEEL	ZEEL	SHADOW
ZEENAT	ZEE-NAT	ORNAMENT
ZILAL	ZEE-LAL	SHADOWS
ZILZAL	ZIL-ZAL	EARTHQUAKE
ZOULAL	ZOO-LAHL	CLEAR COOL PURE WATER
ZUHUR	ZOO-HOOR	FLOWERS

Mouhra (Filly)

ARABIC	PRONUNCIATION	TRANSLATION
ZAIRAH	ZAH-EE-RAH	VISITING GUEST
ZAKEEYEH	ZAH-KEE-YEH	WITTY, INTELLIGENT
ZALAM	ZAH-LAM	DARKNESS
ZAMAN	ZAH-MAN	TIME
ZAMBOUK	ZAM-BOOK	LILY
ZAMILEH	ZAH-MEE-LEH	FRIEND
ZARIFAH	ZAH-REE-FAH	ELEGANT
ZARKAH	ZAR-KAH	BLUE COLOR (HORSE)
ZARKAWI	ZAR-KAH-WEE	BLUE-GRAY COLOR
ZAYEEDAH	ZAH-YEE-DAH	ABUNDANT
ZAYIRAH	ZAH-YEE-RAH	FEMALE VISITOR
ZEEL	ZEEL	SHADOWS
ZEENAT	ZEE-NAT	ORNAMENT, ADORNMENT
ZILAL	ZEE-LAL	SHADOWS
ZINAT	ZEE-NAT	DECORATION
ZOOHR	ZOOHR	NOON
ZOUKRAYAT	ZOOK-RAH-YAT	MEMORIES
ZUHOUR	ZOO-HOOR	FLOWERS
ZUJAJAT	ZOO-JAH-JAT	GLASS CUPS
ZUMURRUD	ZOO-MOO-ROOD	EMERALD

English ~ Arabic

THE ARABIC LANGUAGE
IS BEAUTIFUL
IN BOTH
SOUND
AND
APPEARANCE.

IT IS
DISTINCTLY
POETIC,
AND SUPERBLY
RICH
WITH DIALECT
AND
DESCRIPTIVE WORDS.

Mouher (Colt)

ENGLISH	ARABIC	PRONUNCIATION
\~ A \~		
A BLESSED MOON	HILAL MABROUK	HEE-LAL-MAHB-ROOK
A CHEERFUL SMILE	BASHBASH	BASH-BASH
A GENTLE MOON	HILAL LATIF	HEE-LAL-LAH-TEEF
A HEAVENLY STAR	KOWKAB SAMAHWEE	KOW-CAB-SAH-MAH-WEE
A THOUSAND BLESSINGS	ALF BARAKAH	AHLF-BAH-RAH-KAH
A THOUSAND FRIENDS	ALF SADEEK	AHLF-SAH-DEEK
ABANDON	HAJAR	HAH-JAR
ABANDONED	MATROUK	MAT-ROOK
ABANDONED	SAEB	SAH-EB
ABSOLUTE, DEFINITVE	BATATAN	BAH-TAH-TAN
ABUNDANT	ZAYED	ZAY-YED
ABUNDANT, AMPLE	JAZEEL	JAH-ZEEL
ABYSS	HOOWAHT	HOO-WHAT
ACCESS	MADKHAL	MAH-KHAL
ACCUSATION	ITTEEHAM	IT-TEE-HAM
ACROBATIC	BALAWANI	BAH-LAH-WAH-NEE
ADDICTION	IDMAN	ED-MAN
ADVANCED	MOUTAKADEM	MOO-TAH-KAH-DEM
AERIAL	HAWAHEE	HAH-WAH-EE
AFFIRMATIVE	EJAB	EE-JAB
AGE, ERA	DAHR	DAHR
AGELESS, ETERNAL	AZAHLEE	AH-ZAH-LEE
AGGRESSIVE	SHARESS	SHAH-RESS
ALMOND	LAWZ	LAWZ
ALONE	FARDIYAH	FAR-DEE-YAH
ALPHABETICAL	ABJADEE	AB-JAH-DEE
ALWAYS, FOREVER	DAHIMAN	DAH-EE-MAN
AMBASSADDOR	SAFIR	SAH-FEER
AMBASSADOR	SAFEER	SAH-FEER
AMBER	KAHRAMAN	KAH-RAH-MAN
AMBUSH, TRAP	KAMEEN	KAH-MEEN
AMUSEMENT	LAHOO	LAH-HOO

Mouhra (Filly)

ENGLISH	ARABIC	PRONUNCIATION
~ A ~		
A BEAUTIFUL WORD	KEELMAH HELWAH	KEL-MAH-HEL-WAH
A DANCE	RAKSAT	RAK-SAT
A GENTLE MOON	HILAL LATIFA	HEE-LAL-LAH-TEE-FAH
A KICK	RAFSAT	RAF-SAT
A PROTECTED MOON	HILAL MAHROUSSEH	HEE-LAL-MAH-ROO-SSEH
A SMILE	IBTISSAMAH	IB-TEE-SAH-MAH
A STAR	KOWKABAH	KOW-KAH-BAH
A TENDER WORD	KEELMAH HANOONAH	KEEL-MAH-HAH-NOO-NAH
A THOUSAND BLESSINGS	ALF BARAKAH	ALF-BAH-RAH-KAH
A THOUSAND LOVE'S	ALF HOUB	ALF-HOOB
A THOUSAND THANK YOU'S	ALF SHOUKRAN	ALF-SHOO-KRAHN
A TOWN IN SYRIA (BLACK CONNOTATION)	SUWAIDA	SOO-WAY-DEE-YAH
A WORD	KEELMAT	KEEL-MAT
ABANDONED	MATROUKA	MAT-ROO-KAH
ABBREVIATION	IKHTEESAR	IKH-TEE-SAR
ABDUCTED	MAKHTOUFAH	MAKH-TOO-FAH
ABUNDANT	ZAYEEDAH	ZAH-YEE-DAH
ACCELERATOR	DAWASSAT	DAH-WAH-SSAT
ACCENT	LOUKNAT	LOOK-NAT
ACCENT	NABRAT	NAB-RAT
ACCUSATION	TOUHMAT	TOOH-MAT
ACROBATIC	BAHLAWANIYAH	BAH-LAH-WAH-NEE-YAH
ACTIVE	NASHEETAH	NAH-SHEE-TAH
ADDICTION	IDAHFAT	EE-DAH-FAT
ADMINISTRATOR	MOUDIRAH	MOO-DEE-RAH
ADVANCED	MOUTATAWIRAH	MOO-TAH-TAH-WEE-RAH
ADVANTAGE	FAEDAT	FAH-EE-DAT
ADVICE	NASSIHAT	NAH-SEE-HAT
AERIAL	HAWAHEE	HAH-WAH-EE
AFFECTIONATE	RAOUMAH	RAH-OO-MAH
AFFLUENCE	BOAHBOOHAH	BOAH-BOO-HAH

Mouher (Colt)

ENGLISH	ARABIC	PRONUNCIATION
ANARCHY, CHAOS	FAWDAH	FAW-DAH
ANCESTOR	SALAF	SAH-LAF
ANSWER, REPLY	JAWAB	JAH-WAB
ANVIL	SOUNDAN	SOON-SAN
APPARENT, VISIBLE	BADEE	BAH-DEE
APRIL	NEESAN	NEE-SAN
ARAB HEAD DRESS	KAFIYAH	KA-FEE-YAH
ARBITRATION	TAHKEEM	TAH-KEEM
ARBITRATOR	FAISAL	FAY-SAL
ARISTOCRATIC	ARISTOCRATI	AH-RIS-TOE-CRAH-TEE
ARMISTICE	HOODNAT	HOOD-NAT
ARROW	SAHM	SAHM
ARTICULATE	NATEK	NAH-TEK
ARTIST	FANNAN	FAH-NAN
ASHES	RAMAD	RAH-MAD
AT YOUR SERVICE	LABEYK	LAH-BEYK
ATTENTION	BAL	BAHL
ATTRACTIVE	JAZAB	JAH-ZAB
AUTHENTIC	ASLEE	AHS-LEE
AUTHORIZED	MAEZOUN	MAH-EE-ZOON
AZURE, BLUE OF THE CLEAR SKY	LAZAWARDI	LAH-ZAH-WAR-DEE

~ B ~

BADGE OF HONOR	WEESAM	WEE-SAM
BAILSMAN, ONE WHO GUARANTEES	KAFEEL	KAH-FEEL
BAKER	FARRAN	FAH-RAN
BALANCE	RASEED	RAH-SEED
BALL, GLOBE	KOURAT	KOO-RAT
BARBARIAN	BARBAREE	BAR-BAH-REE
BARREL	BARMIL	BAR-MEEL
BASIS, FOUNDATION	AHSSAHSS	AH-SSAHSS
BEAR	DOUB	DOOB
BEAUTIFICATION	TAJMEEL	TAJ-MEEL
BEAUTIFUL AND ELEVATED	ALI JAMEEL	AH-LEE-JAH-MEEL

Mouhra (Filly)

ENGLISH	ARABIC	PRONUNCIATION
AGE, ERA	JEEL	JEEL
AGELESS, ETERNAL	AZAHLEE	AH-ZAH-LEE
AGGRESSIVE	SHARESSAH	SHAH-REH-SAH
AGILE	RASHEEKAH	RAH-SHEE-KAH
AGITATION	HIYAJJ	HEE-YAJJ
ALFALFA	FISSFISSAT	FISS-FEE-SSAT
ALL OF THEM	KOULOUHOUM	KOO-LOO-HOOM
ALL THE TIME	DAHEEMAN	DAH-EE-MAN
ALLIED	MOUTAHALIFAH	MOO-TAH-HAH-LEE-FAH
ALLOWED	MOUBAHAH	MOO-BAH-HAH
ALTERNATE	MOUTABADILAH	MOO-TAH-BAH-DEE-LAH
AMATEUR	HAWIYAH	HAH-WEE-YAH
AMBASSADOR	SAFIRAH	SAH-FEE-RAH
AMBASSADOR OF THE SOUTH WIND	SAFEERAT AL JANOUBEE	SAH-FEE-RAT-AL-JAH-NOO-BEE
AMBER	KAHRAMAN	KAH-RAH-MAN
AMERICAN (GIRL)	AMERIKIYAH	AH-MEH-REE-KEY-YAH
ANGEL FROM HEAVEN	MALAKEH SAMAWIYAH	MAH-LAH-KAY-SAH-MAH-WEE-YAH
ANNIHILATION	IBADAT	EE-BAH-DAT
ANONYMOUS	MAJHOULAH	MAJ-HOO-LAH
ANSWER	IJAHBAT	EE-JAH-BAT
APPETITE	SHAHIYAT	SHAH-HEE-YAT
APRIL FOOLS	KIZBAT NEESAN	KEEZ-BAT-NEE-SAN
ARGUMENT	JEEDAL	JEE-DAL
ARID	JAFAF	JAH-FAF
ARISTOCRAT	ARISTOCRATEEYAH	AH-RIS-TOE-CRAH-TEE-YAH
ARMY MEMBER (FEMALE)	JOUNDIYAT	JOON-DEE-YAT
ARRANGEMENT	TADBIR	TAD-BEER
ARROW	NABLAT	NAB-LAT
ARROW	NOUSHABAT	NOO-SHAH-BAT
ARTICLES OF LUXURY	KAMAHLIYAT	KAH-MAH-LEE-YAT
ARTIST	FANNANAH	FAH-NAH-NAH
ARTIST, PAINTER (FEMALE)	RASSAMAH	RAH-SAH-MAH
ASSOCIATE	SHARIKAH	SHAH-REE-KAH

Mouher (Colt)

ENGLISH	ARABIC	PRONUNCIATION
BEAUTIFUL SPEECH	KALAHM LAZIZ	KAH-LAHM-LAH-ZEEZ
BEEKEEPER	NAHHAL	NAH-HAL
BEING, EXISTANCE	KAYNOONAT	KAY-NOON-NAT
BELIEF, FAITH	EMAN	EE-MAN
BELIEVER	MOUIMEN	MOO-EE-MEN
BELL, SONG	JARASS	JAH-RASS
BELOVED	MAHBOUB	MAH-BOOB
BEYOND	BEDOUN	BEE-DOON
BEYOND PRICE, PRICELESS	BEDOUN THAMAN	BEE-DOON-THAH-MAN
BIG BELLIED	KIRSH	KIRSH
BIG STAR, PLANET	NIJM	NIJM
BILLBOARD	LAFEETAT	LAH-FEE-TAT
BIRD OF PREY	KASSER	KAH-SER
BITTER ORANGE	ABU SFEIR	AH-BU-SFEIR
BLACK EYED	AKHAL	AHK-HAL
BLACK NIGHTMARE	KABOUSS ASWAD	KAH-BOOSS-AHS-WAD
BLACKBIRD	SHAHROUR	SHAH-ROOR
BLACKNESS	SAWAD	SAH-WAD
BLESSED	MOUBARAK	MOO-BAH-RAK
BLESSED, HAPPY	SAEED	SAH-EED
BLIND	KAFEEF	KAH-FEEF
BLOND, FAIR	ASHKAR	AHSH-KAHR
BLOOD MONEY	DEEYAT	DEE-YAHT
BLOWING WIND	HOUBOUB	HOO-BOOB
BLUE	AZRAK	AHZ-RAK
BODY, PHYSIQUE	BADAN	BAH-DAN
BODYGUARD	MOURAFEK	MOO-RAH-FEK
BOLD, COURAGEOUS	JASSOUR	JAH-SOOR
BOOKLET	KOOTAYAB	KOO-TAH-YEB
BORN DURING THUNDER	MAULOOD BIL RAAD	MAW-LOOD-BIL-RAAD
BORN TO TOUCH	MAULOOD LIL LAMS	MAW-LOOD-LIL-LAMS
BRACELET	SOUWAR	SOO-WAR
BRAVE, BOLD	BASEL	BAH-SEL

Mouhra (Filly)

ENGLISH	ARABIC	PRONUNCIATION
BITTERNESS	MARARAH	MAH-RAH-RAH
BLACK COLORED	SAWDAH	SAW-DAH
BLACK FILLY	MOUHRA SAWDAH	MOOH-RAH-SAW-DAH
BLESSED	MOUBARAKAT	MOO-BAH-RAH-KAT
BLESSED HOUSE	BEIT MOUBARAK	BEIT--MOO-BAH-RAK
BLESSED, HAPPY	SAEIDAH	SAH-EID-AH
BLIND	KAFIFAH	KAH-FEE-FAH
BLISS	NAIMAH	NAH-EE-MAH
BLISS, HAPPINESS	HANA	HAH-NAH
BLONDNESS	SHAKRAT	SHAK-RAT
BLUE COLOR (HORSE)	ZARKAH	ZAR-KAH
BLUE SKY	LAZAWARDI	LAH-ZAH-WAR-DEE
BLUE-GRAY COLOR	ZARKAWI	ZAR-KAH-WEE
BOND	WEESAK	WEE-SAK
BOOKLET	SAKIAT	SAH-KEE-YAT
BOOTS	JAZMAT	JAZ-MATT
BOSSY LADY	SAYYIDAH	SAH-YEE-DAH
BOUNTY FROM PARADISE	REZKAH MIN AL JANNAT	REZ-KAH-MIN-AL-JAH-NAT
BRAID	JADEELAH	JAH-DEE-LAH
BRAVE	JASSOURAH	JAH-SOO-RAH
BRAVERY, COURAGE	BASSALAH	BAH-SAH-LAH
BRIBER	RASHEEYAT	RAH-SHEE-YAT
BRIDLE	LEEJAM	LEE-JAM
BRILLIANT	BAHILA	BAH-HEE-LAH
BROWN COLOR	SAMRAT	SAM-RAT
BUBBLING FOUNTAIN	FAWARAT	FAH-WAH-RAT
BULLET	RASSASSAT	RAH-SAH-SAT
BUNDLE	BALAT	BAH-LAT
BUTTERFLY	FARASHAH	FAH-RAH-SHAH

~ C ~

ENGLISH	ARABIC	PRONUNCIATION
CAMEL (FEMALE)	NAQUAT	NAH-KAT
CANDLE	SHAMAT	SHAM-AT
CAPTURED, TAKEN	ASIRAH	AH-SEE-RAH

Mouher (Colt)

ENGLISH	ARABIC	PRONUNCIATION
CHAMPION, CONQUEROR	NASSER	NAH-SER
CHAMPIONSHIP	BOUTOOLAT	BOO-TOO-LAT
CHANTING, SINGING	SHADOU	SHAH-DOO
CHARITABLE	MOUHSEN	MOOH-SEN
CHARLATAN, IMPOSTER	DAHJJAL	DAH-JAL
CHARMING	MOUHABAB	MOO-HAH-BAB
CHEETAH, LEOPARD	FAHD	FAHD
CHERRY	KARAZ	KAH-RAHZ
CHIEF	WALI	WAH-LEE
CHIEF, LEADER	ZAIM	ZAH-EEM
CHISEL	IZMEEL	IZ-MEEL
CLAW, TALON	BOURTHON	BOOR-THON
CLEAR COOL PURE WATER	ZOULAL	ZOO-LAHL
CLOSE TO SOMEONE	AKRAB	AHK-RAHB
CLOVER, TREFOIL	BIRJEEM	BEER-JEEM
CLOWN, JESTER	HARRAJAH	HAH-RAH-JAH
COAL	JAMR	JAMR
COAST, SHORE	SAHEL	SAH-HEL
COASTAL ROAD	KORNISH	KOR-NEESH
COLD	BARED	BAH-RED
COLLECTION	DEWANN	DEE-WANN
COLONEL	KOLONEL	CO-LO-NEL
COLONY	JALIAT	JAH-LEE-YAT
COLOR, TINT	LOUN	LOWN
COLORFUL	MOUTALAWEM	MOO-TAH-LAH-WEM
COMFORT, CONTENT	NAIM	NAH-EEM
COMICAL	FOUKAHI	FOO-KAH-HEE
COMMANDER, CHIEF	AMER	AH-MER
COMMERCIAL	TEEJARI	TEE-JAH-REE
COMPANION	MOUSSAHEB	MOO-SAH-HEB
COMPANION	SAMIR	SAH-MEER
COMPANION	RAFEEK	RAH-FEEK
COMPANION	RAFEEQ	RAH-FEEK

Mouhra (Filly)

ENGLISH	ARABIC	PRONUNCIATION
CARRIER	NAKEELAH	NAH-KEE-LAH
CAT (FEMALE)	HIRAT	HEE-RAT
CEDAR TREE	AL ARZAH	AL-AHR-ZAH
CELEBRATION	IHTEEFAL	IH-TEE-FAL
CERTAIN, FOR SURE	MOUTAAKIDAH	MOO-TAH-AH-KEE-DAH
CHANT, SONG	TARTILAT	TAR-TEE-LAT
CHAPTER OF THE HOLY KORAN	SURA	SOO-RAH
CHARITABLE	MOUHSEENAH	MOOH-SEE-NAH
CHARMING	KAYISSAH	KAH-YEE-SAH
CHARMING, CUTE	JAZABAH	JAH-ZAH-BAH
CHARMS	MAHASSEN	MAH-HAH-SEN
CHEEK	WAJNAT	WAJ-NAT
CHEERFUL	BASHOOSHAH	BAH-SHOO-SHAH
CHEERFULNESS	BASHASHAH	BAH-SHAH-SHAH
CHERRY	KARAZ	KAH-RAHZ
CHESTNUT COLOR	SHAGRAH	SHAG-RAH
CHICK	KATKOOT	KAHT-KOOT
CHILLED	MOUBARADAH	MOO-BAH-RAH-DAH
CHIVALRY	NAKHWAT	NAKH-WHAT
CHIVALRY	SHAHAMAT	SHAH-HAH-MAT
CHOICE	IKHTEEYAR	IKH-TEE-YAR
CHOICE	NOUKHBAT	NOOKH-BAT
CHOOSY, PARTICULAR	NAYEEQUAH	NAH-YEE-KAH
CITY	MADINA	MAH-DEE-NAH
CLARIFIED, BECOME PURE	MOUBAWAB	MOO-BAH-WAB
CLEANLINESS	NAZAFAT	NAH-ZAH-FAT
CLEVER, SMART	MAHIRAH	MAH-HEE-RAH
CLOSE TO THE HEART, IRRESISTIBLE	MAHDOUMEH	MAH-DOO-MEH
COAL	JAMRAH	JAM-RAH
COLD, ICED	BARIDAH	BAH-REE-DAH
COLLECTION	TAH-SEEL	TAH-SEEL
COLORFUL BEAUTY	JAMEELAT AL ALWAN	JAH-MEE-LAT-AL AL-WAN
COMEDY	KOMIDIAH	KO-MEE-DEE-YAH

Mouher (Colt)

ENGLISH	ARABIC	PRONUNCIATION
COMPANION, FRIEND	NADEEM	NAH-DEEM
COMPANION, PLAYFUL FRIEND	SAHEB	SAH-HEB
COMPASS	BEEKAR	BEE-KAHR
COMPASSION	RAHAFAT	RAH-AH-FAT
COMPLETE	TAM	TAM
COMPREHENSIVE	SHAMEL	SHAH-MEL
COMPULSION	IJBAR	IJ-BAR
COMPULSORY	IJBAREE	IJ-BAH-REE
CONFIDENT, SURE	WATHEQ	WAH-THEK
CONFUSION	IKHTEELAT	IKH-TEE-LAT
CONGRATULATIONS	MABROUK	MAH-BROOK
CONNECTION	ITTEESAL	IT-TEE-SAL
CONQUEST	INTEESAR	IN-TEE-SAR
CONSCIENCE	DAMEER	DAH-MEER
CONSOLATION	SOULWAN	SOOL-WAN
CONSTITUTION	DASTOUR	DAS-TOOR
CONTEMPT	IHTEEKAR	IH-TEE-KAR
CONTINUANCE	DAWAHM	DAH-WAHM
CONVICTION	YAQEEN	YAH-KEEN
COOLED	MOUBARAD	MOO-BAH-RAD
COOLING	TABREED	TAB-REED
CORE	LOOB	LOOB
CORRESPONDENT	MOURASEL	MOO-RAH-SELL
CORRIDOR	DAHLEEZ	DAH-LEEZ
CORRUPT, SPOILED	FASSED	FAH-SSED
COSMOS, WORLD	KOWN	KOWN
COUNCIL	MAJLIS	MAJLIS
COUNSELOR, MENTOR	RASHED	RAH-SHED
COUNTERPART, EQUAL	NAZEER	NAH-ZEER
COUNTRY	WATAN	WAH-TAN
COURTEOUS, POLITE	KAYESS	KAH-YES
CREEK, BROOK	JADWAL	JAD-WAHL
CRICKET	JOUDJOUD	JOOD-JOOD

Mouhra (Filly)

ENGLISH	ARABIC	PRONUNCIATION
COMFORT	MOUASSAT	MOO-AH-SAT
COMICAL	HAZLEE	HAZ-LEE
COMMANDO	FIDAHIYAH	FEE-DAH-EE-YAH
COMMERCE	TEEJARAT	TEE-JAH-RAT
COMMITTEE	LAJNAT	LAJ-NAT
COMMUNITY	JALIAT	JAH-LEE-YAT
COMPANION	MOURAFEEKAH	MOO-RAH-FEE-KAH
COMPANY, ASSOCIATION	ROUFKAT	ROOF-KAT
COMPASSION, MERCY	RAHMAT	RAH-MAT
COMPASSION, PITY	SHAFKAT	SHAF-KAT
COMPASSIONATE	RAOUFAH	RAH-OO-FAH
COMPOSURE	ITTEEZAN	IT-TEE-ZAN
CONCEALED	MASSTOURAH	MASS-TOO-RAH
CONCEITED	MOUTAKABIRAH	MOO-TAH-KAH-BEE-RAH
THE PROUD ONE	AL MOUTAKABIRAH	AL-MOO-TAH-KAH-BEE-RAH
CONDUCT	SEERAT	SEE-RAT
CONFIDENT	AMANAT AL SOUR	AH-MAH-NAT-AHL-SOOR
CONFIDENT, SURE	WATHIQAH	WAH-THEE-KAH
CONFRONTATION	MOUJABAHAH	MOO-JAH-BAH-HAH
CONGRATULATIONS	MABROOKA	MAB-ROO-KAH
CONNECTED	MOUTARABITAH	MOO-TAH-RAH-BEE-TAH
CONNECTION, LINK	RABEETAT	RAH-BEE-TAT
CONSTELLATION	KOWKABAT NOJOUN	KOW-KAH-BAT-NOO-JOON
CONTENT, SATISFIED	RADIYAT	RAH-DEE-YAT
COQUETRY, FLIRT	DALAL	DAH-LAL
CORAL	MERJAN	MER-JAN
CORRESPOND, SUIT, MATCH	RASALAH	RAH-SAH-LAH
CORRESPONDENT	MOURASILAH	MOO-RAH-SEE-LAH
COUNCIL, ASSEMBLY	DEWAHN	DEE-WAHN
COURAGE, BRAVERY	BASSALAH	BAH-SAH-LAH
COURTESY, POLITENESS	KEYASAT	KEY-YAH-SAT
COVER UP	LAFLAF	LAF-LAF
CRAZY	MAJNOUNAH	MAJ-NOON-AH

Mouher (Colt)

ENGLISH	ARABIC	PRONUNCIATION
CRISIS	AZMAH	AHZ-MAH
CRITIC	NAQUED	NAH-QUED
CROSSBREED	HAJEEN	HAH-JEEN
CRYSTAL	BALOOR	BAH-LOOR
CRYSTALLITE	ZABARDAJ	ZAH-BAR-DAJ
CUP	FENJAN	FEN-JAN
CURIOUS	FADOULEE	FAH-DOO-LEE
CURRENT	DAREJ	DAH-REJ
CURRENT	TAYYAR	TAH-YAR

~ D ~

ENGLISH	ARABIC	PRONUNCIATION
DANCER	RAKASS	RAH-KASS
DANCER	RAQUASS	RAH-KAHSS
DARK COLOR	ADHAM	AD-HAM
DARK, DEEP BLACK	DAHMESS	DAH-MESS
DARKNESS	ZALAM	ZAH-LAM
DARLING, FRIEND	HABIBI	HAH-BEE-BEE
DAWN	FAJR	FAJR
DAYTIME	NAHAR	NAH-HAR
DAZZLED	MABHOUR	MAB-HOOR
DAZZLING, BRILLIANT	BAHER	BAH-HER
DEAF	ATRASH	AT-RASH
DECENTRALIZED	LAMARKAZEE	LAH-MAR-KAH-ZEE
DEFEAT	HAZAM	HAH-ZAM
DELICIOUS	LAZEEZ	LAH-ZEEZ
DELIGHTED	FERHAN	FIR-HAN
DELIGHTFUL	MOUBHEJ	MOOB-HEJ
DEMANDING	MOUTATALEB	MOO-TAH-TAH-LEB
DEMON	JINN	JINN
DENSE, THICK	KATHEEF	KAH-THEEF
DEPARTING	RAHEL	RAH-HEL
DEPARTURE	RAHEEL	RAH-HEEL
DEPUTY	NAEB	NAH-EB
DESCRIPTION OF BEAUTY	TAHLEEL AL GAMAL	TAH-LEEL-AL-JAM-AL

Mouhra (Filly)

ENGLISH	ARABIC	PRONUNCIATION
CRESCENT MOON	HILAL	HEE-LAHL
CRICKET	JOUDJOUD	JOOD-JOOD
CRITIC	LAHEEMAT	LAH-EE-MAT
CROSSBREED	HAJEENAH	HAH-JEE-NAH
CROWNED	MOUTAWAJAH	MOO-TAH-WAH-JAH
CUP	FEENJAN	FEEN-JAN
CURIOUS, FOLLOWER	FADOULEH	FAH-DOO-LEH
CURSE	LAHNAT	LAH-NAT
CUSTOM	SHEEMAT	SHEE-MAT

~ D ~

ENGLISH	ARABIC	PRONUNCIATION
DANCE OF THE MOON, MOON DANCE	RAKSAT AL HILAL	RAK-SAT-AL-HEE-LAL
DANCER	RAQUASA	RAH-QUA-SAH
DANCER (FEMALE)	RAKASSAH	RAH-KAH-SAH
DANCER (FEMALE)	RAQUESSAH	RAH-QUE-SAH
DARK COLOR	DAHMA	DAH-MAH
DARK ONE	SAMRAH	SAHM-RAH
DARK SKIN	SAMAR	SAH-MAR
DARK, DEEP BLACK	DAHMISSAH	DAH-MEE-SAH
DARKNESS	DEYJOUR	DEY-JOOR
DARKNESS	ZALAM	ZAH-LAM
DAUGHTER (OF)	BINT	BEENT
DAUGHTER IN LAW	KANNAT	KAH-NAT
DAUGHTER OF THE EAST	BINT AL SHARQ	BEENT-AL-SHARK
DAUGHTER OF THE NORTH	BINT AL SHAMAL	BEENT-AL-SHAH-MAL
DAUGHTER OF THE SOUTH	BINT AL JENOUB	BEENT-AL-JEH-NOOB
DAUGHTER OF THE WEST	BINT AL GHARB	BEENT-AL-GHARB
DAUGHTER OF THE WIND	BINT AL HAWAH	BEENT-AL-HAH-WAH
DAZZLING	BAHIRAH	BAH-HEE-RAH
DEAR	HABBIBAT	HAH-BEE-BAT
DECENDANT	SALILAT	SAH-LEE-LAT
DECORATION	DEECOR	DEE-COR
DECORATION	ZINAT	ZEE-NAT
DECORUM	LABAKAT	LAH-BAH-KAT

Mouher (Colt)

ENGLISH	ARABIC	PRONUNCIATION
DESIRE	RAMAH	RAH-MAH
DESIREABLE	MARGHOUB	MAR-GHOOB
DESIRIOUS	RAGHEB	RAH-GHEB
DESTINATION	MAKSAD	MAK-SAD
DESTINY	NASSEEB	NAH-SEEB
DESTROYER	DAMMAR	DAH-MAR
DESTROYER	MOUDAMER	MOO-DAH-MER
DESTRUCTION	TAKHREEB	TAKH-REEB
DESTRUCTIVE	HADDAM	HAH-DAM
DETERMINATION	HEMMAT	HEE-MATT
DEVIL	SHETAN	SHEE-TAN
DIAMOND	ALMAZ	AHL-MAZ
DIAMOND	ELMASS	ELL-MASS
DIAMOND	MASS	MASS
DICTATOR	ZALEM	ZAH-LEM
DICTATORSHIP	JABROOT	JAB-ROOT
DIFFERENCE	IKHTEELAF	IKH-TEE-LAF
DIGNITY, HONOR	KARAMAT	KAH-RAH-MAT
DIRECTOR	MOUDEER	MOO-DEER
DISBELIEF (IN RELIGION)	KOUFRAN	KOOF-RAN
DISCOVERIES	KOUSHOUF	KOO-SHOOF
DISGUISED	MOUTANAKER	MOO-TAH-NAH-KER
DISGUISED	MOUTASSATER	MOO-TAH-SAH-TER
DISORDERED	FAWDAWEE	FAW-DAH-WEE
DISPATCH	IRSAL	IR-SAL
DISTINGUISHED	MOUMTAZ	MOOM-TAZ
DISTINGUISHED	MOUTAMAYEZ	MOO-TAH-MAH-YEZ
DISTINGUISHED, ELEGANT	NASEEM	NAH-SEEM
DIVINE DESTINY	NASSEEB ELAHI	NAH-SEEB-EE-LAH-HEE
DIVINE, FROM HEAVEN	RABANI	RAH-BAH-NEE
DOMESTIC, TAMED	ALEEF	AH-LEEF
DOMINATING	MOUSAYTAR	MOO-SAY-TAR
DOORMAN, DOORKEEPER	NATOUR	NAH-TOOR

Mouhra (Filly)

ENGLISH	ARABIC	PRONUNCIATION
DEFEAT	HAZEEMAH	HAH-ZEE-MAH
DELAYED	MOUAJALLAH	MOO-AH-JAH-LAH
DELICIOUS	LAZEEZ	LAH-ZEEZ
DELIGHT	LAZAT	LAH-ZAT
DEMANDING	MOUTATALIBAH	MOO-TAH-TAH-LEE-BAH
DEMOLISHER	MOUDAMIRAH	MOO-DAH-MEE-RAH
DEMONSTRATION	TAZAHOURAT	TAH-ZAH-HOO-RAT
DEPENDENCE	ITTEEKAL	IT-TEE-KAL
DESCENDING	HABITAH	HAH-BEE-TAH
DESCENT, ANCESTRY	NAZLAT	NAZ-LAT
DESERT	BADIYAH	BAH-DEE-YAH
DESERT DRESS	JALABIAH	JAH-LAH-BEE-YAH
DESIRED	MARGHOUBAH	MAR-GHOO-BAH
DESIRED	MATLOUBAH	MAT-LOO-BAH
DESTINY, FATE	NASSEEB	NAH-SEEB
DESTITUTE, POOR	FAKEERAH	FAH-KEE-RAH
DESTRUCTION	DAHMAR	DAH-MAR
DESTRUCTIVE	BATTASHAH	BAH-TAH-SHAH
DEVELOPMENT	TATWEER	TAT-WEER
DEVILISH	SHEYTANEE	SHEY-TAH-NEE
DIALECT	LAHJAT	LAH-JAT
DIAMOND	ALMAZAH	AL-MAH-ZAH
DIAMOND	MASSAT	MAH-SAT
DICTATORSHIP	DICTATORIAT	DIC-TAH-TOR-EE-AT
DIGNITY, SOLEMNITY	HAYBAT	HAY-BAT
DIPLOMATIC	DIPLOMASIYAH	DEE-PLO-MAH-SEE-YAH
DIRECTION	JEHAT	JEH-HAT
DIRECTION	NAHIYAT	NAH-HEE-YAT
DIRECTOR	MOUBASHARAT	MOO-BAH-SHAH-RAT
DISAPPEAR	IHTAJAZAH	IH-TAH-JAH-ZAH
DISCIPLINED	NEEZAMIYAH	NEE-ZAH-MEE-YAH
DISCONTENT	SAKITAT	SAH-KEE--TAT
DISCUSSION	MOUBAHATHAT	MOO-BAH-HAH-THAT

Mouher (Colt)

ENGLISH	ARABIC	PRONUNCIATION
DRINK	SHARAB	SHAH--RAB
DRINKER	SHAREB	SHAH-REB
DRINKING FOUNTAIN	SABIL	SAH-BEEL
DRIVER	SAEK	SAH-EK
DRIZZLE	RAZAZ	RAH-ZAZ
DRY	JAHF	JAHF
DRY	YABESS	YAH-BESS
DRYNESS	JAFAF	JAH-FAF
DUALISM, A DOUBLE CHARACTER	IZDEEWAJ	IZ-DEE-WAJ
DURING	BIL	BIL
DURING	IBBAN	IB-BAN
DUTY	WAJEB	WAH-JEB

~ E ~

EAGLE	NISR	NISR
EARTH	TOURAB	TOO-RAB
EARTH, LAND	AHRD	AHRD
EARTHQUAKE	ZILZAL	ZIL-ZAL
EASILY ATTAINED	HAYEN	HAH-YEN
EASTERN	SHARKEE	SHAR-KEE
ECLIPSE	KOUSOUF	KOO-SOOF
EDUCATED	ADEEB	AH-DEEB
EDUCATOR	MOURABI	MOO-RAH-BEE
EFFORT	JAHD	JAHD
ELEPHANT	FEEL	FEEL
ELM TREE	DARDAR	DAR-DAR
ELOQUENCE	FASSAHAT	FAH-SAH-HAT
EMPLOYEE	AJEER	AH-JEER
ENDOWED WITH GOOD EYESIGHT	BASSIR	BAH-SEER
ENERGETIC	NASHEET	NAH-SHEET
ENTITY, BEING	KEYANN	KEY-YAN
ENVOY	WAFD	WAFD
ESCAPE	FERAR	FEE-RAR
ETERNAL	ABADI	AH-BAH-DEE

Mouhra (Filly)

ENGLISH	ARABIC	PRONUNCIATION
DISIRE, WISH	RAGHBAT	RAGH-BAT
DISPOSITION, CHARACTER	FITRAT	FEET-RAT
DISSIMILARITY	IKHTEELAF	IKH-TEE-LAF
DISTINCT	MOUTAMAYIZAH	MOO-TAH-MAH-YEE-ZAH
DISTORTION	TAHRIF	TAH-REEF
DIVINE GIFT	HEBAH ILAHIYAH	HEE-BAH-EE-LAH-HEE-YAH
DIVINE PREDICTION	NOUBOUAT	NOO-BOO-AT
DIVINE SMILE	BASSMAH ILAHIYAH	BAS-MAH-EE-LAH-HEE-YAH
DOLL, TOY	DOUMYAT	DOOM-YAT
DOLPHIN	DARFEEL	DAR-FEEL
DOMINEERING	MOUTASSALITAH	MOO-TAH-SAH-LEE-TAH
DOUBT, SUSPECT	IRTAB	IR-TAB
DOVE	YAMAMAT	YAH-MAH-MAT
DRINKER	SHARIBAH	SHAH-REE-BAH
DRINKS	SHARBAT	SHAR-BAT
DUELING	MOUBARAZAT	MOO-BAH-RAH-ZAT
DYNASTY	SOULALAT	SOO-LAH-LAT

~ E ~

ENGLISH	ARABIC	PRONUNCIATION
EARTHLY, MUNDANE	DUNYAHWIYAH	DUN-YAH-WEE-YAH
EASE	SOUHOULAT	SOO-HOO-LAT
ECHO	SADAH	SAH-DAH
ECLIPSE	KOUSOUF	KOO-SOOF
ECLIPSE OF THE MOON	KOUSOUF AL HILAL	KOO-SOOF-AL-HEE-LAL
ECSTASY	NASHWAT	NASH-WHAT
EDUCATED	ADEEBAH	AH-DEE-BAH
EDUCATION	TARBIYAT	TAR-BEE-YAT
EDUCATOR	MOURABEEYAH	MOO-RAH-BEE-YAH
EGYPT	MASR	MASR
EGYPTIAN	MASRIAH	MASS-REE-YAH
EGYPTIAN VULTURE	RAKHMAT	RAKH-MAT
ELEGANT	ANEEKAH	AH-NEE-KAH
ELEGANT	ZARIFAH	ZAH-REE-FAH
ELOQUENCE	FASSAHAT	FAH-SAH-HAT

Mouher (Colt)

ENGLISH	ARABIC	PRONUNCIATION
ETERNAL	ELA AL ABAD	ELA-AL-AH-BAD
ETERNAL	MOUABBAD	MOO-AH-BAD
ETERNAL	SARMADI	SAR-MAH-DEE
ETERNAL FLAME	NAR AL ABAD	NAR-AL-AH-BAD
ETERNITY	AZAHL	AH-ZAHL
EUROPEAN	FARANJ	FAH-RANGE
EVADE	RAGHAH	RAH-GHAH
EVASIVE	MOUTAHAREB	MOO-TAH-HAH-REB
EVERLASTING	ABADEE	AH-BAH-DEE
EVIDENT, VISIBLE	ZAHER	ZAH-HER
EVIL	LAEIM	LAH-EIM
EVIL	SHAR	SHAR
EXCESSIVE	BAHEZ	BAH-HIZ
EXCESSIVE	FAEK	FAH-EK
EXCHANGE	IBDAL	IB-DAHL
EXCHANGE	TABADOUL	TAH-BAH-DOOL
EXCITED, AGITATED	HAEJJ	HAH-EJJ
EXCITEMENT	HEYAJJ	HEE-YAJJ
EXECUTIONER	JALLAD	JAH-LAD
EXECUTIONER	SAYAF	SAH-YAF
EXECUTIVE	IDAHRI	EE-DAH-REE
EXPLANATION	TAFSEER	TAF-SEER
EXPRESS OPINION	KELMAT	KEEL-MAT
EXPRESSION	LAFAZ	LAH-FAZ
EXQUISITE	ZARIF	ZAH-REEF
EXTREME, UMOST	AKSAH	AHK-SAH
EYE CATCHING	LAFET	LAH-FET
EYES OF THE GUEST	DEIF AL OYOUN	DEIF-AL-OYOON
~ F ~		
FAITH	MAZHAB	MAZ-HAB
FAITHFULNESS, LOYALTY	AMANAH	AH-MAH-NAH
FALCON	SHAHEEN	SHAH-HEEN
FALLING	HABET	HAH-BET

Mouhra (Filly)

ENGLISH	ARABIC	PRONUNCIATION
EMERALD	ZUMURRUD	ZOO-MOO-ROOD
EMPLOYEE, WORKER	AJEERAH	AH-JEE-RAH
ENDOWED WITH EYESIGHT	BASSIRAH	BAH-SEE-RAH
EQUIVALENT, COUNTERPART	NAZEERAH	NAH-ZEE-RAH
ESCAPE	FERAR	FEE-RAR
ESCAPE	NAFDAT	NAF-DAT
ETERNAL	DAYEEMAH	DAH-YEE-MAH
ETERNAL	ELA AL ABAD	ELA-AL-AH-BAD
ETERNAL	SARMADIYAH	SAR-MAH-DEE-YAH
ETERNAL EXISTENCE	ABADIYAH	AH-BAH-DEE-YAH
ETERNITY	AZALIYAH	AH-ZAH-LEE-YAH
EUROPEAN WOMAN	FARANJIYAH	FAH-RUN-JEE-YEH
EVENING	SAHRAT	SAH-RAT
EVERLASTING	MOUABADAH	MOO-AH-BAH-DAH
EXCELLENCE	IJAHDAT	EE-JAH-DAT
EXCEPTIONAL	MOUMTAZAH	MOOM-TAH-ZAH
EXCESSIVE	BAHIZAH	BAH-HEE-ZAH
EXCHANGE	MOUBADALAT	MOO-BAH-DAH-LAT
EXCITEMENT	ITHARAT	EE-THAH-RAT
EXODUS, EMMIGRATION	HOUJRAT	HOOJ-RAT
EXPENSE	NAFKAT	NAF-KAT
EXPERIMENT	TAJREEBAT	TAJ-REE-BAT
EXTREME	MOUTATARIFAH	MOO-TAH-TAH-REE-FAH
EYELASHES	HOODEB	HOO-DEB

~ F ~

ENGLISH	ARABIC	PRONUNCIATION
FACILE, EASILY ACCOMPLISHED	HAYINAH	HAH-YEE-NAH
FAIR	WASEEMAH	WAH-SEE-MAH
FAITHFUL	MOUEELIMAH	MOO-EE-LEE-MAH
FAITHFUL TO ONE'S COUNTRY	WATANIYAH	WAH-TAH-NEE-YAH
FALLING IN LOVE	HIYAM	HEE-YAM
FAMILY, GROUP	FASSEELAT	FAH-SEE-LOT
FAMOUS	SHAHIRAH	SHAH-HEE-RAH
FAMOUS	MASHOORA	MAHSH-HOO-RAH

Mouher (Colt)

ENGLISH	ARABIC	PRONUNCIATION
FAME	SHOUHRAT	SHOO-RAT
FAMOUS	SHAHIR	SHAH-HEER
FAREWELL	WEEDAH	WEE-DAH
FAVORED BY ALL	MOUFADAHL	MOO-FAH-DAHL
FAVORITE PASTURE	HEWAYAT	HEE-WAH-YAT
FEAR	HAYBAT	HAY-BAT
FIDGETY	MOUTAMALMEL	MOO-TAH-MAHL-MEL
FIERY	NAREE	NAH-REE
FINCH	SHOURSHOUR	SHOOR-SHOOR
FINE, VERY GOOD	JAYED	JAH-YED
FIRE	NAR	NAR
FIREFLY	BARAAT	BAR-AAT
FIREFLY	HABAHEB	HAH-BAH-HEB
FIRST (IN FRONT)	AMAHMEE	AH-MAH-MEE
FIRST BORN	BAHKR	BAHKR
FLAME, BLAZE	LAHEEB	LAH-HEEB
FLASK	DAWRAK	DAW-RACK
FLEE	HARABAH	HAH-RAH-BAH
FLOURISHING	MOUZDAHER	MOOZ-DAH-HER
FLOWERS	ZUHUR	ZOO-HOOR
FLOWING	JAREE	JAH-REE
FLUENT	FASSEEH	FAH-SEEH
FOG, MIST	DAHBAHB	DAH-BAHB
FOOTNOTE	HAMESH	HAH-MESH
FOR EVER	KAHLED	KAH-LED
FOREIGN	AJNAHBEE	AHJ-NAH-BEE
FORGIVEN	MOUAZAR	MOO-AH-ZAR
FORM	HAYAT	HAY-AT
FORTUNE TELLER	BASSAR	BAH-SAR
FORTUNE TELLER	MOUBASSER	MOO-BAH-SER
FORUNE TELLING	TABSIR	TAB-SEER
FOUNDER	MOUAHSESS	MOO-AH-SESS
FRAGRANCE, SCENT	AHREEJ	AH-REEJ

Mouhra (Filly)

ENGLISH	ARABIC	PRONUNCIATION
FAMOUS, WELL KNOWN	MAAROUFA	MAH-ROO-FAH
FATE, DESTINY	NASSEEB	NAH-SEEB
FATIGUE, EXHAUSTION	KALALAT	KAH-LAH-LAT
FAVOR, GRACE	FADL	FADL
FAVORED BY ALL	MOUFADALEH	MOO-FAH-DAH-LEH
FEASIBLE	MOUTAYASSIRAH	MOO-TAH-YAH-SEE-RAH
FELONY	JENAYAT	JEH-NAH-YAT
FEMALE AGENT, GUIDE	DALLALAH	DAH-LAH-LAH
FEMALE BEDOUIN	BADAWIYAH	BAH-DAH-WEE-YAH
FEMALE VISITOR	ZAYIRAH	ZAH-YEE-RAH
FEMININE	MOUANASS	MOO-AH-NASS
FIDDLE	KAMANJAT	KAH-MAN-JAT
FIGHTER	MOUHARIBAH	MOO-HAH-REE-BAH
FINENESS, DELICACY	RIKKAT	REE-KAT
FIRE, WARMTH	NAR	NAR
FISHNET	SHABKAT	SHAB-KAT
FLAG	RAYAT	RAH-YAT
FLAVOR	NAKHAT	NAK-HAT
FLOWER	ZAHRA	ZAH-RAH
FLOWER	ZAHRAH	ZAH-RAH
FLOWERS	ZUHOUR	ZOO-HOOR
FLOWING	FIDFAD	FEED-FAD
FLUTE	MIZMAR	MIZ-MAR
FLUTE	SHABABAT	SHAH-BAH-BAT
FOAM, LATHER	RAGHWAT	RAGH-WAT
FOREHEAD	JABHAT	JAB-HAT
FOREIGN	AJNAHBIYAH	AHJ-NAH-BEE YAH
FORELOCK	NASSIYAT	NAH-SEE-YAT
FORGIVENESS	SIMAAH	SEE-MAH
FORMAL	SHAKLEE	SHAK-LEE
FORTUNE TELLER	BASSARAH	BAH-SAH-RAH
FORTUNE TELLER	MOUBASSIRAH	MOO-BAH-SEE-RAH
FOUNDATION	MOUASSASSAT	MOO-AH-SAH-SAT

Mouher (Colt)

ENGLISH	ARABIC	PRONUNCIATION
FRAME	BERWAHZ	BER-WAHZ
FRAMEWORK	ITTAR	EE-TAR
FRANKINCENSE	LOOBAN	LOO-BAN
FRECKLES	NAMASH	NAH-MASH
FREE	BAHLASH	BAH-LAHSH
FREEZING	TAJLEED	TAJ-LEED
FRICTION	IHTEEKAK	IH-TEE-KAK
FRIEND	ZAMEEL	ZAH-MEEL
FRIENDS	HABAYEB	HAH-BAH-YEB
FRIGHTFUL, TERRIFYING	HAELL	HAH-EL
FROM KUWAIT	KUWAITI	KOO-WAY-TEE
FROM SUWAIDAH (MALE)	SUWAIDEE	SOO-WAY-DEE
FUGITIVE	HAREB	HAH-REB
FULL MOON	BADR	BAH-DER
FUNDAMENTAL, BASIC	ASASSEE	AH-SAH-SSEE
FUR (S)	FARWAT	FAR-WHAT

~ G ~

ENGLISH	ARABIC	PRONUNCIATION
GAIN, PROFIT	KASB	KAHSB
GARDEN	KARM	KAHRM
GATHERING	JAMAHEER	JAH-MAH-HEER
GENERATION	JEEL	JEEL
GENEROSITY	JOOD	JOOD
GENEROSITY	KARAM	KAH-RAM
GENEROSITY	SHAHAMAT	SHAH-HAH-MAT
GENEROUS	JAWWAD	JAH-WWAD
GENEROUS, GIVING	KAREEM	KAH-REEM
GENTLE, KIND	LATEEF	LAH-TEEF
GHOST	SHABAH	SHAH-BAH
GIFT	HADIYAT	HAH-DEE-YAT
GIFT	HEBAT	HEE-BAT
GIFTED	MAWHOOB	MAO-HOOB
GIVER	WAHAB	WAH-HAB
GIVING, GENEROUS	KARIM	KAH-REEM

Mouhra (Filly)

ENGLISH	ARABIC	PRONUNCIATION
FOUNTAIN	NAFOURAH	NAH-FOO-RAH
FRAGMENT, FRACTION	KASSRAT	KAHS-RAT
FRECKLED	ANMASH	AHN-MASH
FRESH BREATH OF AIR	NASSMAT	NASS-MAT
FRESHNESS	NADARAT	NAH-DAH-RAT
FRIEND	HABIBA	HAH-BEE-BAH
FRIEND	SAMIRAH	SAH-MEE-RAH
FRIEND	ZAMILEH	ZAH-MEE-LEH
FRIENDLY, TAMED	ANEESAH	AH-NEES-AH
FRIENDS	HABAYEB	HAH-BAH-YEB
FROM GOD	RABANIYAH	RAH-BAH-NEE-YAH
FROM KUWAIT	KUWAITIYAH	KOO-WAY-TEE-YAH
FROM LIBYA	LEEBIYAT	LEE-BEE-YAT
FROM THE KAHLEDIAH	KAHLEDIAH	KAH-LEH-DEE-YAH
FROM THE NORTH	SHAMALIYAT	AHAH-MAH-LEE-YAT
FROM THE TOWN OF MECCA	MEKKAWIYEH	MEE-KAH-WEE-YEH
FROZEN	MOUTAJALIDAH	MOO-TAH-JAH-LEE-DAH
FRUITFUL	MOUMIRAH	MOO-MEE-RAH

~ G ~

ENGLISH	ARABIC	PRONUNCIATION
GAIN	ERADAH	EE-RAH-DAH
GARDEN	BOUSTAN	BOOS-TAN
GARDENER	BOUSTANIYAH	BOOS-TAH-NEE-YAH
GATHERING, SESSION	JALSSAT	JAL-SAT
GAZELLE (FEMALE)	ZABIYAT	ZAH-BEE-YAT
GENEROSITY	KARAMAH	KAH-RAH-MAH
GENEROSITY	SAMAHAT	SAH-MAH-HAT
GENEROUS	JAWWADAH	JAH-WAH-DAH
GENEROUS, GIVER	WAHIBAH	WAH-HEE-BAH
GENEROUS, GIVING	KARIMA	KAH-REE-MAH
GENIUS	NABIGHAH	NAH-BEE-GHAH
GENTLE ONE	LOUTFEEYAH	LOOT-FEE-YAH
GENTLE SMILE, KIND SMILE	IBTISSAMAH ANISA	IB-TEE-SAH-MAH-AH-NEE-SAH
GENTLE, KIND	LATEEFAH	LAH-TEE-FAH

Mouher (Colt)

ENGLISH	ARABIC	PRONUNCIATION
GLASS	ZEEJAJ	ZEE-JAJ
GLORIFIED, EXHALTED	MAJID	MAH-JEED
GLORIOUS, HIGHLY RESPECTED	MAGEED	MAH-JEED
GLORY TO GOD	SUBHAN-ALLAH	SUB-HAN-AL-LAH
GLORY, HONOR	MAJD	MAJD
GOD'S MESSENGER	RASSOUL ALLAH	RAH-SOOL-AL-LAH
GOD'S WILLING	INSHALLAH	IN-SHAH-LAH
GOOD LUCK	SAAD	SAH-AD
GOOD LUCK , GOOD FORTUNE	BAHKTI	BAHK-TEE
GOOD NEWS	BOOSHRAH	BOOSH-RAH
GOOD OMENS	BASHAYER	BAA-SHAH-YER
GOVERNING	SAED	SAH-ED
GRACEFUL	WASIM	WAH-SEEM
GRACEFUL, ELEGANT	RAMIK	RAH-MEEK
GRACEFUL, LOVELY	JAMIL	JAH-MEEL
GRACIOUS (THE)	ROUHMAN	ROOH-MAN
GRACIOUS ONE	LOUTFEE	LOOT-FEE
GRANDFATHER	JIDD	JIDD
GRAPEVINE	KARMAT	KAHR-MAT
GRATUITY	BAKSHEESH	BAHK-SHEESH
GRAY HAIRED	ASHYAB	AHSH-YAHB
GREAT BEAUTY	JAMAL GALEEL	JAH-MAL-JAH-LEEL
GREAT, LARGE	KABEER	KAH-BEER
GREATER, BIGGER	AHKBAR	AHK-BAR
GREATNESS	FAKHAMAT	FAH-KAH-MAT
GREATNESS IN SIZE	KOUBR	KOUBR
GREEDY	NAHEM	NAH-HEM
GUARANTY	KAHFALAT	KAH-FAH-LAT
GUEST	DEIF	DEIF
GUEST	ZAIR	ZAH-ERR
GUIDANCE	IRSHAD	IR-SHAD
GUIDE, LEADER	DAHLIL	DAH-LEEL
GUIDE, LEADER	HADEE	HAH-DEE

Mouhra (Filly)

ENGLISH	ARABIC	PRONUNCIATION
GENTLENESS, KINDNESS	LATAFAT	LAH-TAH-FAT
GIFT FROM GOD	HADIYAH MIN ALLAH	HAH-DEE-YAH-MIN-AL-LAH
GIFT OF THE SOUTH	HADIYAT AL JANOUB	HAH-DEE-YAT-AL-JAH-NOOB
GIFT, PRESENT	TAKDEEMAT	TAK-DEE-MAT
GIVER, GENEROUS	WAHIBAH	WAH-HEE-BAH
GIVING, GENEROUS	KAREEMA	KAH-REE-MAH
GLANCE	LAMHAT	LAM-HAT
GLANCE, A QUICK LOOK	NAZRAT	NAZ-RAT
GLASS CUPS	ZUJAJAT	ZOO-JAH-JAT
GLOBE, SPHERE	KOURAT AL ARD	KOO-RAT-AL-ARD
GLORIOUS, HIGHLY RESPECTED	MAGIDAA	MAH-JEE-DAH
GLORIOUS, HIGHLY RESPECTED	MAJEEDAH	MAH-JEE-DAH
GOAL, AIM	HADDAF	HAH-DAF
GOAT (FEMALE)	MAIZAH	MAH-EE-ZAH
GODDESS	RABBAT	RAH-BAT
GOD'S VISITOR	DEIFALLAH	DEYF-AL-LAH
GOD'S WILLING	INSHALLAH	IN-SHAH-LAH
GOLDEN	ZAHABIYEH	ZAH-HAH-BEE-YEH
GOOD NEWS	BOUSHRAH	BOOSH-RAH
GOOD QUALITY	SHAMILAT	SHAH-MEE-LAT
GOODNESS	JAWDAT	JAW-DAT
GORGEOUS	JAMILAH	JAH-MEE-LAH
GORGEOUS, BEAUTIFUL	BAHIYAH	BAH-HEE-YAH
GRACEFUL	RASHEEDAH	RAH-SHEE-DAH
GRACEFULNESS	RASHAKAT	RAH-SHAH-KAT
GRANDEUR	JALALAH	JAH-LAH-LAH
GRANDMOTHER	JIDDAH	JEE-DAH
GRAPE LEAF	DAWALEE	DAH-WAH-LEE
GRAPEVINE	DAHLIAH	DAH-LEE-YAH
GRAPEVINE	KARMAT	KAHR-MAT
GRATEFUL	SHAKIRAH	SHAH-KEE-RAH
GRAVEYARD	JABANAH	JAH-BAH-NAH
GRAVITY	RASSANAT	RAH-SAH-NAT

Mouher (Colt)

ENGLISH	ARABIC	PRONUNCIATION
~ H ~		
HADBAN TRIBE, HADBAN STRAIN	HADBAN	HAD-BAN
HAIRLESS, BALD	AJRAD	AHJ-RAHD
HALTER	RASAN	RAH-SAN
HAPPINESS	FARAH	FAH-RAH
HAPPY	MABSOOT	MAB-SOOT
HARM, DAMAGE	AZAH	AH-ZAH
HARMONIZER	NAGHEM	NAH-GHEM
HAWK, FALCON	BAHZ	BAHZ
HAY	TABN	TABN
HE	HOOWAH	HOO-WAH
HEAD OF THE HOUSE	WALEE AL BEIT	WAH-LEE-AL-BITE
HEART	FOUAD	FOO-AD
HEGIRA	HEGIRAH	HEH-JEER-AH
(FLIGHT OF MOHAMMAD FROM MECCA)		
HELLO	HALAH	HAH-LAH
HELLO, WELCOME	MARHABAH	MAR-HAH-BAH
HERO	BATAL	BAH-TAL
HEROIC	BOUTOOLEH	BOO-TOO-LEH
HIGH	HAALIK	HAH-LIK
HIGH ONE, ELEVATED	ALI	AH-LEE
HIGH, TALL	BAHSEK	BAH-SEK
HIGHBORN, EXCELLENT	NAJEEB	NAH-JEEB
HIGHLY RESPECTED, GLORIOUS	MAJEED	MAH-JEED
HIGHNESS	SIMOU	SEE-MOO
HOBBYIST	HAWEE	HAH-WEE
HOLIDAY, VACATION	IJAHZAT	EE-JAH-ZAT
HOLY	DEENI	DEE-NEE
HOLY WAR	JIHAD	JEE-HAD
HOME	DAR	DAHR
HONEST, GOOD	FADEL	FAH-DELL
HONOR	SHARAF	SHAH-RAF
HONOR, CONSIDERATION	WAJAHAT	WAH-JAH-HAT

Mouhra (Filly)

ENGLISH	ARABIC	PRONUNCIATION
GREATNESS	AZAMAH	AH-ZAH-MAH
GROUP, BAND	FERQUAT	FER-KAT
GROWING	MOUTAZAYIDAH	MOO-TAH-ZAH-YEE-DAH
GUARANTY, SECURITY	KHAFALAT	KAH-FAH-LAT
GUEST, VISITOR	DEIFAH	DEY-FAH

~ H ~

ENGLISH	ARABIC	PRONUNCIATION
HABIT, CUSTOM	DAYDAN	DAY-DAN
HAIRDRESSER	MASHEETAT	MAH-SHEE-TAT
HALLUCINATION	HALLOUSAT	HAH-LOO-SAT
HALO	HALAT	HAH-LAT
HAPPINESS	FARAH	FAH-RAH
HAPPY, GLAD	FARHANAH	FAR-HAH-NAH
HAPPY, PLEASANT	BAHEEJAH	BAH-HEE-JAH
HAPPY, PLEASED	MABSOUTAH	MAB-SOO-TAH
HEAD DRESS	KAFIAH	KA-FEE-YAH
HEAVENLY STAR	KOWKABAH SAMAHWIYAH	KOW-KAH-BAH-SAH-MAH-WEE-YAH
HEAVENLY, FROM HEAVEN	SAMAWIYAH	SAH-MAH-WEE-YAH
HEGIRA	HEJIRAH	HEE-JEE-RAH
HELLO, WELCOME	MARHABAH	MAR-HAH-BAH
HELM	DAHFFAT	DAH-FAT
HEN	DAJAHJAH	DAH-JAH-JAH
HER HIGHNESS	SEMOU AL AMIRAH	SE-MOO-AL-AH-MEE-RAH
HER SECRET	SEERAH	SEE-RAH
HERITAGE	TOURATH	TOO-RATH
HERO	BATALA	BAH-TAH-LAH
HEROINE, CHAMPION	BATALAH	BAH-TAH-LAH
HIGH REGARD, PERFECT	WEEKAR	WEE-KAR
HIGH TAIL	BASIKAH	BAH-SEE-KAH
HILL, MOUND	HADBAT	HAD-BAT
HOBBY	HIWAYAT	HEE-WAH-YAT
HOLY	MOUKADASSAH	MOO-KAH-DAH-SSAH
HOMEBODY (LIKES TO STAY HOME)	BEITAWIYAH	BEY-TAH-WEE-YAH
HONORABLE	WAHJEEHAH	WAH-JEE-HAH

Mouher (Colt)

ENGLISH	ARABIC	PRONUNCIATION
HONORABLE, SUBLIME	JALEEL	JAH-LEEL
HOOK, CLAMP	KOOLAB	KOO-LAB
HORNET	ZAMBOUR	ZAM-BOOR
HORSE STABLE WORKER	SAESS	SAH-ESS
HORSE, STEED	JAWAD	JAH-WAD
HORSEMAN	FARESS	FAH-RESS
HORSEMEN	FOURSAN	FOOR-SAN
HOT	SOUKN	SOUKN
HUMAN	ADAHMEE	AH-DAH-MEE
HUMMING	WAZWAZAH	WAZ-WAH-ZAH
HURT, PAIN	AHLAM	AH-LAHM

~ I ~

ENGLISH	ARABIC	PRONUNCIATION
ICE BOX	BARRAD	BAH-RAD
IDENTICAL	MASEEL	MAH-SEEL
ILLUSION	WAHM	WAHM
IMAGE	METHAL	MEE-THAL
IMPASSIONED	BASSMAT	BASS-MAHT
IMPROVISATION	IRTEEJAL	IR-TEE-JAL
IN FRONT	AMAM	AH-MAM
INCENSE	BAKHOOR	BAH-KHOOR
INCLINED	MAEL	MAH-EL
INCORPORATION	TAJSEED	TAJ-SEED
INDEPENDENCE	ISTIKLAL	ISS-TIK-LAL
INDIFFERENT	LAMABAL	LAH-MAH-BAL
INFIDEL	KAFER	KAH-FER
INFIDELITY	KOUFR	KOUFR
INFINITY	LANIHAYAT	LAH-NEE-HAH-YAT
INFLUENCE	TAEETHEER	TAH-EE-THEER
INSANE, CRAZY	MAJNOON	MAJ-NOON
INSPECTOR	MOUFATESH	MOO-FAH-TESH
INSPIRATION	SHAHEEK	SHAH-HEEK
INSTANT	FAWREE	FAW-REE
INTELLIGENT	LABEEB	LAH-BEEB

Mouhra (Filly)

ENGLISH	ARABIC	PRONUNCIATION
HOPE	AMAL	AH-MAL
HOPE, WISH	RAJAH	RAH-JAH
HORNET, WASP	DABBOURAH	DAH-BOO-RAH
HORSEWOMAN	FARISSAH	FAH-REE-SAH
HUMAN LIKE	ADAHMIYAH	AH-DAH-MEE-YAH
HUMMING	WAZWAZAH	WAZ-WAH-ZAH
HUMOR, JOKE	FOUKAHAT	FOO-KAH-HAT
HUSH MONEY	RASHWAT	RASH-WHAT
HYMN, SONG	TARNIMAT	TAR-NEE-MAT

~ I ~

ENGLISH	ARABIC	PRONUNCIATION
ICE	JALEED	JAH-LEED
ICON	AYKOUNAH	AYE-KOO-NAH
IDEA, OPINION	FIKRAT	FIK-RAT
IDENTITY	HAWIYAT	HAH-WEE-YAT
IMAGE	MEETHAL	MEE-THAL
IMAGE	SOURAT	SOO-RAT
IMAGE OF HER MOTHER	SOURAT OUMAHAH	SOO-RAT-OOM-MAH-HAH
IMAGE OF THE MOTHER	SOURAT AL OUM	SOO-RAT-AL-OOM
IMPOSTER	NASSABAH	NAH-SAH-BAH
IMPRISONED	MAHBOUSSAH	MAH-BOO-SAH
IMPROVEMENT	TAHSEEN	TAH-SEEN
IN PAIN	MOUTAALIMAH	MOO-TAH-AH-LEE-MAH
INCREASE, GROWTH	IZDEEYAD	IZ-DEE-YAD
INDIGO COLOR	NEELEE	NEE-LEE
INDISPENSIBLE	LAZEEMAT	LAH-ZEE-MAT
INFIDEL	KAFIRAH	KAH-FEE-RAH
INFINITY	LANIHAYAT	LAH-NEE-HAH-YAT
INFLEXIBLE, UNYIELDING	MOUTASHADIDAH	MOO-TAH-SHAH-DEE-DAH
INFLUENCE	NOUFOUZ	NOO-FOOZ
INFLUENCE	SATWAT	SAT-WHAT
INGREDIENT	MADDAT	MAH-DAT
INITIATIVE	MOUBADARAT	MOO-BAH-DAH-RAT
INNER SELF	SARIRAT	SAH-REE-RAT

Mouher (Colt)

ENGLISH	ARABIC	PRONUNCIATION
INTERMEDIARY	WASSIT	WAH-SEET
INVENTION	IBTIKAR	IB-TEE-KAR
IVY	LIBLAB	LIB-LAB

~ J ~

ENGLISH	ARABIC	PRONUNCIATION
JAILER	SAJJAN	SAH-JAN
JESTER, CLOWN	BALOOL	BAH-LOOL
JEWEL	JAWHARAH	JAW-HA-RAH
JONAH	YOUNEES	YOO-NEES
JOY	SEEROUR	SEE-ROOR
JOY, DELIGHT	BAHJAT	BAH-JAT
JOYFUL	BAHIJ	BAH-HEEJ
JOYFUL	MARAH	MAH-RAH
JULEP	JALAB	JAH-LAB
JUSTIFICATION	TABRIR	TAB-REER
JUSTIFIED	MOUBARAR	MOO-BAH-RAR

~ K ~

ENGLISH	ARABIC	PRONUNCIATION
KICKER	RAFASS	RAH-FASS
KIDNAPPED	MAKHTOUF	MAKH-TOOF
KINDLY, PLEASE	LOUTFAN	LOOT-FAN
KINGFISHER	RAFRAF	RAF-RAF
KNOWN FOREVER	MAAROUF LIL ABAD	MAA-ROOF-LIL-AH-BAD

~ L ~

ENGLISH	ARABIC	PRONUNCIATION
LACKS COURAGE, COWARD	JABAN	JAH-BAN
LADDER	SOULOUM	SOO-LOOM
LAKE, BODY OF WATER	BOOHAYRAH	BOO-HAY-RAH
LAND	BARR	BARR
LARGE BELLY	AKRASH	AHK-RASH
LAST JUDGEMENT	DAYNOONAT	DAY-NOON-NAT
LAST, FINAL	AKHEER	AH-KHEER
LASTING, PERMANENT	DAYEM	DAH-YEM
LAW, CODE	NAMOUSS	NAH-MOOS
LEADER, PRESIDENT	RAYESS	RAH-YESS
LEAN	HAZEEL	HAH-ZEEL

Mouhra (Filly)

ENGLISH	ARABIC	PRONUNCIATION
INQUIRY	ISTIFSAR	ISS-TIF-SAR
INQUISITIVE	FADOULIYA	FA-DOO-LEE-YAH
INSTRUCTIONS	TAHLIMAT	TAH-LEE-MAT
INTEGRITY, FAIRNESS	NAZAHAT	NAH-ZAH-HAT
INTELLIGENCE	FITNAT	FEET-NAT
INTELLIGENCE	NABAHAT	NAH-BAH-HAT
INTELLIGENT, WITTY	ZAKEEYEH	ZAH-KEE-YEH
INTENSE	KATHEEFAH	KAH-THEE-FAH
INTRIGUE	DASSISSAH	DAH-SEE-SAH
INTRIGUE	MOUAMARAT	MOO-AH-MAH-RAT
IRRISTIBLE, CLOSE TO THE HEART	MAHDOUMEH	MAH-DOO-MEH
ISLAMIC	ISLAME	ISS-LAH-MEE
ISLAND	JAZEERAH	JAH-ZEE-RAH

~ J ~

JASMINE	YASMIN	YAH-MEEN
JEWEL	HOULIYAT	HOO-LEE-YAT
JEWEL, PRECIOUS STONE	JAWHARAH	JOUW-HAH-RAH
JEWELRY	JAWAHER	JAH-WAH-HER
JOKE	NOUKTAT	NOOK-TAT
JOURNEY	JAWLAT	JAW-LAT
JOURNEY	RAHLAT	RAH-LAT
JOURNEY	SAFRAT	SAF-RAT
JOVIAL, HAPPY	MARAH	MAH-RAH
JOYFUL	MOUBHIJAH	MOOB-HEE-JAH
JUBILATION	IBTIHAJ	IB-TEE-HAJ

~ K ~

KIND SOUL	JINSS	JINSS
KISS	BAWSAT	BAW-SAT
KISS	LASMAT	LAS-MAT

~ L ~

LADY	SAYIDAT	SAH-YEE-DAT
LADY	SITT	SEETT
LAKE, BODY OF WATER	BOOHAYRAH	BOO-HAY-RAH

Mouher (Colt)

ENGLISH	ARABIC	PRONUNCIATION
LEASE, RENT	EJAR	EE-JAR
LENIENT	RAHEEM	RAH-HEEM
LIBERAL	MOUTAHARER	MOO-TAH-HAH-RER
LIGHT RAIN, SHOWER	MATTAR	MAH-TAR
LIGHT, BRIGHT	FATEH	FAH-TEH
LIGHT, GLEAM	NOOR	NOOR
LILY (FLOWER)	SOUSAN	SOO-SAN
LION	LAYTH	LAYTH
LION CUB	SHIBEL	SHI-BEL
LOFTY, HIGH	SAMEK	SAH-MEK
LONER	NASEK	NAH-SEK
LONGER	ATWAHL	AT-WALL
LOVE	HAWAH	HAH-WAH
LOVE, AFFECTION	WEEDAD	WEE-DAD
LOVER	MOUHEB	MOO-HEB
LOVING	MOUHIB	MOO-HEEB
LOVING, TENDER	RAOUM	RAH-OOM
LOWER	ASFAL	AS-FAL
LUKEWARM	FATER	FAH-TER

~ M ~

ENGLISH	ARABIC	PRONUNCIATION
MADLY IN LOVE WITH	MOUTAYAM	MOO-TAH-YAM
MAGIC	SIHR	SIHR
MAGICIAN	SAHER	SAH-HER
MAGNANIMOUS	SHAHEM	SHAH-HEM
MAGNIFICENCE	JALAL	JAH-LAL
MAJESTIC	MOULOUKI	MOO-LOO-KEE
MAJORITY	AKTARIYAH	AHK-TAH-REE-YAH
MANE OF A LION	LOOBDAT	LOOB-DAT
MANHOOD	REJOULAT	REE-JOO-LAT
MANY	ADEED	AH-DEED
MANY GREETINGS (HELLOS)	SALAMAT	SAH-LAH-MAT
MARCH (MONTH)	AZAR	AH-ZAR
MARK, BLEMISH	SHAEB	SHAH-EB

Mouhra (Filly)

ENGLISH	ARABIC	PRONUNCIATION
LAST JUDGEMENT	DAYNOONAT	DAY-NOO-NAT
LAW	SHARIAH	SHAH-REE-AH
LAZY, INACTIVE	KASLAHNAH	KAHS-LAH-NAH
LEASED	MOUAJAHRAH	MOO-AH-JAH-RAH
LEFT HANDED	YASSARIAH	YAH-SAH-REE-YAH
LEMON	LEYMOON	LEY-MOON
LENIENCY	HAWADAT	HAH-WAH-DAT
LETTER, NOTE	REESALAT	REE-SAH-LAT
LIAISON	IRTEEBAT	IR-TEE-BAT
LIBERATED	MOUTAHARIRAH	MOO-TAH-HAH-REE-RAH
LIBERATION	TAHRIR	TAH-REER
LICENSE, PERMIT	ROUKHSAT	ROOKH-SAT
LIGHT SEARCHER	KASHEEFAT AL NOOR	KAH-SHEE-FAT-AL-NOOR
LIGHT, BRIGHT	FATIHAH	FAH-TEE-HAH
LILY	ZAMBOUK	ZAM-BOOK
LINGUISTIC	LEESANI	LEE-SAN-EE
LIONESS	LABOUAT	LAH-BOO-AT
LIQUIDITY	SOUYOULAT	SOO-YOO-LAT
LIVELIHOOD	RIZKAT	RIZ-KAT
LONG WALK	MASSIRAT	MAH-SEE-RAT
LONLINESS	WEHDAT	WEH-DAT
LOOK ALIKE	SHABIHAT	SHAH-BEE-HAT
LOVE, AFFECTION	WEEDAD	WEE-DAD
LOVEABLE	MOUHABABAH	MOO-HAH-BAH-BAH
LOVED ONE, DARLING	MAHBOUBA	MAH-BOO-BAH
LUKEWARM	FATIRAH	FAH-TEE-RAH
LUXURIOUS	KAMAHLEE	KAH-MAH-LEE
	~ M ~	
MADE OF BRONZE	BRONZIYAH	BRON-ZEE-YAH
MADNESS, FOOLISHNESS	JENOON	JEH-NOON
MAGICAL	SIHREE	SIH-REE
MAGNIFICENCE	FAHKHAMAT	FAH-KAH-MAT
MAIDEN	BATOOL	BAH-TOOL

Mouher (Colt)

ENGLISH	ARABIC	PRONUNCIATION
MARTYR	FEDAEE	FEE-DAH-EE
MASTER	SAYYED	SAH-YED
MASTER OF THE WIND	SAYYED AL HAWAH	SAH-YED-AL-HAH-WAH
MASTERFUL	MOUTASSALET	MOO-TAH-SAH-LET
MATERIAL	MAHDEE	MAH-DEE
MAY	NAWAR	NAH-WAR
MEDIATOR	WASSEET	WAH-SEET
MEDICINE	DAWAH	DAH-WAH
MELODY	LAHN	LAHN
MELODY	NAGHAM	NAH-GHAM
MELON	SHAMAM	SHAH-MAM
MERCHANT	MOUTAJER	MOO-TAH-JER
MERCHANT, SHOP KEEPER	TAJER	TAH-JER
MERCIFUL	RAOUF	RAH-OOF
MERCIFUL	SHAFOUK	SHAH-FOOK
MERCIFUL	RAHOUM	RAH-HOOM
MERIT	FADL	FADL
MESSENGER	RASSOUL	RAH-SOOL
MILK	LABAN	LAH-BAN
MINDFUL	MOUBAL	MOO-BAL
MINE	LEE	LEE
MINISTER	WAZEER	WAH-ZEER
MINORITY	AKALIYAH	AH-KAH-LEE-YAH
MISCHIEVOUS	RAZEEL	RAH-ZEEL
MOLASSES	DIBSS	DIBSS
MONASTERY	DEIR	DEIR
MONEY	DEERHAM	DEER-HAM
MONK	RAHEB	RAH-HEB
MOON	HILAL	HEE-LAL
MORAL, ETHICAL	ADAHBEE	AH-DAH-BEE
MORALS, DECENCIES	ADAHB	AH-DAB
MORE THAN	AKTAR	AHK-TAHR
MORSELS	FOUTTAT	FOO-TAT

Mouhra (Filly)

ENGLISH	ARABIC	PRONUNCIATION
MAIDEN, UNSPOILED	BIKRAH	BIK-RAH
MAJOR	RASHIDAT	RAH-SHEE-DAT
MAJORITY	AKTHARIYAH	AHK-THA-REE-YAH
MANKIND, PEOPLE	BASHARIYAH	BAH-SHAH-REE-YAH
MANY GREETINGS	SALAMAT	SAH-LAH-MAT
MANY TREASURES	KOUNOOZ	KOO-NOOZ
MARBLE	ROUKHAM	ROO-KHAM
MARE	FARAS	FAH-RAS
MARK, SCAR	NADBAT	NAD-BAT
MEDIATOR	WASEETAH	WAH-SEE-TAH
MEDICATED	JAHILAH	JAH-HEE-LAH
MEDICINE	DAWAH	DAH-WAH
MEMORIES	ZOUKRAYAT	ZOOK-RAH-YAT
MERCY	RAAHFAT	RAH-AH-FAT
MERIT, VIRTUE	FADEELAT	FA-DEE-LAT
MESSENGER (FEMALE)	RASSOULAH	RAH-SOO-LAH
MIDDAY	NISF AL NAHR	NISF-AL-NAHR
MIDDAY, NOON	HAJEERAH	HAH-JEE-RAH
MIDDLE AGE	KOUHOULAT	KOO-HOO-LAT
MIDDLE EASTERN DANCE	DABKA	DAB-KAH
MIDDLE WOMAN, BROKER	SIMSARAH	SIM-SAH-RAH
MIDNIGHT	NISF AL LEIL	NISF-AL-LAY-IL
MILITANT	MOUTAHARIBAH	MOO-TAH-HAH-REE-BAH
MINISTER	WAZEERAH	WAH-ZEE-RAH
MINORITY	AKAHLIYAH	AH-KAH-LEE-YAH
MIRACLE	MOUJIZAH	MOO-JEE-ZAH
MIRACLE, WONDER	AHYAT	AH-YAHT
MISFORTUNE, DISASTER	DAHIYAT	DAH-HEE-YAHT
MIXED	MAMZOUJAH	MAM-ZOO-JAH
MODESTY	IHTEESHAM	IH-TEE-SHAM
MOISTENED, SLIGHTLY WET	MABLOULAH	MAB-LOO-LAH
MOMENT	HOUNAYHAT	HOO-NYE-HAT
MOMENT	LAHZAT	LAH-ZAT

Mouher (Colt)

ENGLISH	ARABIC	PRONUNCIATION
MORTAL ENEMY	LADOOD	LAH-DOOD
MOUNTAIN	JABAL	JAH-BAL
MUCH, MANY	KATEER	KAH-TEER
MURKY	MOOSHAWASH	MOO-SHAH-WAHSH
MY BROTHER	AKHEE	AH-KEE
MY COUNTRY	WATANI	WAH-TAH-NEE
MY FRIEND	SADIQUI	SAH-DEE-KEE
MY HOME	DAREE	DAH-REE
MY LAND, TERRESTIAL	AHRDEE	AHR-DEE
MY LIFE	YA-HAYATI	YAH-HAH-YAH-TEE
MY LIGHT	NOORI	NOO-REE
MY MYSTIC	SEERI	SEE-REE
MY PRINCE	AMIRI	AH-MEE-REE

~ N ~

ENGLISH	ARABIC	PRONUNCIATION
NATIVE	BALADI	BAH-LAH-DEE
NATURAL, NATIVE	FAHTRI	FAHT-REE
NAVY BLUE	KOOHLEE	KOOH-LEE
NEAR TO SOMEONE	ADNAH	AHD-NAH
NEATNESS	HINDAM	HIN-DAM
NECESSARY	LAZEM	LAH-ZEM
NEEDY	FAKEER	FAH-KEER
NEIGHBOR (MALE)	JAR	JAR
NEVER	ABADAN	AH-BAH-DAN
NEW, MODERN	JADEED	JAH-DEED
NIGHTINGALE	BULBUL	BOOL-BOOL
NIGHTINGALE	HAZZAR	HAH-ZAR
NIGHTMARE, FRIGHTENING DREAM	KABOUSS	KAH-BOOSS
NO CONDITION	LASHART	LAH-SHART
NOBILITY	NOUBL	NOOBL
NOBLE	SHARIF	SHAH-REEF
NOBLE PARTNER	SHAREEK MAJEED	SHAH-REEK-MAH-JEED
NOBLEMAN	NABIL	NAH-BEEL
NOCTURNAL	LAYLEE	LAY-LEE

Mouhra (Filly)

ENGLISH	ARABIC	PRONUNCIATION
MORNING	SABBAH	SAH-BAH
MORSEL	LEKMAT	LEK-MATT
MOUNTAIN	JABBAL	JAH-BAL
MOUNTAINOUS	JABALEE	JAH-BAH-LEE
MY COMPANION	RAFEEKATI	RAH-FEE-KAH-TEE
MY FAVORITE	MOUFADALLAH	MOO-FAH-DAH-LAH
MY LADY	SAYIDATEE	SAH-YEE-DAH-TEE
MY LIFE	YA HAYATI	YAH-HAH-YAH-TEE
MY LIFE COMPANION	SHARIKAT HAYATI	SHAH-REE-KAT-HAH-YAH-TEE
MY PRINCESS	AMEERATI	AH-MEE-RAH-TEE
MY TREASURE	KANZEE	KAHN-ZEE

~ N ~

ENGLISH	ARABIC	PRONUNCIATION
NARGILEH (EGYPTIAN)	SHISHAH	SHEE-SHAH
NATIONALITY	JENSIYAT	JEN-SEE-YAT
NATURAL DISPOSITION	JABLAT	JAB-LAT
NATURAL DISPOSITION	SAJIYAT	SAH-JEE-YAT
NECESSITY	LOUZOUM	LOO-ZOOM
NECESSITY, NEED	DAHROURAT	DAH-ROO-RAT
NEEDLE	IBRAT	IB-RAT
NEW, MODERN	JADEEDAH	JAH-DEE-DAH
NIGHT, EVENING	LAYLA	LAY-LAH
NIGHT, EVENING	LEILA	LAY-LAH
NIGHT, EVENING	LEYLAH	LEY-LAH
NIGHTINGALE	BULBULAH	BOOL-BOO-LAH
NIGHTINGALE	HAZZAR	HAH-ZAR
NO SUBSTITUTE	BALA BADEEL	BAH-LAH-BAH-DEEL
NOBLE	SHARIFAH	SHAH-REE-FAH
NOBLE AND KIND	KAREEMAT AL SHARAF	KAH-REE-MAT-AL-SHAH-RAF
NOBLE WOMAN	NABILAH	NAH-BEE-LAH
NOCTURNAL	LAYLIYAH	LAY-LEE-YAH
NOISE	JALBAT	JAL-BAT
NOMAD (FEMALE)	RAHALAT	RAH-HAH-LAT
NOMADS, WANDERERS	HAJJARAH	HAH-JAH-RAH

Mouher (Colt)

ENGLISH	ARABIC	PRONUNCIATION
NOMAD, BEDOUIN	BADAWI	BAH-DAH-WEE
NON-ARAB	AJAHME	AA-JAH-ME
NORTH	SHAMAL	SHAH-MAL
NORTH WIND	SHAMALEE	SHAH-MAH-LEE
NOTEBOOK	DAHFTAR	DAHF-TAR
NUMBER	RAKM	RAKM

~ O ~

ENGLISH	ARABIC	PRONUNCIATION
OAK	BALOOT	BAH-LOOT
OATH	YAMEEN	YAH-MEEN
OBSCURE	MOUBHAM	MOOB-HAM
OBSCURITY	IBHAM	IB-HAM
OBSERVER	RAKEEB	RAH-KEEB
OBSERVER	RASED	RAH-SED
OBSESSION	HAJESS	HAH-JESS
OCCUPATION	IHTEELAL	IH-TEE-LAL
OF THE HEGIRA	HOUGREE	HOOJ-REE
OFFENSIVE	HOUJOUM	HOO-JOOM
OFFICER (IN THE MILITARY)	RATEB	RAH-TEB
OFFICIAL	RASSM	RASSM
OH! BEAUTIFUL ONE	YA-JAMEEL	YAH-JAH-MEEL
OH! MOTHER	YA-OUMEE	YAH-OO-MEE
OLD FASHIONED	MOUTAGHASSEB	MOO-TAH-GHA-SSEB
ONE	AHAD	AH-HAD
ONE	WAHED	WAH-HED
ONE WHO BRINGS GOOD NEWS	MOUBASHER	MOO-BAH-SHER
ONE WHO PLEADS A CAUSE	WAKEEL	WAH-KEEL
ONLY SON	WAHEED	WAH-HEED
OPIUM	AFYOUN	AHF-YOON
OPTIMISTIC	MOUTAFAEL	MOO-TAH-FAH-EL
ORANGE (COLOR)	BOURTOOKALEE	BOOR-TOO-KAH-LEE
ORANGE (FRUIT)	BOURTOOKAL	BOOR-TOO-KAL
ORBIT	FALAK	FAH-LAK
ORIGIN	AHSEL	AH-SEL

Mouhra (Filly)

ENGLISH	ARABIC	PRONUNCIATION
NOON	ZOOHR	ZOOHR
NORTHERLY	SHAMALEE	SHAH-MAH-LEE
NUN	RAHIBAT	RAH-HEE-BAT

~ O ~

ENGLISH	ARABIC	PRONUNCIATION
OBSERVER	RASEEDAH	RAH-SEE-DAH
OBSERVER (FEMALE)	RAKEEBAH	RAH-KEE-BAH
OCCUPATION FORCES	IHTEELAL	IH-TEE-LAL
OF NOBLE BIRTH	HASIBAH	HAH-SEE-BAH
OF NOBLE ORIGIN	ASSILAH	AH-SEE-LAH
OF THE HEGIRA	HOUGREE	HOOJ-REE
OH! BEAUTIFUL	YA JAMEELA	YAH-JAH-MEE-LAH
OH! DARLING	YA HABIBTI	YAH-HAH-BEEB-TEE
OH! LOVE	YA HAWAH	YAH-HAH-WAH
ONCE	MARRAT	MAH-RAT
ONE OF A KIND	FARIDAH	FAH-REE-DAH
ONE OF A PAIR	FARDAT	FAR-DAT
ONE WHO PLEADS A CAUSE	WAKEELAH	WAH-KEE-LAH
ONLY DAUGHTER	WAHEEDAH	WAH-HEE-DAH
OPPRESSIVE	JAIRAT	JAH-EE-RAT
OPTIMAL	IKHTEEYAREE	IKH-TEE-YAH-REE
OPTIMISTIC	MOUTAFAHILAH	MOO-TAH-FAH-EE-LAH
ORIENTAL	SHARKIYAH	SHAR-KEE-YAH
ORIGIN	MASSDAR	MASS-DAR
ORIGINAL, FIRST	ASSAHSSIYAH	AH-SSAH-SSEE-YAH
ORNAMENT, ADORNMENT	ZEENAT	ZEE-NAT
ORPHAN	YATEEMAH	YAH-TEE-MAH
OVERWHELMED	MABHOURAH	MAB-HOO-RAH
OWL	BOUMAH	BOO-MAH

~ P ~

ENGLISH	ARABIC	PRONUNCIATION
PACKAGE	RIZMAT	RIZ-MAT
PAMPERED	MOUDALALAH	MOO-DAH-LAH-LAH
PARADISE	FERDOUS	FER-DOWS
PARADISE	JANNAT	JAH-NAT

Mouher (Colt)

ENGLISH	ARABIC	PRONUNCIATION
ORIGINALITY	ASAHLAH	AH-SAH-LAH
ORNAMENT	ZEENAT	ZEE-NAT
ORPHAN	YATIM	YAH-TEEM
OUTLAW	MOOJREM	MOOJ-REM
OVERALL	IJMAHLEE	IJ-MAH-LEE
OWL	BOUM	BOOM

~ P ~

ENGLISH	ARABIC	PRONUNCIATION
PAINTER	DAHHAN	DAH-HAN
PAINTER, ARTIST	RASSAM	RAH-SAM
PALACE	EWAN	EE-WAN
PALE	SHAHEB	SHAH-HEB
PALE, NOT COLORFUL	BAHEET	BAH-HEET
PALM TREE	NAKHL	NAKHL
PARADISE	FERDOUS	FER-DOWS
PARADISE	JANNAT	JAH-NAT
PARTIAL DARKNESS, GLOOMY	DAJJEN	DAH-JEN
PARTICIPATION	ISHTEERAK	ISH-TEE-RAK
PARTNER	SHAREEK	SHAH-REEK
PARTY	MARAJAN	MAH-RAH-JAN
PASSAGE (ACT OF PASSING THROUGH)	MOUROUR	MOO-ROOR
PASSIVE	HEYAM	HEE-YAM
PAST	MADEE	MAH-DEE
PASTURE	MARJ	MARJ
PATCHWORK	KASHKOOL	KASH-KOOL
PATERNAL	ABAHWEE	AH-BAH-WEE
PATH, ROUTE	MASSAR	MAH-SAR
PEACE	SALAM	SAH-LAM
PEARLS	LOULOU	LOO-LOO
PERFECT, COMPLETE	KAMEL	KAH-MEL
PERFECTION	KAMAL	KAH-MAL
PERIOD, TIME	FATTRAT	FAH-TRAT
PERMISSIBLE	JAEZ	JAH-EZ
PERMISSION	IZN	IZN

Mouhra (Filly)

ENGLISH	ARABIC	PRONUNCIATION
PARENTLESS	LATEEMAT	LAH-TEE-MAT
PASSION	HAWAH	HAH-WAH
PASSWORD	KEELMAT AL SIR	KEEL-MAT-AL-SIR
PATROL	DAWREEYAT	DAW-REE-YAT
PEACE	SALAM	SAH-LAM
PEACEFUL	SALMEE	SAL-MEE
PEARL	DOURRA	DOO-RAH
PEARL	DOURRAT	DOO-RAT
PEARLS	LOULOUIYAT	LOO-LOO-EE-YAT
PEASANT LADY	FALLAHAH	FAH-LAH-HAH
PERFECT	KAMEELA	KAH-MEE-LAH
PERFECT	KAMILAH	KAH-MEE-LAH
PERFECT	KHAMILAH	KAH-MEE-LAH
PERIODIC, REGULAR	DAWREE	DAW-REE
PERMITTED	MAEEZOUNAH	MAH-EE-ZOO-NAH
PERSIAN	FARISSEE	FAH-REE-SEE
PERSONALITY	SHAKHSIYAT	SHAKH-SEE-YAT
PHILOSOPHY	FALSAFAT	FAL-SAH-FAT
PICK POCKET, THIEF	NASHALAT	NAH-SHAH-LAT
PIGTAIL	DAHFIRAT	DAH-FEE-RAT
PLAYING CARDS	KOTCHINAH	KO-TCHEE-NAH
PLEASURE	SEROUR	SEE-ROOR
POLITICS	SIYASSAT	SEE-YAH-SAT
POMEGRANITE	ROUMANAT	ROO-MAH-NAT
POPCORN	FOUSHAR	FOO-SHAR
POPULAR	DAREEJAH	DAH-REE-JAH
POSITIVE	EJABIYAH	EE-JAH-BEE-YAH
POSSIBILITY	IHTEEMAL	IH-TEE-MAL
POWDER	BOODRAH	BOO-DRAH
POWERFUL	AL JABBARAH	AL-JAH-BAH-RAH
PRAISE THE LORD	SUBHAN ALLAH	SUB-HAN-AL-LAH
PRECEDENT	SABIKAH	SAH-BEE-KAH
PRECIOUS	TOHFA	TOH-FAH

Mouher (Colt)

ENGLISH	ARABIC	PRONUNCIATION
PERSIAN	FARISSI	FAH-REE-SEE
PERSISTANT, DILIGENT	DAHOUB	DAH-OOB
PERSON, INDIVIDUAL	NAFAR	NAH-FAR
PHILOSOPHY	FALSAFAT	FAL-SAH-FAT
PHYSICAL	BADANEE	BAH-DAH-NEE
PICKPOCKET	NASHAL	NAH-SHALL
PIN	DABBOUSS	DAH-BOOSS
PIPER	ZAMMAR	ZAH-MAR
PISTACHIO	FOUSTOK	FOOS-TOC
PITCHER, JUG	IBREEK	IB-REEK
PLAY	HAZAL	HAH-ZAL
PLEASED, CONTENT	RADEE	RAH-DEE
PLEASURE	LAZAT	LAH-ZAT
PLOT	MOUAMARAT	MOO-AH-MAH-RAT
POET	SHAER	SHAH-ER
POLICEMAN	DAHRAKEE	DAH-RAH-KEE
POLITICIAN	DIPLOMACEE	DEE-PLO-MAH-SEE
POPCORN	FOUSHAR	FOO-SHAR
PORCUPINE	DOULDOUL	DOOL-DOOL
POSITIVE	EJABEE	EE-JAH-BEE
POWERFUL	AJAJ	AH-JAJ
PRAISED	MAHMOOD	MAH-MOOD
PRAYER	IBTIHAL	IB-TEE-HAL
PREACHING	TABSHEER	TAB-SHEER
PREMATURE	MOUBKER	MOOB-KER
PREVIOUS	SABEK	SAH-BEK
PREY	FAREESAT	FAH-REE-SAT
PRICE	THAMAN	THAH-MAN
PRINCE OF ESCAPE	AMIR AL FERAR	AH-MEER-AL-FEE-RAR
PRISON	SIJN	SIJN
PRISONER	SAJEEN	SAH-JEEN
PRISONER, CAPTIVE	ASEER	AH-SEER
PROOF, EVIDENCE	BOORHAN	BOOR-HAN

Mouhra (Filly)

ENGLISH	ARABIC	PRONUNCIATION
PRECIOUS STONE, JEWEL	JAWHARAH	JOUW-HAH-RAH
PREFACE	DEEBAJAT	DEE-BAH-JAT
PREJUDICED	MOUTAHAZIBAH	MOO-TAH-HAH-ZEE-BAH
PREMATURE	MOUBKIRAH	MOOB-KEE-RAH
PREPARED	JAHIZAH	JAH-HEE-ZAH
PRESENT, DONATION	HEBAT	HEE-BAT
PRESENT, GIFT	HADIYA	HAH-DEE-YAH
PRESTIGE	WAJAHAT	WAH-JAH-HAT
PRETTY, BEAUTIFUL	JAMEELAH	JAH-MEE-LAH
PREVIOUSLY	SABIKAN	SAH-BEE-KAN
PRICELESS, BEYOND VALUE	NAFISSAH	NAH-FEE-SAH
PRIDE, ARROGANCE	TAKABOUR	TAH-KAH-BOOR
PRINCESS	AMEERAH	AH-ME-RAH
PRINCESS OF THE MOUNTAIN	AMIRAT AL JABAL	AH-MEE-RAT-AL-JAH-BAL
PRINCESS, LEADER OF THE TRIBE	BASHANA	BAH-SHAH-NAH
PRIORITY	AWLAHWIYAH	AW-LAH-WEE-YAH
PRISON	NAZARAT	NAH-ZAH-RAT
PRISONER	SAJEENAT	SAJ-JEE-NAT
PRISONER (OF)	RAHINAT	RAH-HEE-NAT
PRISONER, CAPTIVE	ASIRAH	AH-SEE-RAH
PRIZE, REWARD	JAIZAT	JAH-EE-ZAT
PROMENADE	NAZHAT	NAZ-HAT
PROPHECY	NOUBOUWAT	NOO-BOO-WHAT
PROSPEROUS	YASIRAT	YAH-SEE-RAT
PROTECTED	MAHROUSSEH	MAH-ROO-SSEH
PROTECTED ONE	MAHFOUZAH	MAH-FOO-ZAH
PROUD	FAKHOURAH	FAH-KOO-RAH
PROUD, DISDAINFUL	ANOUF	AH-NOOF
PRUDENT, CAUTIOUS	MOUTAZINAH	MOO-TAH-ZEE-NAH
PSYCHOLOGICAL	NAFSANI	NAF-SAH-NEE
PUBLICATION, A PUBLISHED WORK	NASHRAT	NASH-RAT
PUNCH, A QUICK STRIKE	LAKMAT	LAK-MATT
PURE	NAZEEFAH	NAH-ZEE-FAH

Mouher (Colt)

ENGLISH	ARABIC	PRONUNCIATION
PROPERTY	MELK	MELK
PROPHET	NABEE	NAH-BEE
PROPHETIC	NABAWI	NAH-BAH-WEE
PROPRIETOR	MALEK	MAH-LEK
PROSPERITY	IZDEEHAR	IZ-DEE-HAR
PROSPEROUS	YASERR	YAH-SERR
PROTEST, OBJECTION	IHTEEJAJ	IH-TEE-JAJ
PROUD, ARROGANT	MOUTAKABER	MOO-TAH-KAH-BER
PROVOCATION	ISTIFZAZ	ISS-TIF-ZAZ
PULSE	NABAD	NAH-BAD
PURE	SAFI	SAH-FEE
PURE LIGHT	SAFI-NOUR	SAH-FEE-NOOR
PURE, CLEAN	NAZEEF	NAH-ZEEF
PURE, CLEAR	NAHKI	NAH-KEE
PURPOSE	HADDAF	HAH-DAF
PYRAMID	HARAM	HAH-RAM

~ Q ~

QUANTITY, AMOUNT	KAMIYAT	KAH-MEE-YAT
QUESTION	ISTIFHAM	ISS-TIF-HAM

~ R ~

RACE	SEEBAK	SEE-BAK
RACE (WITH HORSES)	MOUSABAKAT	MOO-SAH-BAH-KAT
RADICAL	MOUTATAREF	MOO-TAH-TAH-REF
RAINY	MATTER	MAH-TER
RANGE	NEETAK	NEE-TAK
RARE	NADIR	NAH-DEER
READY	JAHEZ	JAH-HEZ
READY	MOUTAHAHEB	MOO-TAH-AH-HEB
REAR	MOUAKHAR	MOO-AH-KHAR
REASON	ROOSHD	ROOSHD
REBELLIOUS	MOUTAMARED	MOO-TAH-MAH-RED
RECEPTION	ISTIKBAL	ISS-TIK-BAL
RECREATION, FUN	ISTIJMAM	ISS-TIJ-MAM

Mouhra (Filly)

ENGLISH	ARABIC	PRONUNCIATION
PURE, CLEAR	SAFINA	SAH-FEE-NAH
PURPOSE	NEEYAT	NEE-YAT
PYRAMIDICAL	HARAMI	HAH-RAH-MEE

~ Q ~

QUEEN OF THE FIELD	MALIKAT AL BOUSTAN	MAH-LEE-KAT-AL BOOS-TAN
QUIET	HAMIDAH	HAH-MEE-DAH

~ R ~

RAIN WATERS	MIYAH AL AMTAR	MEE-YAH-AL-AM-TAR
RAISING	RAFIAT	RAH-FEE-AT
RANSOM	FADEEYAT	FAH-DEE-YAT
RARE JEWEL	ALMASAH JASSIRAH	AL-MAH-SAH-JAH-SEE-RAH
RARE JEWEL	JAWHARAH NADIRAH	JOUW-HAH-RAH-NAH-DEE-RAH
RARELY, SELDOM	NADEERAN	NAH-DEE-RAN
RARITY	NOUZRAT	NOOZ-RAT
READY	MOUTAAHIBAH	MOO-TAH-AH-HEE-BAH
REALIZATION	IDRAK	EE-DRAHK
REBEL	MOUTAMARIDAH	MOO-TAH-MAH-REE-DAH
RECEIVER	MOUTASSALIMAH	MOO-TAH-SAH-LEE-MAH
RED PEPPER	FOULAYFOULAH	FOO-LAY-FOO-LAH
RED ROSES	WARD AHMAR	WARD-AH-MAR
REDDISH	HAMRAH	HAM-RAH
REFRESHMENT	KAZOOZAH	KAH-ZOO-ZAH
REJECTING	RAFEEDAH	RAH-FEE-DAH
RELATIVE	NASSEEBAH	NAH-SEE-BAH
RELIABLE	JADEERAH	JAH-DEE-RAH
RELIABLE	WASSIKAH	WAH-SEE-KAH
RELIGION	DEEYAHNAT	DEE-YAH-NAT
RENEWED	MOUTAJADIDAH	MOO-TAH-JAH-DEE-DAH
RENOWN	SHOURAT	SHOOH-RAT
REPEAT	RADADAH	RAH-DAH-DAH
REPENTANT	TAIBAT	TAH-EE-BAT
REPUBLIC	JAMHOURIAT	JAM-HOO-REE-YAT
REQUIEM	JOUNAZ	JOO-NAZ

Mouher (Colt)

ENGLISH	ARABIC	PRONUNCIATION
REJOICING	MOUBTAHEJ	MOOB-TAH-HEJ
RELATION, LIASON	IRTEEBAT	IR-TEE-BAT
RELATIVE OF THE SAND	HAFEED AL RAML	HAH-FEED-AL-RAML
RELEVANT	SADEED	SAH-DEED
RELIABLE	WASSEK	WAH-SEK
RELIANCE	ITTEEKAL	IT-TEE-KAL
RENEWED	MOUTAJADED	MOO-TAH-JAH-DED
REPENTANT	NADEM	NAH-DEM
REPENTANT	TAHEB	TAH-EB
RESERVE	RADEEF	RAH-DEEF
RESPECT	WEEQUAR	WEE-KAR
RESPONSIVE	MOUTAJAWEB	MOO-TAH-JAH-WEB
RETURN	EYAB	EE-YAB
REVERAND FATHER	ABOUNAH	AH-BU-NAH
RIBBON	REBAT	REE-BAT
RIFLEMAN	RAMEE	RAH-MEE
RIOT	SHAGHAB	SHAH-GHAB
RIVER	NAHR	NAHR
ROAR	HADARAH	HAH-DAH-RAH
ROAR OR RUMBLE OF A WATERFALL	HADEER	HAH-DEER
ROOT	JIZR	JIZR
ROTATING, REVOLVING	DAWAHR	DAH-WAHR
ROTATION	DAWAHRAN	DAH-WAH-RAN
RUBY	YAKOUT	YAH-KOOT
~ S ~		
SADDLE	SOURJ	SOURJ
SAFETY, SECURITY	AMAN	AH-MAN
SAILOR, SEAMAN	BAHHAR	BAH-HAR
SAINT	MAR	MAR
SALTY	MALEH	MAH-LEH
SAND	RAML	RAML
SATIRIZE	HAJAH	HAH-JAH
SATISFYING THE THIRSTY ONE	MIRWI AL AATSHAN	MEER-WEE-AL-AAT-SHAN

Mouhra (Filly)

ENGLISH	ARABIC	PRONUNCIATION
RESCUE	NAJAT	NAH-JAT
RESIGNATION	ISTEEKALAT	ISS-TEE-KAH-LAT
RESOLUTION	HIMMAT	HEE-MATT
RESPECT	KARAMAT	KAH-RAH-MAT
RESPECTED	MOUHTARAMAH	MOOH-TAH-RAH-MAH
RESPONSIBLE	WALIYAH	WAH-LEE-YAH
RESPONSIVE	MOUTAJAWIBAH	MOO-TAH-JAH-WEE-BAH
RESTLESS	MOUTAMALMILAH	MOO-TAH-MAL-MEE-LAH
RESULT, OUTCOME	NATEEJAT	NAH-TEE-JAT
RETURN	EYAB	EE-YAB
RIGHT GUIDANCE	HOODAH	HOO-DAH
RIGHTEOUS	FADILAH	FAH-DEE-LAH
RIGID	JAMEEDAH	JAH-MEE-DAH
ROAR OF A WATERFALL	HADEER	HAH-DEER
ROARING, LOUD	HADER	HAH-DER
ROBBERY	SATTOU	SAH-TOO
ROCKING	HAZZAZ	HAH-ZAZ
ROSE COLORED	WARDI	WAR-DEE
ROSES	WOUROUD	WOO-ROOD
ROUND	DAWRAT	DAW-RAT
ROUSED, EXCITED	HAEEJJAH	HAH-EE-JAH
RUNAWAY	HARABAT	HAH-RAH-BAT
RUNAWAY	HAREEBAH	HAH-REE-BAH
	~ S ~	
SAFETY PIN	DABBOUSS ZAINEE	DAH-BOOSS-ZAI-NEE
SALUKI (DOG)	SALUKI	SAH-LOO-KEE
SANDY	RAMLEE	RAM-LEE
SATISFACTION	IRTEEYAH	IR-TEE-YAH
SATISFIED, CONTENT	RADEEYAH	RAH-DEE-YAH
SCANDAL	FADEEHAT	FA-DEE-HAT
SCHOLAR	DAREESSAH	DAH-REE-SSAH
SCHOOL TEACHER	MOUDARISSAH	MOO-DAH-REE-SAH
SEARCHER	KASHEEFAH	KAH-SHEE-FAH

Mouher (Colt)

ENGLISH	ARABIC	PRONUNCIATION
SAVAGE	HAMAJEE	HAH-MAH-JEE
SEARCHER	KASHEF	KAH-SHEF
SECRETIVE	SOURRI	SOO-RREE
SEED	BIZREH	BIZ-REH
SELECTED	MOUKHTAR	MOOK-TAR
SELF-EVIDENT, OBVIOUS	BADEEHI	BAH-DEE-HEE
SEPARATE, TO PART WITH	FAREK	FAH-REK
SEPARATION	FEERAQ	FEE-RAK
SERGEANT	SHAWISH	SHAH-WISH
SESAME	SOUMSOUM	SOOM-SOOM
SESAME OIL	SIRJ	SIRJ
SHADOW	ZEEL	ZEEL
SHADOWS	ZILAL	ZEE-LAL
SHAWL	SHAL	SHALL
SHINING, SPARKLING	BARRAK	BAH-RAK
SHOOTING STAR	SHEEHAB	SHEE-HAB
SHORT STORY	AKSOUSSAH	AHK-SOO-SAH
SHORTER	AKSAHR	AHK-SAR
SHOWN, COME TO VIEW	BAYAN	BAH-YAN
SIDE TEAM	FAREEQ	FAH-REEK
SIGHT	NAZAR	NAH-ZAR
SIGN (OF THE ZODIAC)	BOORJ FALAKI	BOORJ-FAH-LAH-KEE
SIGN, INDICATION	DALEEL	DAH-LEEL
SILENCE	SEEKOUT	SEE-KOOT
SILENCE	SOUKOUT	SOO-KOOT
SILK GARMENT	DEEBAJ	DEE-BAJ
SILVER	FEEDAT	FEE-DAT
SINGER	SHADI	SHAH-DEE
SITTING DOWN	JOULOUSS	JOO-LOOS
SKILLED	MAHER	MAH-HER
SKY	SAMAH	SAH-MAH
SLEEP	NAWM	NAWM
SLEEP	ROUKAD	ROO-KAD

Mouhra (Filly)

ENGLISH	ARABIC	PRONUNCIATION
SECRECY	SERRIYAT	SEH-REE-YAT
SECURE, TRUSTED, FAITHFUL	AMEENAH	AH-ME-NAH
SEDUCE	RAWADAH	RAH-WAH-DAH
SEDUCTION, APPEAL	FOOTNAT	FOOT-NAT
SEED	NAWAT	NAH-WHAT
SELF CONSCIOUS, SHY	BADAHAH	BAH-DAH-HAH
SELF EVIDENT	BADIHIYAH	BAH-DEE-HEE-YAH
SENDER	MOUSILAH	MOO-SEE-LAH
SEPARATION	FEERAQ	FEE-RAK
SEPTEMBER (MONTH)	AYLOOL	AYE-LOOL
SESAME	SOUMSOUM	SOOM-SOOM
SET OF SAME KIND	WAJBAT	WAJ-BAT
SEVERAL, MANY	JOUMLAT	JOOM-LAT
SHADOWS	ZEEL	ZEEL
SHADOWS	ZILAL	ZEE-LAL
SHAPE, APPEARANCE	HAYAT	HAY-AT
SHE IS BLESSED	MARZOUKAH	MAR-ZOO-KAH
SHEEP (FEMALE)	NAAJAT	NAH-JAT
SHEER SPLENDOR	BAHRAJAT	BAH-RAH-JAT
SHELTER	MAEEWAH	MAH-EE-WAH
SHELTER	SAKIFAT	SAH-KEE-FAT
SHIELD	SITR	SITR
SHORT STORY	AKSOUSSAH	AHK-SOO-SAH
SHOUTING	HOOTAF	HOO-TAF
SHOW, SPECTACLE	FOURJAT	FOOR-JAT
SHRUB	SHOUJAIRAT	SHOO-JAY-RAT
SHY	KAJLANEH	KAJ-LAH-NEH
SIGN OF BEAUTY	ISHARAT AL JAMAL	EE-SHAH-RAT-AL-JAH-MAL
SIGN, INDICATION	BADIRAH	BAH-DEE-RAH
SIGN, MARK, SYMBOL	ISHARAT	EE-SHAH-RAT
SIGN, TOKEN, SYMBOL	AYAT	AH-YAT
SIGNIFICANCE	DALAHLAT	DAH-LAH-LAT
SILK BROCADE	DEEBAJ	DEE-BAJ

Mouher (Colt)

ENGLISH	ARABIC	PRONUNCIATION
SLOW GLITTER OR SPARKLE	BASSISS	BAH-SEESS
SLY, CRAFTY	SHATER	SHAH-TER
SLY, CUNNING	MAHKER	MAH-KER
SMALLER, YOUNGER	AHZGAHR	AHZ-GAHR
SMART, INTELLIGENT	FAHEEM	FAH-HEEM
SMART, INTELLIGENT	ZAKEE	ZAH-KEE
SMILE	IBTASSEM	IB-TAH-SEM
SMILING	BASEM	BAH-SEM
SMILING	MOUBTASSEM	MOOB-TAH-SEM
SMILING, BRIGHT FACE	BASHOOSH	BAH-SHOOSH
SMOKE	DOUKHAN	DOO-KHAN
SMUGGLE	HARRAB	HAH-RAB
SNOWBALL	KOURAT THALJ	KOO-RAT-THALJ
SOLDIER	JOUNDEE	JOON-DEE
SOLID, HARD	JAMED	JAH-MED
SON OF	IBN	IBN
SONG OF PRAISE, ANTHEM	NASHEED	NAH-SHEED
SOONER	AJLAN	AHJ-LAN
SOPHISTICATED	MOUTATAWIAR	MOO-TAH-TAH-WEE-AR
SOUL, SPIRIT	NAFS	NAFS
SOUTH	JANOUB	JAH-NOOB
SOUTHERN	JANOUBEE	JAH-NOO-BEE
SOUVENIR	TEZKAR	TEZ-KAR
SPARROW	BASHEK	BAH-SHEK
SPEAKER	MOUTAKALEM	MOO-TAH-KAH-LEM
SPECIAL	MOUTAMAYEZ	MOO-TAH-MAH-YEZ
SPECIALIZATION	IKHTEESAS	IKH-TEE-SAS
SPECTATOR	MOUTAFAREJ	MOO-TAH-FAH-REJ
SPEECH	KALAHM	KAH-LAHM
SPIRIT OF THE NILE	NAFS AL NIL	NAFS-AL-NEEL
SPLASH	RASHASH	RAH-SHASH
SPY	JASSOUSS	JAH-SOOS
SPYING	JASSOUSSIAT	JAH-SOO-SEE-YAT

Mouhra (Filly)

ENGLISH	ARABIC	PRONUNCIATION
SILVER	FIDAT	FEE-DAT
SIMPLY HONEST	DARWISHAH	DAHR-WEE-SHAH
SINCERITY, HONESTY	IKHLASS	IKH-LASS
SISTER	SHAKIYKAT	SHAH-KEE-KAT
SKILLED	MOUJIDAH	MOO-JEE-DAH
SKINNY, THIN, POOR	HAZEELAH	HAH-ZEE-LAH
SKULL	JOUMJOUMAH	JOOM-JOO-MAH
SMART, EXPERIENCED	SHATIRAT	SHAH-TEE-RAT
SMILE	BASSMAH	BAHS-MAH
SMILE	IBTASSEM	IB-TAH-SEM
SMILING	IBTISSAN	IB-TEE-SAN
SMILING	MOUBTASSIMAH	MOOB-TAH-SEE-MAH
SMOOTH, SLEEK	AMLAHSIYAH	AHM-LAH-SEE-YAH
SNAPSHOT	LAKTAT	LAHK-TAT
SNOW BALL	KOURAT THALJ	KOO-RAT-THALJ
SOFTNESS	LOUYOUNAT	LOO-YOU-NAT
SOLAR	SHAMSEE	SHAM-SEE
SOLEMN	JALEELAH	JAH-LEE-LAH
SOLEMN	RAZEENAT	RAH-ZEE-NAT
SOLEMNITY	RAZANAT	RAH-ZAH-NAT
SONGSTRESS	MOUTRIBAH	MOO-TREE-BAH
SORCEROR	SAHIRAT	SAH-HEE-RAT
SOULS, SPIRITS	NOUFOUS	NOO-FOOS
SOUND OF WIND	ZAFEER	ZAH-FEER
SOUND, UNHARMED	SALIMAH	SAH-LEE-MAH
SOUTHERN WIND	JENOUBEE	JEH-NOO-BEE
SOUVENIR	TEZKAR	TEZ-KAR
SPANISH	ISBANIAH	ISS-BAH-NEE-YAH
SPARKLING, SHINY	BARRAKAH	BAHR-RAH-KAH
SPARKS	SHARARAT	SHAH-RAH-RAT
SPARROW	DOURI	DOO-REE
SPEAKER	MOUTAKALIMAH	MOO-TAH-KAH-LEE-MAH
SPECIAL	MOUTAMAYIZA	MOO-TAH-MAH-YEE-ZAH

Mouher (Colt)

ENGLISH	ARABIC	PRONUNCIATION
STAR	KOWKAB	KOW-CAB
STEEL	FOOLAZ	FOO-LAZ
STILL, CALM	HAMED	HAH-MED
STINGY, SPARING	BAKHEEL	BAHK-KHEEL
STORK	LEEKLAK	LEEK-LAK
STORM	REIH	REEH
STORYTELLER	RAWEE	RAH-WEE
STRENGTH	MATANAT	MAH-TAH-NAT
STRONG, MIGHTY	JABBAR	JAH-BAR
STRONG, POWERFUL	SHADID	SHAH-DEED
STRUGGLE	NEEDAL	NEE-DAL
STRUGGLER	MOUJAHED	MOO-JAH-HED
STUDENT	DARESS	DAH-RESS
SUBSTITUTE, REPLACEMENT	BADEEL	BAH-DEEL
SUBSTITUTION	ISTIBDAL	ISS-TIB-DAL
SUCCESS	NAJAH	NAH-JAH
SULTAN, SOVEREIGN	SULTAN	SUL-TAN
SUMMED UP	IJMAHL	IJ-MAHL
SUNFLOWER	DAWAHR AL SHAMS	DAH-WAHR-AL-SHAMS
SUNRISE	SHOUROUK	SHOO-ROOK
SUPERINTENDANT, DIRECTOR	NAZER	NAH-ZER
SUPPORTER	MOUAYED	MOO-AH-YED
SURGE OF THE FLAME	MAHAB AL LAHEEB	MAH-HAB-AL-LAH-HEEB
SURGE OF THE STORM	MAHAB AL REIH	MAH-HAB-AL-REEH
SURGING	MAEJJ	MAH-EJJ
SURPRISED	MOUNDAHESH	MOON-DAH-HESH
SWALLOW	SOUNOUNOU	SOO-NOO-NOO
SWEET, SUGAR	SUKKAR	SOO-KAR
SWINDLER	NASSAB	NAH-SAB
SWORD FISH	ABU MINSHAR	AH-BU MIN-SHAR
SYSTEM	JEHAZ	JEE-HAZ

~ T ~

TAKING OUT	IKHRAJ	IKH-RAJ

Mouhra (Filly)

ENGLISH	ARABIC	PRONUNCIATION
SPECKLE	NOOKTAT	NOOK-TAT
SPECTATOR	MOUTAFARIJAH	MOO-TAH-FAH-REE-JAH
SPINNING TOP	DAWAHMAH	DAH-WAH-MAH
SPINNING, TURNING	DAWAHRAN	DAH-WAH-RAN
SPIRAL	LAWLAB	LAW-LAB
SPIRITS OF THE NILE	NOUFOUS AL NIL	NOO-FOOS-AL-NEEL
SPITE, ANNOYANCE	NEEKAYAT	NEE-KAH-YAT
SPLASH	RASHASH	RAH-SHASH
SPOILED, CORRUPTED	FASSIDAH	FAH-SEE-DAH
SPONSOR	KAFEELAH	KAH-FEE-LAH
SPROUTING PLANT	NABTAT	NAB-TAT
SPY	JASSOUSSAH	JAH-SOO-SAH
SPYING	JASSOUSSIAT	JAH-SOO-SEE-YAT
SQUANDERER	MOUBAZIRRAH	MOO-BAH-ZEE-RAH
STAR	NEJMAT	NEJ-MATT
STEEL	FOOLAZ	FOO-LAZ
STEPDAUGHTER	RABEEBAH	RAH-BEE-BAH
STOCKINGS	JAHWAHREB	JAH-WAH-REB
STORYTELLER (FEMALE)	RAWIYAT	RAH-WEE-YAT
STRIKING	LAFITAH	LAH-FEE-TAH
STRONG	JABBARAH	JAH-BAH-RAH
STRUGGLE	MOUJAHIDAH	MOO-JAH-HEE-DAH
SUBSTITUTE	BADILAH	BAH-DEE-LAH
SUBSTITUTE	RADEEFAT	RAH-DEE-FAT
SUBSTITUTION	IBDAL	IB-DAHL
SUFFICIENT	KIFAYAT	KEE-FAH-YAT
SUGAR	SUKKARAH	SOO-KAH-RAH
SUGAR BOWL	SOUKRIYAT	SOOK-REE-YAT
SULTANATE	SULTANAT	SUL-TAH-NAT
SUMMIT	HAMAT	HAH-MATT
SUNFLOWER	DAWAHR AL SHAMS	DAH-WAHR-AL-SHAMS
SUNRISE	SHOUROUK	SHOO-ROOK
SUPERIOR	NAJEEBAH	NAH-JEE-BAH

Mouher (Colt)

ENGLISH	ARABIC	PRONUNCIATION
TALL PARTNER, TALL FRIEND	SHAREEK TAWEEL	SHAH-REEK-TAH-WEEL
TEACHER	MOUDARESS	MOO-DAH-RESS
TEMPLE	HAYKAL	HAY-KAL
TENDERNESS, GENTLENESS	LAYEN	LAH-YEN
TERROR	IRHAB	IR-HAB
TERRORIST	IRHABE	IR-HAH-BEE
THANKFUL	SHAKER	SHAH-KER
THE BATTLE FRONT	JABHAT	JAB-HAT
THE BLACK EYED ONE	ASWAD AL OUYOUN	AS-WAD-AL-OO-YOON
THE CLEAR COLORS	BARED AL ALWAN	BAH-RED-AL-AL-WAN
THE CONQUEROR OF THE MOUNTAIN	KAHAR AL JABAL	KAH-HAR-AL-JAH-BAL
THE CONQUEROR OF THE NORTH	NASSER AL SHAMAL	NAH-SER-AL-SHAH-MAL
THE CONQUEROR, THE VICTOR	FATEH AL BELAD	FAH-TEH-AL-BEE-LAD
THE DESERT MOON	HILAL AL SAHRAH	HEE-LAL-AL-SAH-RAH
THE EARLY ONE	AL MOUBAKKER	AL-MOO-BAH-KER
THE EAST	AL SHARQ	AL-SHARK
THE FARM OF THE MOON	ISTABEL AL HILAL	IS-TAH-BEL-AL-HEE-LAL
THE FIRE	AL NAR	AL-NAR
THE FIRE OF MARCH	NAR AZAR	NAR-AH-ZAR
THE FIRE OF THE MOON	NAR AL HILAL	NAR-AL-HEE-LAL
THE FIRE OF THE SUN, THE SUN FIRE	NAR AL SHAMS	NAR-AL-SHAMS
THE FIRST ONE	AL AHWAHL	AL-AH-WAHL
THE GIVER	AL WAHAB	AL-WAH-HAB
THE GREEK	EL GRECO	EL-GREY-CO
THE GUARDIAN OF MY SECRET	AMEEN-SEYREE	AH-MEEN-SAY-REE
THE HERO, THE FEARLESS ONE	AL BATTAL	AL-BAH-TAL
THE HONORABLE GIVING ONE	KAREEM AL SHARAF	KAH-REEM-AL-SHAH-RAF
THE JOY OF THE HADBAN TRIBE	MASSARAT HADBAN	MAH-SAH-RAT-HAD-BAN
THE KIND HEARTED ONE	ROUHAYEM	ROO-HAH-YEM
THE LIGHT OF THE CHESTNUT ONE	NOOR AL SHAGRA	NOOR-AL-SHAG-RAH
THE LIGHT OF THE SAND	NOUR AL RAML	NOOR-AL-RAML
THE LIGHT SEARCHER	KASHEF AL NOOR	KAH-SHEF-AL-NOOR
THE MAGNIFICENT CHESTNUT	JALEEL AL ASHKAR	JAH-LEEL-AL-ASH-KAR

Mouhra (Filly)

ENGLISH	ARABIC	PRONUNCIATION
SUPPORT	RAFEEDAT	RAH-FEE-DAT
SUPPORTER	MOUAYIDAH	MOO-AH-YEE-DAH
SURGE, BOOM	FAWRAT	FAW-RAT
SURPRISED	MOUNDAHISHAH	MOON-DAH-HEE-SHAH
SURRENDER	ISTISLAM	ISS-TIS-LAM
SUSPICION	SHABHAT	SHAB-HAT
SWEATER	KANZAT	KAHN-ZAT
SWEET	SUKKARAH	SU-KAH-RAH
SWEETHEART	MAHBOUB	MAH-BOOB
SWEETLY BEAUTIFUL	HELWEH	HEL-WEH
SWINDLER	DAJAHLAH	DAH-JAH-LAH
SYMBOL	DALEELAH	DAH-LEE-LAH
SYMBOLIC	RAMZEE	RAM-ZEE
SYRIAN (FEMALE)	SOURIYAH	SOO-REE-YAH
SYSTEM	JEHAZ	JEH-HAZ

~ T ~

ENGLISH	ARABIC	PRONUNCIATION
TAKEN	MAKHOUZAH	MAH-KHOO-ZAH
TAME, DOMESTICATED	DAJJINAH	DAH-JEE-NAH
TAMED, DOMESTICATED	ALEEFAH	AH-LEE-FAH
TANK	DABAHBAH	DAH-BAH-BAH
TEENAGER	MOURAHIKAH	MOO-RAH-HEE-KAH
TEMPLE	HAYKAL	HAY-KAL
TENDER HEART	RIKKAT AL QUALB	REE-KAT-AL-QUALB
TENDER TALK	KALAHM HANOON	KAH-LAHM-HAH-NOON
TERRACE	SATIHAT	SAH-TEE-HAT
TERRESTRIAL	BARRIYAH	BAH-REE-YAH
TESTAMENT	WASSIYAH	WAH-SEE-YAH
THE BEAUTIFUL ONE	AL HELWAH	AL-HEL-WAH
THE BEAUTIFUL TIGRESS	AL NEEMRAH JAMEELA	AL-NEEM-RAH-JAH-MEE-LAH
THE BEDOUINS	AL BADOU	AL-BAH-DOO
THE BEE OF MY LIFE	NAHLAT HAYATEE	NAH-LAT-HAH-YAH-TEE
THE BEGINNING	AL BEEDAYAH	AL-BEE-DAH-YAH
THE BRIDE	AL AROUSS	AL-AH-ROOS

Mouher (Colt)

ENGLISH	ARABIC	PRONUNCIATION
THE MARKED ONE	AL MALHOUZ	AL-MAL-HOOZ
THE MYSTIC	EL SOURRI	EL-SOO-REE
THE ONE WHO LIGHTS THE FLAME	AL LAHAB	AL-LAH-HAB
THE ONE WHO STANDS WITH PRIDE	AL SAMED	AL-SAH-MED
THE ONE WITH PERFECT FEATURES	KAMEL AL AWSAF	KAH-MEL-AL-AW-SAF
THE PERFECT ONE	AL KAMEL	AL-KAH-MEL
THE PERFECTION OF PERFECTION	KAMAL AL KAMAL	KAH-MAL-AL-KAH-MAL
THE PRIDE OF THE WEST	AMEER AL GHARB	AH-MEER-AL-GHARB
THE PROPHET	AL RASSOUL	AL-RAH-SOOL
THE PURE HERO	BATAL ASIL	BAH-TAL-AL-AH-SEEL
THE PURE WARRIOR	AL MOUHAREB AL ASIL	AL-MOO-HAH-REB-AL-AH-SEEL
THE RARE NORTH WND	NADIR AL SHAMALEE	NAH-DEER-AL-SHAL-MAH-LEE
THE SAND OF THE DESERT	RAML AL SAHRAH	RAML-AL-SAH-RAH
THE SHINING ONE	LAHMEH	LAH-MEH
THE SKIN	JEELD	JEELD
THE SMART LOVED ONE	ZAKEE AL MOUHIB	ZAH-KEE-AL-MOO-HIB
THE SOUTH WIND	AL JANOUBEE	AL-JAH-NOO-BEE
THE SPONSOR OF MY LIFE	KAFEEL OUMRI	KAH-FEEL-OUM-REE
THE STUBBORN ONE	AL ANEED	AL-AH-NEED
THE SURGE	AL MAHAB	AL-MAH-HAB
THE TOUCH OF FIRE	LAMSAT AL NAR	LAM-SAT-AL-NAR
THE VICTORIOUS, THE CONQUEROR	AL MOUNTASSER	AL-MOON-TAH-SER
THE WAR HORSE	AL FARASS AL HARBI	AL-FAH-RAHS-AL-HAR-BEE
THE WEST	AL GHARB	AL-GARB
THE WIND OF THE DESERT	HAWAH AL SAHRA	HA-WAH-AL-SAH-RAH
THEOLOGY	LAHOOT	LAH-HOOT
THIEF	LISS	LEESS
THIRSTY	AATSHAN	AAT-SHAN
THREAT	TAHDEED	TAH-DEED
THUNDER	RAED	RAH-ED
THUNDEROUS	HADER	HAH-DER
TIGER	NIMR	NIMR
TIP	BAHKSHISH	BAHK-SHEESH

Mouhra (Filly)

ENGLISH	ARABIC	PRONUNCIATION
THE CLOSER ONE	AL AKRAB	AL-AHK-RAB
THE COMPANION FOR LIFE	SHAKIRAT AL OMR	SHAH-KEE-RAT-AL-OMR
THE CONCERN	AL IHTEEMAM	AL-IH-TEE-MAM
THE CONSCIENCE OF THE HEART	DAMEER AL WEJDAN	DAH-MEER-AL-WEJ-DAN
THE DANCING PRINCESS	AL AMEERA AL RAQUASSA	AL-AH-MEE-RAH-AL-RAH-QUAH-SSAH
THE DAUGHTER OF THE DESERT	BINT AL BADIYAH	BEENT-AL-BAH-DEE-YAH
THE DAUGHTER OF THE GREAT ONE	BINT AL KABIR	BEENT-AL-KAH-BEER
THE DAUGHTER OF THE HOME	BATALAT AL DAR	BAH-TAH-LAT-AL-DAHR
THE DAUGHTER OF THE KING	BINT AL MALIK	BEENT-AL-MAH-LEEK
THE DAUGHTER OF THE OLD WISE ONE	BINT AL AJOUZ	BEENT-AL-AH-JOOZ
THE DAUGHTER OF THE SOUL	BINT AL NEFOUS	BEENT-AL-NEH-FOOS
THE DESERT	AL BADEEYAH	AL-BAH-DEE-YAH
THE DESERT SUN	SHAMS AL SAHRAH	SHAMS-AL-SAH-RAH
THE DIAMOND OF THE EYE	ALMAZAT AL OYOUN	AL-MAH-ZAT-AHL-OU-YOON
THE DREAM OF A LIFETIME	AHLAM AL OUMR	AH-LAM-AL-OOMR
THE EAST	AL SHARK	AL-SHARK
THE END	NEHAYAT	NEE-HAH-YAT
THE ETERNAL EXISTENCE	AZAHLEEYAT AL WOUJOOD	AH-ZAH-LEE-YAHT-AL-WOO-JOOD
THE EXPENSE OF THE DREAMS	KOULFAT AL AHLAM	KOOL-FAT-AL-AH-LAM
THE FRAME OF MY HEART	BERWAHZAT ALBEE	BER-WAH-ZAHT-AL-BEE
THE GIFT OF MY LIFE	HADIYAT HAYATI	HAY-DEE-YAT-HAH-YAH-TEE
THE GIFT OF THE SAND	HADIYAT AL RAML	HAH-DEE-YAT-AL-RAML
THE GLIMPSE OF HOPE	BASSISSAT AL AMAL	BAH-SEE-SAT-AL-AH-MAL
THE GLORIOUS ONE	AL MAJEEDAH	AL-MAH-JEE-DAH
THE HOPE OF MY EXISTANCE	KAYNOUNAT AMALEE	KAY-NOON-NAT-AH-MAH-LEE
THE IMPRINT OF THE SOUL	BASSMAT AL NEFOUS	BAS-MAT-AL-NEH-FOOS
THE ISLAND	AL JAZIRAH	AL-JAH-ZEE-RAH
THE JEWEL OF THE NILE	HOULIYAT AL NIL	HOO-LEE-YAT-AL-NEEL
THE LESSON, THE EXAMPLE	AL OUMTHOULAH	AL-OUM-THOO-LAH
THE LIGHT OF THE CHESTNUT MARE	NOOR AL HAMRA	NOOR-AL-HAM-RAH
THE LIGHT OF THE CHESTNUT ONE	NOOR AL SHAGRA	NOOR-AL-SHAG-RAH
THE LIGHT OF THE DAY	BAYAHD AL NAHAR	BAH-YAD-AL-NAH-HAR
THE LONG AWAITED ONE	AL MOUNTAZARAH	AL-MOON-TAH ZAH-RAH

Mouher (Colt)

ENGLISH	ARABIC	PRONUNCIATION
TO AGGRAVATE	FAQUEM	FAH-KEM
TO ATTACK	HAJEM	HAH-JEM
TO BE IN TOUCH WITH	LAMESS	LAH-MESS
TO BE KIND TO	LOUTF	LOUTF
TO BECOME GREATER	MAZEED	MAH-ZEED
TO BICKER WITH	MAHEK	MAH-HEK
TO BLESS	BARAKAH	BAH-RAH-KAH
TO BREAK, FRACTURE	KASSAR	KAH-SAR
TO CHARM	FATN	FATN
TO CROSS	IJTAZ	IJ-TAZ
TO DOMINATE	HAYMANAH	HAY-MAH-NAH
TO EMBRACE ISLAM	ASLAMAH	AHS-LAH-MAH
TO EMIGRATE	HAJER	HAH-JER
TO EVACUATE	AJLAH	AHJ-LAH
TO EXCEL	AJAHD	AH-JAHD
TO FLATTER	DAHHEN	DAH-HEN
TO FOCUS ON	ABRAZAH	AHB-RAH-ZAH
TO GUIDE	HADAH	HAH-DAH
TO HONOR	KARRAM	KAH-RRAM
TO HOPE	RAJAH	RAH-JAH
TO INVENT	IKHTALAKAH	IKH-TAH-LAH-KAH
TO KISS	BAHSSAH	BAH-SAH
TO MAKE PEACE WITH	SALEM	SAH-LEM
TO PAMPER, TO SPOIL	DALLALAH	DAH-LAH-LAH
TO PREFER	FADDAL	FAH-DAL
TO PROVOKE	TAHAROUSH	TAH-HAH-ROOSH
TO REGRET	AHSEF	AH-SEF
TO REJOICE AT	ABSHARAH	AHB-SHAH-RAH
TO RELIEVE	FARAJ	FAH-RAJ
TO RISE EARLY	BAKKAR	BAH-KAHR
TO SARIFICE	FADI	FAH-DEE
TO SEE, TO LOOK AT	ABSAHRAH	AHB-SAH-RAH
TO SEEK DECISION	IHTAKAMAH	IH-TAH-KAH-MAH

Mouhra (Filly)

ENGLISH	ARABIC	PRONUNCIATION
THE MIDDLE	AL AWSAT	AL-AW-SAT
THE MOON OF LIFE	BADR AL HAYAT	BADR-AL-HAH-YAT
THE MOON OF MY LIFE	BADR HAYATI	BADR-HAH-YAH-TEE
THE OLDEST ONE, LARGE	KABEERAH	KAH-BEE-RAH
THE ONE TRUSTED WITH MY LIFE	AMINAT HAYATEE	AH-MEE-NAT-HAH-YAH-TEE
THE ONE WHO BREAKS THINGS	KASSARAH	KAH-SAH-RAH
THE ONE WITH PERFECT FEATURES	KAMEELAT-AL-AWSAF	KAH-MEE-LAT-AL-AW-SAF
THE PLAYFUL GRAY	NASHEETA-EL-ZARKA	NAH-SHEE-TAH-EL-ZAR-KAH
THE PRISONER OF THE HEART	ASEERAT AL ALB	AH-SEE-RAT-AL-ALB
THE PROUD AND GENTLE ONE	ZAHRA AL MOUTAKAHBIRAH	ZAH-RAH-AL-MOO-TAH-KAH-BEE-RAH
THE QUEEN OF SEPTEMBER	AMIRAT AL AYLOUL	AH-MEE-RAT-AL-AY-LOOL
THE SAND OF THE DESERT	RAML AL SAHRAH	RAML-AL-SAH-RAH
THE SHAKE, THE SWING	AL IHTEEZAZ	AL-IH-TEE-ZAZ
THE SONG	AL OUGNEEYAH	AL-OUG-NEE-YAH
THE SPONSOR OF MY LIFE	KAFEELAT OUMRI	KAH-FEE-LAT-OOM-REE
THE SUBSTITUTE OF THE EYES	BADILAT AL OYOUN	BAH-DEE-LAT-AL-OYOUN
THE SUBSTITUTE OF THE SWEET ONE	BADILAT AL MAHBOOB	BAH-DEE-LAT-AL-MAH-BOOB
THE SUN	SHAMS	SHAMS
THE SUN OF PARADISE	SHAMS AL JANNAT	SHAMS-AL-JAH-NAT
THE TIMID ONE	AL KHAJOULEH	AL-KAH-JOO-LEH
THE TREASURE OF THE EYES	KANZ-AL-OUYOUN	KANZ-AL-OU-YOON
THE TRUST OF THE HEART	AMEENAT AL ALB	AH-ME-NAT-AHL-ALB
THE WIND OF THE DESERT	HAWAH AL SAHRAH	HAH-WAH-AL-SAH-RAH
THE WORD OF LIFE	KEELMAT AL HAYAT	KEEL-MAT-AL-HAH-YAT
THE WORLD, LIFE	DOUNIA	DOO-NEE-YAH
THEOLOGICAL	LAHOUTEE	LAH-HOO-TEE
THIEF, PICK POCKET	NASHALAT	NAH-SHAH-LAT
THIN, SLIM	NAHIFAT	NAH-HEE-FAT
THRILLING, BEAUTIFUL	FATINAH	FAH-TEE-NAH
TIDINESS	HINDAM	HIN-DAM
TIME	ZAMAN	ZAH-MAN
TIME TABLE, SCHEDULE	JADWAL	JAD-WAHL
TO ATTRACT	IJTAZABAH	EEJ-TAH-ZAH-BAH

Mouher (Colt)

ENGLISH	ARABIC	PRONUNCIATION
TO SHINE	YATAHALAK	YAH-TAH-AH-LAK
TO SHOW	DALLAH	DAH-LAH
TO SMILE	TABASSOUR	TAH-BAH-SOOR
TO STRIKE	JAHADAH	JAH-HAH-DAH
TO TOUCH THE MOON	LAMESS EL AMAR	LAH-MESS-EL-AH-MAR
TO TREAT WITH KINDNESS	LATAFAH	LAH-TAH-FAH
TO TUCK	SHAMMAR	SHAH-MAR
TO TURN	DAWAHMAH	DAW-WAH-MAH
TO TWIST	LAWAH	LAH-WAH
TOMB	LAHED	LAH-HED
TORRENTIAL	FAYAD	FAH-YAD
TORRENTIAL	MEDRAR	MED-RAR
TOUGH	AHSEE	AH-SEE
TOURIST	SAEH	SAH-EH
TOWEL	FOOTAH	FOO-TAH
TOWER	BOORJ	BOORJ
TRADE	TABDIL	TAB-DEEL
TRAGEDY	MAESSAT	MAH-EE-SAT
TRAINER	MOUDAREB	MOO-DAH-REB
TRANSLATOR	TOURJOUMAN	TOOR-JOO-MAN
TRAVELER	RAHAL	RAH-HAL
TREASURE	KENZ	KENZ
TROOP, GROUP	KOUKABAT	KOW-KAH-BAT
TROT, JOG	HARWALAH	HAR-WAH-LAH
TRUE FRIEND	SHAREEK ANEES	SHAH-REEK-AH-NEES
TRUMPET	NAFEER	NAH-FEER
TRUSTWORTHY	AMEEN	AH-MEEN
TUNNEL	NAFAK	NAH-FAK
TURNIP	LEEFT	LEEFT

~ U ~

ENGLISH	ARABIC	PRONUNCIATION
UNIQUE	FAREED	FAH-REED
UNJUST, UNFAIR	JAERR	JAH-ERR
UNKNOWN	MAJHOUL	MAJ-HOOL

Mouhra (Filly)

ENGLISH	ARABIC	PRONUNCIATION
TO BE IMPOSSIBLE	ISTEEHAL	ISS-TEE-HAL
TO CARESS	RAEEMAT	RAH-EE-MAT
TO CHANT	DANDANAH	DAN-DAH-NAH
TO COMMIT	IRTAKABAH	IR-TAH-KAH-BAH
TO CONCLUDE	ISTAFADAH	ISS-TAH-FAH-DAH
TO CONTROL	HAYMANAH	HAY-MAH-NAH
TO COO (DOVES)	HADALAH	HAH-DAH-LAH
TO DISAGREE	IKHTALAFAH	IKH-TAH-LAH-FAH
TO FACILITATE	HAWANAT	HAH-WAH-NAT
TO FAVOR, LIKE	ISTAHSANAH	ISS-TAH-SAH-NAH
TO FIGHT	JAHADAH	JAH-HAH-DAH
TO FLOURISH	IZDAHARAH	IZ-DAH-HAH-RAH
TO GROWL	HADARAH	HAH-DAH-RAH
TO HAVE FUN	MAHZEEHAH	MAH-ZEE-HAH
TO JOG	HARWALAH	HAR-WAH-LAH
TO LEAN ON	IRTAKAHZAH	IR-TAH-KAH-ZAH
TO MURMER	DAMDAMAH	DAM-DAH-MAH
TO REJOICE	IBTIHAJAH	IB-TEE-HA-JAH
TO RESPOND TO	ISTEEJAB	ISS-TEE-JAB
TO SEEK PROTECTION	IHTAMAH	IH-TAH-MAH
TO TALK SWEETLY	DAHINAH	DAH-HEE-NAH
TO TEAR, DESTRUCTIVE	HADDAMAH	HAH-DAH-MAH
TO TERRIFY	HAWALAT	HAH-WAH-LAT
TOTAL, ENTIRE	IJMAHLEE	IJ-MAH-LEE
TOURISM	SIYAHAT	SEE-YAH-HAT
TOURIST	SAEEHAH	SAH-EE-HAH
TOWEL	FOOTAH	FOO-TAH
TOWERING	SAMIKAH	SAH-MEE-KAH
TRADER	MOUTAJIRAH	MOO-TAH-JEE-RAH
TRAGEDY	MAISSAT	MAH-EE-SAT
TRAINER	MOUDARIBAH	MOO-DAH-REE-BAH
TRANSLATOR	TOURJOUMANEH	TOOR-JOO-MAH-NEH
TRANSPARENT	SHAFFAF	SHAH-FAF

Mouher (Colt)

ENGLISH	ARABIC	PRONUNCIATION
UNSUCCESSFUL	FASHELL	FAH-SHELL
UPROAR	ZAJAL	ZAH-JAL

~ V ~

ENGLISH	ARABIC	PRONUNCIATION
VALLEY	WADI	WAH-DEE
VALUABLE TREASURE	KENZ GAHLEE	KENZ-GAH-LEE
VAPOR, STEAM	BOOKHAR	BOO-KHAR
VERTIGO	DOUWAHR	DOO-WAHR
VERY MUCH	KATEERAN	KAH-TEER-RAN
VICTORIOUS	ZAFER	ZAH-FER
VICTORY	FAWZ	FAWZ
VICTORY	NASR	NASR
VIOLET	BANAFSAJ	BAH-NAF-SAJ
VIOLIN	KAMAM	KAH-MAM
VIRGIN, PURE	BATOOL	BAH-TOOL
VISITOR FROM ALLAH	DEIF ALLAH	DEIF-AL-LAH
VISUAL, OPTICAL	BASSAREF	BAH-SAH-REF
VIVIDNESS	ZAHAWAT	ZAH-HAH-WHAT
VOID	BATTEL	BAH-TEL
VOLCANO	BOURKAN	BOOR-KAHN
VOW	NAZR	NAZR

~ W ~

ENGLISH	ARABIC	PRONUNCIATION
WALKER	SAER	SAH-ER
WALKING	MASHEE	MAH-SHEE
WALL	JEEDAR	JEE-DAR
WANDERER	MOUTAJAWAL	MOO-TAH-JAH-WAL
WANDERER	SHARED	SHAH-RED
WANTED	MATLOUB	MAT-LOOB
WANTED	MOUROD	MOO-ROD
WAR SHIP, BATTLE SHIP	BAREEJAH	BAH-REE-JAH
WARRIOR OF THE NOBLE ONE	ANTAR AL MAJEED	AN-TAR-AL-MAH-JEED
WARRIOR, FIGHTER	MOUHAREB	MOO-HAH-REB
WASP	DABBOUR	DAH-BOOR
WATER FOUNTAIN	FAWAR	FAH-WAR

Mouhra (Filly)

ENGLISH	ARABIC	PRONUNCIATION
TRAVELER	MOUSSAFIRAH	MOO-SAH-FEE-RAH
TRAVELLING	MOUTAJAWALAH	MOO-TAH-JAH-WAH-LAH
TREE	SHAJRAT	SHAJ-RAT
TREMBLE	RAJFAT	RAHJ-FAT
TRUCE	HOUDNAT	HOOD-NAT
TRUST	AMANAT	AH-MAH-NAT
TRUSTED WITH A JOB	WAKEELAT	WAH-KEE-LAT
TRUSTWORTHY	MOUTAMINAH	MOO-TAH-MEE-NAH
TUMBLE DOWN	DAHWARAH	DAH-WAH-RAH
TURQUOISE, PRECIOUS STONE	FAYROUZ	FAY-ROOS
TWISTED	MAJDOULAH	MAJ-DOO-LAH

~ U ~

UNEQUALED, ONE OF A KIND	FAREEDAH	FAH-REE-DAH

~ V ~

VACANCY	SHOUGHOUR	SHOO-GOOR
VACATION	EJAZAH	EE-JAH-ZAH
VAGUE	MOUBHAMAH	MOOB-HAH-MAH
VALUABLE	NAFEESAT	NAH-FEE-SAT
VASTNESS	RAHABAT	RAH-HAH-BAT
VAULT	SER-DAB	SER-DAB
VEIL	NIKKAB	NEE-KAB
VEIL	SITTAR	SEE-TAR
VEILED	MOUTASSATIRAH	MOO-TAH-SAH-TEE-RAH
VERIFICATION	ITHBAT	ITH-BAT
VICTIM, PREY	FAREESAT	FAH-REE-SAT
VILLA	DAHRAT	DAH-RAT
VIOLET COLOR	BANAFSAJIYAH	BAH-NAF-SAH-JEE-YAH
VISION	ROUIYAT	ROO-EE-YAT
VISITING GUEST	ZAIRAH	ZAH-EE-RAH
VIVIDNESS	ZAHAWAT	ZAH-HAH-WHAT

~ W ~

WALNUT	JAWZAT	JAW-ZAT
WANDERER	SHARIDAH	SHAH-REE-DAH

Mouher (Colt)

ENGLISH	ARABIC	PRONUNCIATION
WATERED	MIRWI	MEER-WEE
WATERFALL	SHAGHOUR	SHAH-GOOR
WATERFALL	SHALLAL	SHAH-LLAL
WATERS	MEYAH	MEE-YAH
WEAPON	SILAH	SEE-LAH
WEAVER	NASSAJ	NAH-SAJ
WELL	JOUB	JOOBB
WELL RESPECTED	BASHA	BAH-SHAH
WHEEL	DOULAB	DOO-LAB
WHIRLPOOL	DOURDOUR	DOER-DOER
WHISPER	HAMASAH	HAH-MAH-SAH
WHITE HAIR	SHAIB	SHAH-EB
WHITE LIE	KEZBAH BAYDAH	KEEZ-BAH-BAY-DAH
WHITISH	MOUBYAD	MOOB-YAD
WIDE, LOOSE	FEEFAD	FEED-FAD
WIDESPREAD	RAEJ	RAH-EJ
WINNER	FAYEZ	FAH-YEZ
WINNER	RABBEH	RAH-BEH
WINNER, CHAMPION	KASSEB	KAH-SEB
WINTERY	SHATAWI	SHAH-TAH-WEE
WISE, USES CAUTION	MOUTAZEN	MOO-TAH-ZEN
WITH HONOR	WAJEEH	WAH-JEEH
WITHOUT, DEPRIVED OF	FAQUED	FAH-KED
WITNESS	SHAHED	SHAH-HED
WORLDLY	DUNYAHWEE	DUN-YAH-WEE
WORSHIPPING	SEEJOUD	SEE-JOUD
WORTHY	JADEER	JAH-DEER
WRINKLES	TAJAEID	TAH-JAH-EID
WRITER	KATEB	KAH-TEB
WRITER, AUTHOR	AHDEB	AH-DEB

~ Y ~

YOUNG MAN	FATTAH	FAH-TAH
YOUTHFULNESS	FOUTOUWAHT	FOO-TOO-WHAT

Mouhra (Filly)

ENGLISH	ARABIC	PRONUNCIATION
WANDERING, AMBULENT	DAWAHR	DAH-WAHR
WARMTH, HEAT	SOUKOUNAT	SOO-KOO-NAT
WATCHER	RASIDA	RAH-SEE-DAH
WATER PIPE FOR TOBACCO	NARGHILEH	NAR-JEE-LEH
WELCOME	AHLAN WASAHLAN	AH-LAN-WA-SAH-LAN
WELCOME, TO GREET	RAHABAH	RAH-HAH-BAH
WELCOMING	TARHEEB	TAR-HEEB
WELL BEING	RAFAHAT	RAH-FAH-HAT
WELL KNOWN, FAMOUS	MAAROUFA	MAH-ROO-FAH
WELL REFINED	JAYIDDAH	JAH-YEE-DAH
WHIRLPOOL	DORDOUR	DOUR-DOUR
WHISPER	HAMSAT	HAM-SAT
WHITISH	MOUBYADAH	MOOB-YAH-DAH
WICKED	SHEERIRAH	SHEE-REE-RAH
WICKED, SORDID	LAEEMAH	LAH-EE-MAH
WINNER	FAYEEZAH	FAH-YEE-ZAH
WINNER	KASSIBAH	KAH-SEE-BAH
WISE, JUDICIOUS	LABEEBAH	LAH-BEE-BAH
WISH, HOPE	RAJAH	RAH-JAH
WISHFUL	RAGHIBAH	RAH-GHEE-BAH
WITH DIFFERENT COLORS	MOUTALAWINAH	MOO-TAH-LAH-WEE-NAH
WITNESS	SHAHIDAT	SHAH-HEE-DAT
WITTY, INTELLIGENT	ZAKEEYEH	ZAH-KEE-YEH
WITY, FOXY	MAHKKAR	MAH-KAR
WOMAN FROM SUWAIDAH	SUWADAWIYAH	SOO-WAY-DAH-WEE-YAH
WOOD SHAVINGS	NEJJARAT	NEH-JAH-RAT
WORTH, MERIT	JADARAT	JAH-DAH-RAT
WRITER	KATIBAH	KAH-TEE-BAH

~ Y ~

ENGLISH	ARABIC	PRONUNCIATION
YESTERDAY	AL AMS	AL-AHMS
YOGURT	LABAN	LAH-BAN
YOUNG WOMAN	SHABAT	SHAH-BAT
YOUNGSTER	NASHEEAT	NAH-SHEE-AT

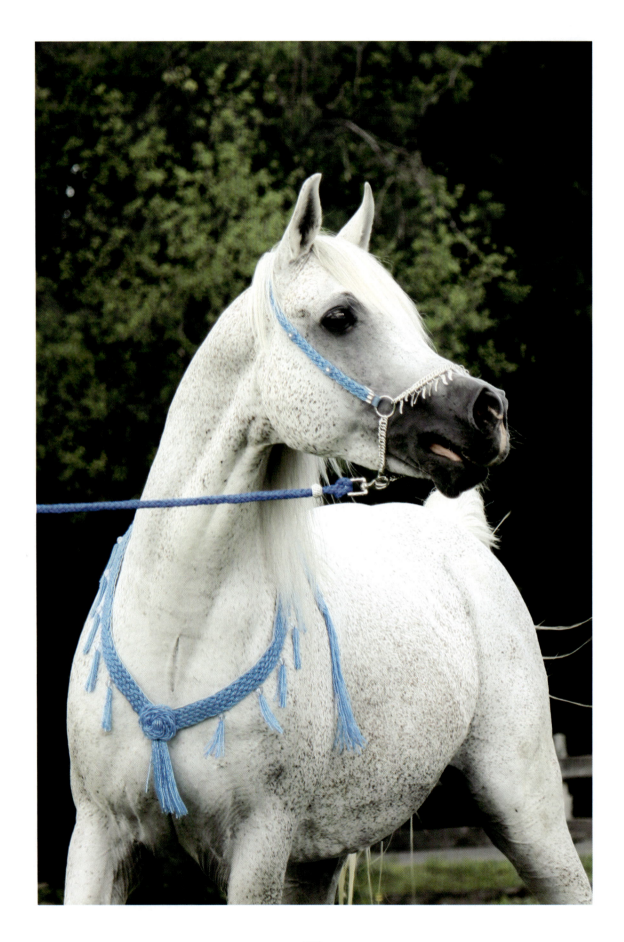

Picture Credits

I am eternally thankful to the world renowned photographers Gigi Grasso, Darryl Larson, Nasr Marei, and Rik Van Lent Jr., and to one of the greatest equine artists in the world Mr. Ali Al Mimar, for allowing the publication of their works in *Authentic Arabian Horse Names*, Volume II. I would also like to extend a special recognition and thank you to my dear friends Gary Kenworthy and Robin Lee, as well as my co-author Kellie Kolodziejczyk, for their exquisite photographic contributions. The talents of these special people have captured the sheer essence and beauty of the desert Arabian horse beyond description.

Page	Credit
Front Cover/1	© Ali Al Mimar, *Maan Ela Al Abad*, Oil on canvas, Painted 2007
2	© Gary Kenworthy, Courtesy of Mr. and Mrs. Gary Kenworthy, PARADISE ARABIANS, www.paradisearabians.com
6-7	© Ali Al Mimar, *Farouk*, Oil on canvas, Painted 2006
9	© Gigi Grasso, Courtesy of Mr. and Mrs. C.R. Watts, HALSDON ARABIANS, www.halsdonarabians.com
10	©Ali Al Mimar
11	© Perry Kolodziejczyk
12	© Nasr Marei
16	© Kellie Kolodziejczyk
22-23	© Kellie Kolodziejczyk
24	© Kellie Kolodziejczyk
30-31	© Ali Al Mimar, *Al Raqsat*, Oil on canvas, Painted 2009
33	© Darryl Larson
42	© Ali Al Mimar, *Al Tawaem*, Oil on canvas, Painted 2006
44	© Nasr Marei
50-51	© Ali Al Mimar, *Nouzhat Fee Al Badiah*, Oil on canvas, Painted 2003
52	© Nasr Marei
60-61	© Ali Al Mimar, *Raqsat Ma Al Shams*, Oil on canvas, Painted 2008
63	Bachir Bserani Collection
65	Bachir Bserani Collection (Both Photos)
66	Bachir Bserani Collection
68	© Robin Lee, Courtesy of Robin Lee, ALEAH ARABIANS, www.aleaharabians.com
70	© Kellie Kolodziejczyk
74	© Kellie Kolodziejczyk
142	© Gigi Grasso, Courtesy of Mr. and Mrs. DeShazer, DESHAZER ARABIANS, www.deshazer.com
210	© Kellie Kolodziejczyk
214-215	© Rik Van Lent, Jr.
Back Cover	© Ali Al Mimar, *Harakat Hourrah*, Oil on canvas, Painted 2002
Endsheets	© Art Resource, NY/Réunion des Musées Nationaux. By Horace Vernet, French artist, (1789-1863), *The Gathering of the Members of Parliament*, Painted 1834. Oil on canvas, 0.980 x 0.520 m. PE438. Photo R. G. Ojeda. Original painting located at the Musée Condé, Chantilly, France

About the Artists and Photographers

Ali Al Mimar
Equine Artist

Ali Al Mimar is one of the most well known and highly acclaimed equine artists in the world. His magnificently beautiful artwork is truly a gift to mankind. The paintings of Ali Al Mimar provoke in those that view his work, a deep respect for the beauty and nobility of the Arabian horse, as well as the Arab culture which is reflected in his art. Whether it be his expression through the strictest detail and realism, or through his abstract style of painting, in each of his works there is a most poignant story being told.

Ali Al Mimar was born in Bagdad, Iraq in 1965. He graduated from the Institute of Fine Arts, Bagdad in 1985 and the College of Fine Arts, Bagdad in 1991 with honors. During this time Ali worked closely with and was mentored by the famous Iraqi artist, Fa'ik Hassan, who first introduced Ali to the painting of Arabian horses and helped him to develop his remarkable talent. In 1985, at the Al Shabab Festival in Iraq, Ali was awarded the highly coveted Fa'ik Hassan Golden Medal for painting. Since then Ali has won numerous other awards for his paintings and is considered by his peers, as well as judges in the field, to be one of the foremost equine artists, and also one of the most talented painters of the Arabian horse in the world. Original paintings by Ali Al Mimar are greatly valued. Most are kept in private collections and institutions throughout the United States and Europe, as well as the Royal Palaces of the Sheiks in the Middle East and Egypt.

    For more information please contact:
    Website: www.magicoforiginality.com or E-mail: almimar1@hotmail.com

Nasr Marei
Egyptian Arabian Horse Breeder, Equine Photographer, International Arabian Horse Show Judge, Advisor

Nasr Marei is owner of the highly influential Egyptian Arabian breeding farm, Albadeia Stud in Giza, Egypt producing some of the most desired horses in the world. Established in 1935 by the Marei family, it is one of the oldest farms in Egypt. These beautiful and treasured horses were threatened with near extinction in the 1960's as the new socialistic regime of Egypt had planned to disallow ownership of Arabians as well as any other valuable property. Entire herds were dispersed. Sayed Marei, Nasr's father, who was then the Minister of Agriculture of Egypt, was in a position to approach the new leader, and was able to prove to him the value of the Egyptian Arabian horse not only to the individual, but to the country of Egypt and to the world. The breeding programs were allowed to continue. The Marei family later acquired the most exquisite Arabian mares and stallions and brought them to their breeding farm Albadeia Stud. Nasr continues this tradition of breeding and showing. Horses from the Albadeia Stud have been and continue to be a significant influence to Egyptian Arabian breeding programs throughout the Middle East and the USA, as well as Europe and Australia.

Nasr Marei is also an advisor and international Arabian horse show judge. He also holds a Doctorate from the University of California Davis in Agricultural Sciences. And his talents extend to the camera lens as well as a keen photographer, and among his favorite subjects is the Arabian horse. His ability to capture the beauty and essence of the Arabian horse is extraordinary. A compilation of the photography of Nasr Marei including a history of the Arabian horse can be seen in his book *The Arabian Horse of Egypt*. Also included in this work is a Foreword by HRH Princess Alia Bint Al Hussein, and Historical Introduction by Cynthia Culbertson.

    For more information please contact:
    Website: www.albadeia.net or E-mail: info@albadeia.net

Gigi Grasso
Arabian Horse Photographer, Breeder, Artist

Gigi Grasso is known around the world for his stunning images of the Arabian horse. His ability to capture the natural spirit and emotions of the Arabian is truly remarkable. Gigi Grasso has produced some of the world's most captivating and poetic images of the Arabian horse ever seen. A compilation of his work can be seen in the book *Gigi Grasso - 20 Years of Photography*.
    For more information please contact:
    Websites: www.gigigrasso.com or www.arabianessence.com
    E-mail: info@arabianessence.com

Darryl Larson
Equine Photographer and Videographer, Breeder, Equestrian

Darryl Larson is an award winning equine photographer and videographer known in the United States and abroad for her exceptionally creative and romantic imagery of the Arabian horse in both still photos and video. Her expertise is highly sought after by some of the most influential Arabian horse breeders and owners in the industry. Darryl Larson's work appears regularly in American, European and International Arabian horse publications and media.
    For more information please contact:
    Website: www.darryllarson.com or E-mail: darryllarson@gmail.com

Rik Van Lent, Jr.
Photographer, Arabian Horse and Middle Eastern Culture Enthusiast

Rik Van Lent Jr is one of the most famed photographers of the Arabian horse in the world. His breathtaking and often candid images capture the natural beauty and spirit of the Arabian, and the culture that surrounds it. To experience the photography of Rik Van Lent is to experience the true essence of the Arabian. A compilation of his photography along with the photography of his father Rik Van Lent Sr., can be seen in their book titled *Arabians*. Also included is a Foreword by Hossein Amirsadeghi, Introduction by H.H. Sheikh Zayed bin-Sultan al-Nahyan, and Text and Captions by Peter Upton and Hossein Amirsadeghi. This book was originally published in Great Britain under the title *The Arabian Horse, History, Mystery and Magic*.
    For more information please contact:
    E-mail: visualart@qatar.net.qa

Gary Kenworthy
Photography Enthusiast, Egyptian Arabian Horse Owner and Breeder
    For more information please contact:
    Website: www.paradisearabians.com or E-mail: info@paradisearabians.com

Kellie Kolodziejczyk
Photography Enthusiast, Arabian Horse Owner and Breeder
    For more information please contact:
    Website: www.abmoracres.com or E-mail: abmoracres@yahoo.com

Robin Lee
Photography Enthusiast, Egyptian Arabian Horse Owner and Breeder
    For more information please contact:
    Website: www.aleaharabians.com or E-mail: aleaharabians@yahoo.com

Horace Vernet
French Artist (1789-1863). Many of the paintings by Horace Vernet are on display at the Musée Condé located in Chantilly, France.

"Behold, there were brought before Him, at eventide, coursers of the highest breeding, and swift of foot.

And He said, 'Truly do I love the love of good with a view to the Glory of Allah.'"

– The Holy Koran

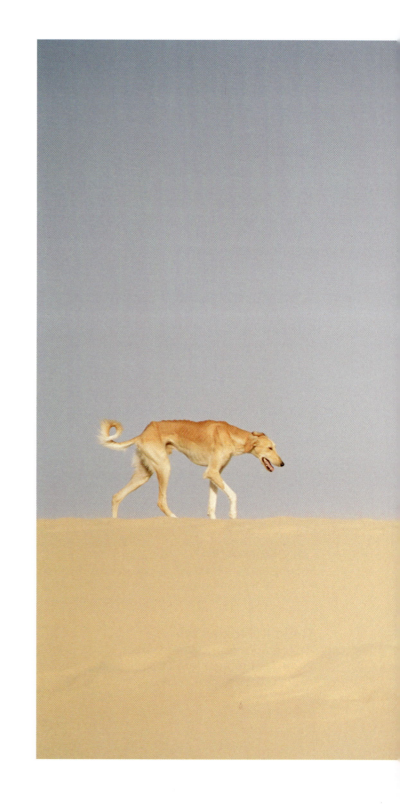